DALTON CAMP

Whose Country Is This Anyway?

Douglas & McIntyre
Vancouver/Toronto

Douglas & McIntyre
1615 Venables Street
Vancouver, British Columbia
V5L 2H1

Canadian Cataloguing in Publication Data
Camp, Dalton, 1920–
  Dalton Camp

  ISBN 1-55054-467-5

  1. Canada—Politics and government—1993–* 2. Canada—
Social conditions—1971–* I. Title.
FC635.C35 1995   971.064'8   C95-910574-3
F1034.2.C35 1995

Editing by Nancy Pollak
Cover design by Michael Solomon
Text design and typesetting by Val Speidel
Printed and bound in Canada
Printed on acid-free paper

The publisher gratefully acknowledges the assistance of the Canada Council and of the British Columbia Ministry of Tourism, Small Business and Culture.

For Andrew, Emma, Amy, Jamie, Caroline,
Sophie, Teddy, and Thomas

Contents

PART III   Somewhat Uplifting

PART IV   News and Reviews

Acknowledgments

Some of this material originally appeared in a previous incarnation of *Saturday Night*; in a magazine produced by the *Globe and Mail*, now defunct; and in a CBC radio commentary. Most of the material appeared originally in the *Toronto Star* and through the Toronto Star Syndicate. I thank Patricia Aldana, who encouraged this book and has since fled to France, and my editor and copy editors at the *Star*, who have been unfailingly cheerful and supportive from creation to publication.

Introduction

> The essayist is a self-liberated man, sustained by the childish belief that everything he thinks about, everything that happens to him, is of general interest. Only a person who is congenitally self-centered has the effrontery and the stamina to write essays.
>
> — E. B. WHITE, *Essays of E. B. White*

Writing newspaper columns can be a liberating personal experience but also an exercise in self-indulgence. The columnist becomes the publisher of his own opinion. The effrontery comes with the belief that others will be interested in what he has to say. When the columnist conspires with his publishers to make a book of his columns, the effrontery is brazen.

I have been more or less a columnist most of my life. While a school boy at Horton Academy, in Wolfville, Nova Scotia, I edited the *Hortonian* (an annual) and wrote an opinion piece. (It was about Munich.) When I went on to Acadia University before the war, I wrote a column, along with a friend, in the campus newspaper. After the war, at the University of New Brunswick, I edited the *Brunswickan* and wrote editorials.

One editorial caught the eye of the Liberal premier of New Brunswick. The consequences were considerable: I became a Liberal and a columnist for the party newspaper, the *Liberal Review*. Thus began a half-century's involvement in politics, as activist, advisor, observer, and finally as columnist, with the *Toronto Telegram*, until it folded, then the *Toronto Star*, and then the *Toronto Sun* for a time, before rejoining the *Star*.

Along the way, I became a student of other columnists. I grew up in a California home filled with newspapers. When the family "went east" during the summers, I could read the *New York Herald Tribune*, the *Boston Post*, and the *Bangor Daily News*. In California, the newspaper fare included the *Oakland Tribune*, the *San Francisco Chronicle*, the *San Francisco Examiner*, and the *Call Bulletin*.

For good reason, which I will explain later, my father loathed the

Hearst press and refused to allow the *Examiner* in the house. But my mother enjoyed the theatre and movie reviews in the *Examiner*, so the paper boy was instructed to leave it in the fuse box at the side of the house. While I supported my father's boycott of the *Examiner*, I continued to read its forbidden columns, passed on by my mother.

I was raised on Walter Lippmann whom I began reading in the *New York Tribune* when I was twelve. Also Bob Ruark, Grantland Rice, the Alsop brothers, "Red" Smith, Joe Palmer, Herb Caen, Jimmy Cannon, and A. J. Liebling; Henry MacLemore and Bugs Baer, both of whom wrote humour, were special favourites.

Every columnist had his own style; this was of greater interest to me than the content. Joe Palmer, for instance, was the racing correspondent for the *Tribune* as was Audax Minor for the *New Yorker* magazine. Although I knew nothing about the subject of their expertise, I devoured their columns as avidly as a tout.

Jimmy Cannon, who wrote for the *New York Post*, provided a good example of how not to be a columnist. His columns were notoriously florid, melodramatic, and discursive, but he was widely read. "Red" Smith recalls a colleague telling Cannon, "You remind me of a young left-handed pitcher with all the speed in the world and no control." Hemingway said of him, "What Jimmy doesn't understand is that that stuff up top is just the warm-up. You write it all, then you throw away those first paragraphs."

But if Cannon, in Hemingway's description, "wrote to end writing," A. J. Liebling wrote to inspire it. Liebling wrote on boxing for the *New Yorker* magazine. More interesting to me, he also wrote critical pieces on print journalism under the title "The Wayward Press." He was the first and best of journalism's iconoclasts in a world begging for them. Witty, urbane, and ironic, Liebling's irreverent critiques of the press created a cult of admirers at the Columbia Graduate School of Journalism, where the style book was that of the *New York Times* and journalism was rarely a laughing matter.

Many of the students at the Columbia School were war veterans and more worldly than most of the faculty members. There was occasional friction, along with an underlying cynicism about journalism that we wore almost as an article of clothing and that addressed adversary relationships to come, with newspaper owners, publishers, and managing editors. Liebling was our hero; had any of us been able to choose our place in journalism, we would have liked Liebling's job.

Since life at the Columbia School was largely one of virtual reality journalism, we had a make-believe "Press Club." During the first term I was its president, with the major responsibility of hosting a Press Club beer night with an invited speaker of sufficient solemnity and stature to draw a crowd and impress the faculty of our serious intentions.

As guest speaker for the occasion, A. J. Liebling was the unanimous first choice, though no one thought he would accept our invitation. It would be like inviting Dean Witter to speak to your dollar-averaging investment club. But I called the *New Yorker*, asked to speak to "Mr. Liebling" and, miraculously, he came on the line. Recovering my poise, I stated my business, describing him as the sole choice of the entire student body to address them on beer night. To my astonishment, he accepted.

"You may not want to hear what I'm going to say," he told me.

"Say anything you like," I reassured him.

"I should tell you," he said, "I think journalism schools are a waste of time."

"So do we," I said, my heart leaping with joy.

Liebling appeared at the school on a sodden, late fall evening, his trench coat dark with rain, his hair matted, his glasses steaming. Like so many people I later would come to know who wrote heroic prose, Liebling's appearance was unprepossessing. He was short, rotund, nondescript, plainly shy. While greeted with great deference, it was unclear who was the most impressed—he by us, or we by him.

When Liebling spoke, however, we sat silent and enthralled. I don't know what you're doing here, he began, because if you want to know about journalism, you could learn more in a month working for a weekly newspaper than you'll learn here in a year. Besides, those of you who are veterans enjoy the beneficence of grateful governments willing to finance your education so long as you want to learn. You are wasting your good fortune attending a journalism school, he said, when you could be enriching your minds and broadening your experience studying Renaissance literature (or anything else) in France.

By the end of Liebling's sardonic elegy in the Pulitzer School's

Press Club, his audience held him in ever higher esteem, bordering on the rapturous. Following tumultuous applause, questions and comments were invited. At the back of the room throughout Liebling's performance, Dean Baker had stood listening, his head down, a frown of concentration on his youthful features.

Now, casually, in a manner suggesting nonchalance, Baker began to thank Liebling, on behalf of those present and those unavoidably absent, the latter including Dean Ackerman, the head of the school. Baker also thanked Liebling for his interesting remarks, going on to praise him for his unique contribution to journalism, through the columns of the *New Yorker* magazine, which had brought such great satisfaction and pride to the school, particularly since—and here is a little known fact—A. J. Liebling was a distinguished graduate of the Columbia School of Journalism!

Dean Baker's intervention removed a lot of oxygen from the room. Soon after, there being no further questions and the hour growing late—some had trains to catch—we saw our favourite columnist and fellow Columbian down the elevator and out the door, watching him recede in the night, the thin slanting rain falling upon the quiet street, our protracted expressions of gratitude trailing on the winds behind him.

Still, the Columbia School was an experience. If not much like a year in Paris studying the works of Rabelais or Pierre de Ronsard, it was fulfilling enough. We were not only taught journalism by the *New York Times* style book, but taught by the man who wrote it, Teddy Bernstein, not yet the icon he would become. Marquis Childs—is there a better name for a columnist?—taught us about writing columns. I was an avid listener, even though I thought him dull as a columnist.

Bennett Cerf visited the school to talk about book publishing; Herb Mays, who published *Good Housekeeping*, came to speak of magazine writing.

Meanwhile, we roamed the streets of New York City looking for stories of our own or covering those assigned us. Politicians held "press conferences" in the school's lecture theatre. These included Senator Howard Taft, Postmaster General and master pol Jim Farley, former New York Governor Tom Dewey and putative presidential candidate, General Dwight D. Eisenhower. I remember, nearly four decades later, Taft's ingenuous, earnest conservatism (he spoke against the war trials at Nuremberg). I recall Farley's nearly overwhelming geniality; he autographed his book for me (*Jim Farley's Story: The Roosevelt Years*), in green ink:

> To Dalton Camp, with all good wishes I do hope you find this story interesting and informative.
> — JAMES A. FARLEY, May 19, 1948

Tom Dewey struck me as hard edged, the eternal attorney for the prosecution. As for Eisenhower, he became the first public figure I had encountered up close who had charisma, before the word came to be linked to politicians.

Meanwhile, we roamed the city looking for news to file with our overseers. My most memorable story came out of an interview with Alabama Governor James "Kissin' Jim" Folsom, conducted at a mid-town hotel in a room sparsely attended by real journalists, though with several photographers present and a few women, apparently hired for the occasion, who were routinely bussed by "Kissin' Jim" amidst exploding flash bulbs. I have not, since then, had a high opinion of Alabama governors, Alabama football coaches, Alabama drum majorettes, or for that matter, Alabama.

After speaking briefly with the governor of Alabama, I filed my story as a column. I could sense my superiors at the "city desk" considered this an act of breathtaking presumption, but, fortunately for me, it was a good column and I got away with it. The gist of the piece, I need hardly say, was to describe in some detail a politician who admitted to an uncontrollable urge to kiss every woman he met. These days, he would have been locked up.

But I have gotten ahead of the story.

There is a belief, instilled in many of us in childhood, that we can pretty well become what we want. You need only to believe, strive, persevere, keep on truckin'. It is not said that you also need some luck.

I graduated from the University of New Brunswick even though I did poorly in chemistry. In fact, I flunked it. But my chemistry prof, also the dean of arts, called me in to say he had determined that, since I was not likely even to see a chemistry book again in my life, and because my other marks were high, and because I was a veteran, he would not let anything like Chemistry 100 stand in the way of my future.

My debt to Dr. Francis Toole, who many merchant princes of Fredericton once suspected was a Communist (he read books written by British socialists), remains eternal; his son, who later became Richard Hatfield's deputy minister of federal-provincial relations, has been a close friend of many years. After Toole's dispensation, I was free to perform my task as the elected valedictorian of the Class of '47. One of my valedictory topics was about luck. While all of us, as graduates, could look forward to lives of personal fulfillment, I said, none could expect to be rich or famous without a modicum of luck.

The valedictory was delivered in the presence of Lord Beaverbrook, installed that same day as the university's chancellor. His lordship's speech followed mine. He promptly challenged my opinion that fame and fortune need rely on so frail and ephemeral a thing as luck. I did not then know that Beaverbrook believed himself a Calvinist, nor would I have known what a Calvinist was. For Beaverbrook, it was a faith rooted in the doctrine of predestination, that one's fate was predetermined at birth by God.

Not everyone took Lord Beaverbrook's reproach to my views kindly. A woman from Gagetown, down river, who had designed the New Brunswick tartan and woven a lap rug for the Queen, and who had heard the graduation ceremonies on radio, told me she was indignant over Beaverbrook's behaviour. Magnanimously, I demurred.

I could not tell her that my luck was only beginning. On becoming chancellor, Beaverbrook instituted a series of lavishly generous overseas graduate scholarships, tenable at London University. Impressed by my valedictory, perhaps pleased with his own part in it, he instructed the selection committee to appoint me a scholar in the following year. I departed the University of New Brunswick campus with my B.A. degree, an overseas scholarship in hand, each bestowed under a lucky star. Soon after, I had my acceptance at the Columbia Graduate School of Journalism.

Of course, life is a matter of choices and one always hopes, as life goes on, to make better ones. It is also true that much of one's life is spent in preparation for the chance one yearns for, or the opportunity one covets. But we know it does not always come.

Because I loved to read, I wanted to write. It is not much more complicated than that. And for a considerable time, I wanted to write a column, to air my own opinion, provoke controversy, hold up to readers matters of interest and turn them in the light, under the illumination of my own words.

In Toronto, one of my closest friends was George Hogan, a successful businessman who was also a client of my Toronto advertising agency. We lunched Thursdays, almost every week, at One Benvenuto Place, off Avenue Road. The restaurant was on the lower floor of an exclusive apartment building. Philanthropist and publisher Floyd Chalmers lived there, as did Glenn Gould. Hogan and I would see Gould occasionally in the restaurant. He wore gloves to the table but dined without them; he always dined alone.

Hogan was a young Tory in his thirties, articulate, thoughtful, and full of fun. He had published a book on Ontario conservatism and he wrote a weekly column for John Bassett's *Toronto Telegram*. Part of the agenda for our two-hour lunches was to discuss George's column of the week; he sometimes read it to me. He was the only man I have known who dictated his columns into a machine. (Since childhood, I have beat out my words on a typewriter, presently a Canon ES3-11 electric). But for the most part, Hogan and I discussed politics and political personalities. We had each run for Parliament and lost. We were both on the executive of the national party; he was the Ontario vice-president, and I was the party's president. We both enjoyed martinis.

One Thursday during lunch at One Benvenuto Place, George showed me a train ticket from New York to Miami. The next day, he was going to fly to New York and take the train south. Trains were a passion with Hogan; I had once spent a weekend in London following him about, exploring train stations. He had an attic full of electric trains.

While George would be flying to New York, I would be flying to Ottawa to attend a party executive meeting. Diefenbaker had taken to his bed. Hogan said the move was strategic and the leader's health would improve as soon as the party executive left town on Sunday. (He was right.)

I returned from Ottawa late Sunday night and thought of phoning

George but put it off. Early Monday morning, the phone rang beside my bed. It was George's wife.

"I have to tell you something," she said. "Are you alone?"

"No," I said. My wife was lying beside me.

"Promise me you won't say anything when I tell you," she said.

"Okay. I won't."

"George is dead."

"I don't understand," I said.

"He killed himself."

"My God."

My wife sat up in bed. "What's wrong?" she asked.

"Don't tell anyone," George Hogan's wife said. "I have to see you right away."

About two weeks after Hogan's funeral, Arnold Agnew of the *Telegram* phoned and asked if I would like to write a weekly column. With the exception of a sabbatical in the Privy Council Office, a couple more in Portugal, and one week following heart surgery, I have been writing columns ever since.

> It's just wonderful to be a pariah. I really owe my success to being a pariah . . . To be a pariah is to be left alone to see things your own way, as truthfully as you can. Not because you're brighter than anyone else is—or your own truth so valuable. But, because, like a painter or a writer or an artist, all you have to contribute is the purification of your own vision, and add that to the sum total of the other visions.
>
> To be regarded as nonrespectable, to be a pariah, to be an outsider, this is really the way to do it. To sit in your tub and not want anything.
> — I. F. STONE, the *Nation*, July 10, 1989

I have a somewhat more understated, private version of my own, in which I need to say that writing for newspapers as a nonconnected, unaligned, freelance, syndicated columnist is not without its desideratum, that I'm not suggesting I'm any great hell as a journalist, only that I'm doing and saying pretty well what I want and not everyone can say that. And if I later decide to become a novelist and write the great Canadian classic, I hope to be as lucky in my choice of mentors, sponsors, publishers, and audiences.

As I began writing columns, I began identifying myself. Writing gives one added dimension, revealing other sides. People who knew me as a partisan, a Progressive Conservative, now saw me as a columnist, someone who occupied valuable space from which he could launch his own opinions. A subtle change ensued in my relations with people, especially those in public life, so that discourse became not so much strained as cautious. People would often say, "I don't want to be quoted on this."

McKenzie Porter, a *Toronto Telegram* reporter and the city's social arbiter (who once wrote no man should wear a white shirt until after six o'clock in the evening), had written of me that I was a potential prime minister. After I became a columnist, Porter wrote a column advising me to give it up since no future prime minister should be engaged in so lowly a task.

In the process of self-definition, rising out of the practice of the regular public expression of personal opinion, there were unforeseen developments. One was described by Stephen Lewis, of Peter Gzowski's *Morningside* troika of Eric Kierans, Lewis and myself. On *Morningside* each Tuesday, we would together discuss major topics of the day. We were given twenty-four-hours notice on the subjects to be raised by Gzowski, presumably to give us time for research, and for pondering and composing our positions and responses. It didn't always work that way. As Lewis said, he sometimes could hardly wait to hear what he thought. I often heard myself saying things contrary to my earlier views.

In the act of public expression, one must be prepared to go beyond the mere assertion of personal bias. It is easy to be an opinionated private person; less easy to expound in public.

Putting one's mouth where one's mind is would make much of private discourse impossible. For people talking at a bar or over morning coffee or at the nineteenth hole, speech can be a careless exercise in outrageous or mindless opinion; many would sooner be found dead than see their words printed in the daily newspaper under their name.

While I was writing for the *Telegram*, much of the stuff I wrote was supportive of my party and meant to be so. It had been Bassett's purpose to open his pages to unbridled partisan comment, from identifiable partisans—Liberal, NDP, or Tory. For me, it was like writing years ago for the *Liberal Review*.

It was easy writing for the *Telegram*; no one said "you can't say that." No one said anything. It was, for me, a good place to start. Then the *Telegram* suddenly folded. I was without a paper.

A friend called to ask if I would consider writing for the *Globe and Mail*. He said he would advise the editor-in-chief of my availability. The next day my friend phoned to tell me he had spoken to the editor who had told him, "Dalton Camp will never write for the *Globe and Mail*." (He was wrong.)

My relations with the upper floor personnel of the *Globe* have always been troubled. But I have always admired the *Globe* for its editorial vigour. One of its columnists, George Bain, was in my view the inventor of the modern political column, for many years the only columnist in Canada to blend wit with style and substance in his writing. But I found a number of those with high titles at the *Globe* to be pompous bores and full of themselves. I suppose the ultimate indictment of them lies in the ultimate truth: None was found fit to become publisher of the paper when the position became vacant in 1994.

On one occasion, I lunched with the publisher of the *Globe* in his apartment on the upper storey of the paper's offices on King Street. I was then president of my advertising agency and he was hopeful of selling me an advertising promotion. After lunch, he saw me to the door of his suite. I thanked him for lunch, expressing surprise the likes of him, a newspaper publisher, would have so much time for the likes of me, the humble president of an advertising agency.

"Mr. Camp," he said engagingly, putting a hand on my shoulder, "all newspaper publishers are whores."

Val Sears, whom I had known for many years as the *Toronto Star*'s parliamentary reporter and a devout skeptic, asked if I would be interested in writing for the *Star*, and if so, if I would meet with the paper's managing editor, Martin Goodman. When I met with Goodman, we discussed the matter of frequency. I had been writing once a week for the *Telegram*; Goodman proposed twice a week. "You will never become established as a columnist writing one column a week," he told me.

For a long time, the *Star* covered its ankles by adding an editorial caveat to my columns—lest it be thought I was promulgating *Star* editorial policy—informing readers I was a "former president of the

Progressive Conservative Party" and, later on, a "former senior advisor to the Mulroney government." For some, this would help explain why my opinions struck them as heretical; for others, it explained nothing but raised the question: How could a loyal, devoted Tory say things like that?

Along the way, having departed my career in advertising and begun disengaging myself from partisan politics, I could feel free to offend anyone. On arriving in Ottawa to serve in the Privy Council Office, I had resigned my ex-officio seat on the Tory party's national executive, torn up my party card, and commenced reading the *Ottawa Citizen*. Studied efforts to become nonpolitical were often frustrated, however, by my being surrounded by civil servants who thought and acted very much like the politicians I had known, and who weighed each significant issue of public policy on the scales of public opinion polls and likely media response. There were, I once told the prime minister, four parties operating in Ottawa: Conservative, Liberal, and NDP in Parliament and the PCO Party in the Langevin Building.

Ottawa soon became a nightmare because of my failing heart and a failing marriage. Still, I would not have missed the opportunity to observe how governments worked or didn't work. I emerged from the experience a wiser man.

Once again settled into the role of columnist and commentator, I felt that all I had done before had been an apprenticeship for what I am now doing. I had been the president of a national party, been seriously engaged in some twenty-seven federal and provincial general election campaigns. I had been a senior civil servant in a position to observe at first hand the cabinet system, the role of the prime minister within it, and the complex interrelationships among the government in power, its caucus, and the Parliament of Canada.

I occasionally boast of the ultimate listing in my C.V.: I have shared political platforms with five men who were, or became, prime ministers of Canada (Mackenzie King, John Diefenbaker, Mike Pearson, Joe Clark, and Brian Mulroney).

Besides any of that, there was the advantage of an American experience: a childhood in Connecticut and California, and later, graduate school in New York. And a seminal intellectual foray at the London School of Economics where I was taught and inspired by Harold Laski, who guided me through the *Communist Manifesto* of

Karl Marx into the greener fields of readings on Disraeli and Burke.

These years formed habits of thought and a system of values that helped steer a less erratic course and temper erratic opinion. It also helped make the writer comfortable in his own skin, less likely to be imitative, more likely to resist supporting opinion that was merely fashionable.

A part of that experience made me a deep believer in party politics and a romantic admirer of those ordinary and sensible people who maintain and assure the vitality of partisanship. It is a pity so few journalists understand the requirement for partisan politics and its role in a democracy. But it is difficult to educate or enlighten people who do not, as we used to say in Carleton County, "know their arse from their elbow" about politics, but delight in disparaging its practices and defaming its practitioners. I have in mind the children, fresh out of school, who bring to their new work a long-practised cynicism and an unearned world-weariness.

I had become fiercely proud of my country and jealously devoted to its institutions. I had no doubt Canadians had created a society exemplary to the world for its civility and tolerance.

For someone who longs for a British title, or to be an American-style tycoon, life in Canada might be a limiting experience. But another very good thing about Canada is that any of its citizens is always free to leave, having been raised in good health, educated in an atmosphere where learning is valued, and brought up to respect others and, for at least a time, to know the benefits of a personal humility and the need for kindness and charity.

This, at any rate, is how it used to be, how many of us were raised. In the formative years, as I believe one's childhood is described, I went to school in the United States but spent all of my summers, save one, in Canada, travelling the continent each year from Oakland to Boston, stopping often in Chicago and New York for shopping, baseball games, or visits with family friends.

But the highlight of each year was the Canadian summer, spent in the small New Brunswick town of Woodstock that was my parents' home, or at the primitive, isolated cottage on the shores of Skiff Lake where each day we canoed, fished, and swam, and ran the gravel roads and searched the woods for the higher adventures of imagination.

Along the way, through those years, I began to notice in myself differences in attitude and perception between the California boy in Canada and the Canadian boy in California. One of the differences seemed to be the atmospherics, in the way life was lived in New Brunswick in the town of Woodstock; the gentleness of speech, the lessening of tension, the pace. Later on, the Maritime lifestyle would become stereotyped for its "slow pace," but the pace was never slow, simply unhurried, a distinction forever lost upon those who equate important tasks with the frenzy so importantly vested in completing them.

As a Canadian living in America, I knew Americans talked incessantly of being first, coming first, striving for first, leading the world, being more powerful, more prosperous, more fortunate than any other nation on earth. It was important to them to see themselves as first and best, as eternally superlative. But the more I knew about America, the less I envied Americans. There would come a time, living in California, when I would be homesick for Canada, for the quiet, unhurried, sunlit small corner of it that I knew in New Brunswick.

Among my father's books, I found something written by Petrarch. It read: "You see, often second place is both safer and more advantageous. Ahead of you is someone to absorb envy's first blows, to show you the way at the risk of his own reputation, whose steps will teach you what to avoid and what to follows . . ."

It has been to our advantage to have America be first. It has been our blessing to remain uncelebrated, unenvied, and undiscovered. For generations, foreigners, including those next door, knew only vaguely where we were; no one knew who we were or what we were doing. Better still, no one cared.

Throughout history, dignitaries and celebrities have come to see our Rockies and to visit Niagara Falls (our Niagara Falls are wider than America's Niagara Falls, but theirs are higher). Winston Churchill came; someone said he bought a ranch in Alberta. The Prince of Wales came and built a hunting lodge on the shores of the Bedford Basin, outside Halifax; the next Prince of Wales came and broke hearts, from coast to coast. Babe Ruth arrived in New Brunswick to hunt bear and, legend has it, to father a child on the southwest fork of the Miramichi. Ted Williams came later to buy a fishing lodge and fish salmon. People who came to New Brunswick to hunt and fish were called "sports." Ruth, according to legend, was a poor sport, a drunk, and a womanizer. But an American hero.

While Americans are raised on myths, we are raised on clichés. For a long time, what people came to Canada to do—shoot moose and bear, kill salmon, and look at the scenery—defined us. The national stereotype could have been the postcard of a man in a red coat seated on a black horse, standing in snow.

I don't mind. Clichés seldom hurt anyone, but mythic histories can be deadly. The truth may be hard and elusive, but our own truth is we are a better nation and a better people for not being American.

The deeply ingrained sense of what we are not—so often attributed to our anti-Americanism—is the inheritance of an unlearned history created out of the great confluence of two abandoned and isolated peoples, the French in Lower Canada and the United Empire Loyalists in the Maritimes and Ontario.

"Were it not for the United States," Hugh MacLennan wrote, "Canada would never have been a nation at all, much less the kind it is." So what else might we have been, other than American?

It is perhaps more simple and less cryptic than that. It was the Québec Act of 1774 and the Constitution Act of 1867 that would provide the framework that shaped the Canadian character (were there such a thing) and created a unique society, in a world of societies where none is quite like another.

Frank Underhill, in a Founder's Day Address given at the University of New Brunswick thirty-three years ago, spoke of the difficulty of describing Canadians to non-Canadians. He quotes a British travel writer who was observing tourists visiting Saint Mark's in Venice. He saw tourists from all over the world.

"The Australians," he noted, "are unmistakable, the Canadians are undistinguishable."

Underhill quotes Henri Joly de Lobtinière, a Québec legislator, speaking 130 years ago about how Canada might be represented by a symbol. Lobtinière proposed the rainbow, because "by its lack of consistence—an image without substance—the rainbow would represent the solidity of our Confederation."

We may lack for an agreed-upon, mandated sense of ourselves, as Canadians, but we still know a thing or two about who we are. It is not all mystery. McLuhan, our guru, described us as "the only country in the world that knows how to live without an identity."

But we knew our place. We are also the only country in the world that never did envy America—even knowing we were coming in second, but knowing we were not American and glad of it! The exuberance is in the awareness of not caring, the daily enjoyment of knowing what is, which surrounds us, and what isn't, but might have been.

On Grand Manan Island, on the Bay of Fundy, I was standing at a hotel desk this summer, exchanging pleasantries with the hotel owner. The morning's CTV news infiltrated our small talk. From the anchor desk came word that, for the third year out of four, the United Nations had cited Canada as the best nation in the world in which to live, in terms of health, education, personal security, income, and other general criteria composing the quality of life.

"We already knew that," I remarked to the owner. He concurred.

A young woman, standing nearby listening to this exchange, seemed suddenly distressed by the news and by our comments. Briefly, her face reflected dismay, then indignation, finally resentment. An American tourist, plainly, visiting just inside the world's longest undefended border, but suddenly never before feeling so far from home, hearing this news—or purported news—in the presence of strangers.

Anyway, how would they know? The publication of such propaganda would help explain the contempt of the American right for the United Nations and its endless talk and compulsive do-goodism, the babbling tongues and all the shades of black, and the bureaucratic scandals and loose morals, and the terrible impotence of its peacekeepers. Would you want your boy to serve under a Canadian general?

How would she know, the perplexed Yankee tourist? It may well be true, this recurrent rumour of our reigning national virtues, the repeated triumph of our lifestyle. Now living at an age when there is a clear excess of recollection over expectation, there is an accumulation of evidence about a life configured and richly embellished by Canada's exquisite ambience, a conjunction of history, geography, and what my mother called "kismet."

My ancestors were Loyalists, driven out of the American Colonies —in this instance, from New Haven—during the revolution.

Abiathar Camp and son John brought three boatloads of Loyalists to Saint John and were later given land grants by the king in the areas of Jemseg and Gagetown, in what is now Queens County.

Family lore records Abiathar's dismissal from Yale because he refused to revoke his oath of loyalty to George III. Later, he would be instrumental in persuading Benedict Arnold to switch sides and betray the revolution.

The Camps were of sturdy stock: loyal, stubborn, principled, and Ivy League. And Tory. They came to these woods and waters more than two centuries ago; they, and their heirs, are buried all around me. They have left me a good inheritance.

While my father was in Europe in July of 1936, his family summered in Woodstock and at nearby Skiff Lake. On his return, I found him full of dark foreboding about Germany and shaken by the poverty he had witnessed on the streets of London. He was convinced there would be a second world war.

He returned to California and began speaking out about what he had seen of Hitler's Germany and how certain he was that fascism meant war in Europe. It was then that he was attacked by the Hearst press and the family ban on Hearst papers was issued.

During this time, the Italian Fascists conquered the hapless Ethiopians—guns against spears—while the fascist Falange of General Franco began the civil war to overthrow the second Spanish republic. I watched these events and heard my father's voice, from a distance, a gulf of incomprehension between myself and the vague emerging shapes of the convulsions and tragedy to come.

I am nearly at the end of my narrative. I have gone to such lengths, I suppose, in order to display my bona fides, exampling White's description of the essayist, to expose my "congenitally self-centered" self. Still, a reader may be better off for knowing of whom he or she reads. And a columnist better off admitting his biases. Growing up, I developed an instant sympathy for the underdog, for the put-upon, the unemployed, the disadvantaged, and the luckless. And for the Spanish republicans and the German Jews.

My generation is the last with any memory of the Second World War and the Great Depression. I have clear memories of men coming to the door of our home in Oakland to ask for work in exchange for food. I remember their sunburned, unshaven faces and sad eyes, and their soiled clothes, and how much they looked, except for their desperate condition, like anyone else, like my own father or any of his friends.

At the end of summer of 1939, when the war came, I was in Canada, in the town of Woodstock, and almost immediately the jobless men who hung about the town bridge, the stables, and the vacant lots along the side streets, disappeared from sight. I next saw them in uniform, strutting about town in the evenings in their new army boots and wearing army caps with infantry badges.

When the war was over, public policy launched upon a prolonged process of social reform. It was as though the generation that had endured the Depression and fought the war had determined upon the establishment of a new Canadian society based upon compassion and caring and a gathered resolve that life could be made better for all Canadians by governments committed to principles of tolerance, fairness, and equity.

Today, Canadians are being told there is no longer enough to go around. We have been too generous to one another. The children of those who rebuilt Canadian society after the war are now engaged in dismantling it, urged on by their children of the second postwar generation. These efforts are being pressed by the economic interests of a new and more formidable autocracy, who not only own the resources and means of production and the new technologies, but own, to an increasing degree, the means of communication. This has not yet given us a new world but only a view of what it might look like.

It looks like hell. American economist Lester Thurow told a conference assembled at Muskoka last June that "within a few years, Western governments will have to abandon the income tax entirely, relying on sales taxes and VATs." This is the result of the behaviourial patterns of today's multinationals who are banking their money in such tax-free havens as the Grand Cayman Islands.

Corporations today earn and produce at home but bank abroad. And, embarrassed by their profits, many of them (IBM, PepsiCo) are spending their spare cash buying back shares from their shareholders. While values rise (but never enough) on Wall Street and profits soar, new product and research investment declines. So do tax revenues.

It has become clear that multinational corporatism and new patterns of cartelization have forever altered the longstanding relationships between business and society, between employer and employee, and between the nation state and the outside world.

The result has been what we see around us: structural employment, falling incomes, a vanishing middle class, all in a climate of fear, anger, and disillusion. In Ben Carniol's book on Canada's present social services system, a presumed beneficiary is quoted as saying, "I'm a single mom. I use the food bank. My child is too proud to come to a food bank with me. He holds me responsible for my poverty."

As well he should, having heard the rhetoric of the mother's accusers, the political prattle of the pontificating right. It is simply a disgrace that the failure of capitalism—its chaotic dysfunction and its disastrous default of social responsibility—has made a civic virtue of selfishness and turned the middle class upon the victims of its failure.

It would have seemed impossible, a decade ago, that Conservatives and Liberals would be joined in their abandonment of the poor. But worse is to come. Having bought the case for a capitalism beyond accountability—which agrees to sell, barter, or trade any principle or program for the public good in the interest of more satisfactory tax rates, less tedious regulation, and private sector dominance over the public interest—there is little left of politics other than the self-satisfaction of Liberals or Conservatives, who betray their people rather than disappoint the bondsmen and the bankers and the conglomerate press.

Nietzsche put it perfectly, in *The Will to Power*: "The great majority of men have no right to existence, but are a misfortune to higher men." This is a codicil for the comfortable, the affluent, and the obscenely rich in our time, as it was the inspiration for fascism earlier in our century.

The new order is not without its coterie of apologists and intellectual dandies. Indeed, it even has a political party of its own, called— irony of ironies—the "Reform" Party. Their models and values, as their political heroes, are American—the latter including such established mountebanks as Newt Gingrich, Al D'Amato, and Jesse Helms, and the ubiquitous pair of shabby parsons on the Christian right. Among these trend-setting followers of the new conservatism, American style, are rising hosts of Canadian imitators and cross-breeders, fervently devoted to the reduction of government and the elevation of the oligarchy.

It seems to me a mistake to call neo-conservatism anything other than the enemy of the society those of my generation built over the years since the war. The differences are irreconcilable; there is no common ground. As a Tory Canadian, neo-conservatism is as alien to me as is Marxism or fascism or dadaism. It rejects the idea of Canada and the ideals that have, for so long, been the inspiration for the kind of society that has become a political wonder of the world.

Maj. Gen. Lewis MacKenzie, formerly our man in command of the United Nations forces in Sarajevo, has warned, "We must not undervalue our God-given blessings as a nation to such an extent that we let them be taken from us as we sleep."

Peter Lougheed, for many years the all-conservative quarterback in our nation's politics, has warned the Tory party not to set its face against the poor. He has also expressed his unease with the increased "Americanization" of our country.

For some time, while writing the columns in this book, I seemed to be alone in my concerns. This is no longer true. The general and the former Alberta premier may not agree with any of my views, but they share my concerns. They would, I am sure, put things differently; how differently, I cannot know.

But it is the function of the columnist to say what he thinks and to say it with grace, preferably with wit, and with the full strength of his conviction. And it helps when he can write with authority earned from his own experience, so that whatever his opinion—and it can seldom be more than that—it becomes "the purification" of his own vision.

Northwood
Queens County, New Brunswick
August 1995

PART I

Carpet Bombing the Deficit

The Second Book of Genesis

MAY 25, 1985

Who liked Michael Wilson's first budget? The business community, for whom the document was supposedly drawn, has showered the finance minister with faint praise. The Liberal leader, John Turner, who is only beginning to talk this way, called the budget "gutless and sneaky." The NDP leader, Ed Broadbent, promised war to the knife, as usual.

It has been a long time since we've had a popular budget and there was no way this one could break the spell. Even so, I thought that Wilson's presentation was engaging for its earnestness, and the rationale given for his emphasis upon the difficulties created by the deficit was compelling and credible.

The finance minister is fortunate to be preaching to a new generation of taxpayers who are more worldly and sophisticated than any in Canadian history. It will be more difficult for Wilson's critics to persuade the taxpayers they have been unjustly treated than it would have been a generation ago, when most people believed government services were truly free and that wealth could be created in the mint.

There had been, as we know, a good deal of artful orchestration prior to the budget, including many dire warnings of tough measures —which could only be translated as indicating increased personal taxation—along with several inspired leaks out of finance, some of which even turned out to be accurate.

The prime minister toured the West, preparing public opinion for the worst that could be imagined as the result of being both tough and fair at the same time. When the finance minister finally got to his feet in the Commons on Thursday to let us in on his secrets, the country seemed as much bemused by the whole business as apprehensive.

There is always a lot of bunk in budget speeches and strategies, and Wilson's budget was faithful to the genre. The present minister of finance stands in a long line of predecessors who have showered incentives upon businesses—big and small—while exhorting them to invest, employ, compete, and profit. Have we ever had a finance minister who has told them anything else?

But the business community, a likely misnomer if a familiar one, has always been quick to say, while pocketing the benefits, that they really don't go far enough. Michael Wilson, it already turns out, hasn't gone far enough either, which sounds to me, as it always has, that businessmen are profoundly reluctant to accept the burden of responsibility for economic recovery.

I also believe there is an important semantic distinction between "living beyond our means," which the government insists we've been doing, and not living up to our obligations, which is more like it. No one who is not either richly insane or insanely rich wants to do away with government health services, not many want to see the federal government reduce its commitment to post-secondary education, and only the selfish would encourage the government towards any drastic reduction of transfer payments, including equalization, for the poorer provinces.

These all represent major government expenditures—a far greater "sacred trust" than so archaic a practice as welfare universality—but they do not constitute profligacy. Instead, they speak to the fact that successive federal governments have lacked the moral courage and integrity to ask Canadians to pay for services rendered, to bear the cost, so to speak, of being Canadian.

The deficit has not been the creation of the taxpayers, but a monument to the practised deception of past governments that could not bear to tell taxpayers the truth.

This may have been the best of all reasons for getting rid of the governing party responsible for this protracted reign of fiscal irresponsibility. Fundamentally, the Wilson budget is an attempt, however reluctant, to bring revenues closer to the level of expenditures by going to the nearest productive source—the individual taxpayer.

This may resemble Thatcherism more than Reaganomics but at least it's honest. As such, it ought to be welcomed as an appropriate way of marking the final passage of a bankrupt liberalism.

Wilson's budget can be celebrated as an indication of a government's willingness to come to terms with the real cost of governance; part of that is the cost of lost illusions. If there were pipe dreams about how much the deficit could be reduced by simply cutting spending, these have been dispelled by an acquaintance with the limits to arbitrary power. The notion that increased taxation might risk too great a decrease in consumption seems also to have been dispelled.

This leaves only the last and most romantic of the finance minister's dreams, which is that of the nation being rescued from penury by seven hundred thousand small businessmen, all of them summoned to action, inspired by the generosity of his faith in them. No one should doubt he believes it or even that some of them believe it too.

The truth is, and I say so reluctantly, most people think it's a crock. Meanwhile, we're at least beginning to pay our way, in itself a small matter of business between ourselves and the government of Canada and likely, in the end, the quickest way for us to get the country out of hock.

Putting the Country on Hold

DECEMBER 27, 1994

Unlike the year before, 1994 has been a difficult one. It seems to me that I have become a party of one, out of the mainstream, no longer so much an interpreter as a dissenter. The year 1993 was a strange one in Canadian politics, even though most of what happened made sense, and even though the second largest party in the House of Commons was separatist, and the third largest was Reform, which is not a party but a congregation. But these anomalies held their own logic and it was easily possible to accept their meaning and enjoy the contradictions, especially since they seemed to promise an interesting future.

This has not been so. Politics in Canada has seldom been duller, not because the issues are dull or not worthy of debate. The trouble is there is no one to debate; this narrow focus and concentration bearing on a single aspect of public policy has thrust all other considerations aside.

The single aspect of public policy is, of course, fiscal, having to do with debt and taxes. For months—month after month after month—the Canadian public has been bullied and belaboured by its government, by the Liberal-Reform parties, or party, in the House, and by the business community, its household institutes, and other spokespersons, and by the corporate media complex, all plucking on the one string, hammering the same key, and hollering the same note.

It is absolutely clear, even to the deaf, that the government's only policy is to wrestle the deficit to the ground. Apart from the deficit, all else is platitude. All else suffers from a want of commitment, a lack of energy, a loss of memory. Did we promise that? Do we need to act? Can't it wait?

The country has long since been mesmerized by this singular performance. It is easier now to live as some sort of bookkeeper, rather than as a Canadian in a country with a national agenda within a lively, ongoing political context. It is now becoming easier to consider forgoing the accepted standards of social services, to accept the argument that the Americans have known better all along about these matters, and that while the bankruptcy of social policy is inevitable, society's needs can safely be left to charity.

As we know, public policy should be a matter of choice in a free society. But there is no choice to be made between the Liberals and Reform; one could hardly articulate the scant differences among these men—mostly men—who have already agreed on their priorities. What is the difference, really, between Reform and the Liberals with regard to the strengthening of Canadian culture, the arts, and communications? As to the consideration of laws to protect gays from discrimination, what is the difference between the caucus of the Liberals and that of Reform?

Anyway, there is, by agreement, not enough time for subjects of lesser importance. Still, one might have thought the gun control measures might have been advanced more expeditiously, or the regulations on lobbying. But it is the sense of this Parliament that doing nothing is either good politics (Liberal) or good orthodoxy (Reform), and there is no dissenting voice to be heard amidst the tumult of agreement.

We could easily make it unanimous: The government has no more important task than that of bringing the deficit into balance. But most governments, particularly ones with a good majority, have been able to walk and chew gum at the same time. Besides, this much-heralded, highly hyped budget soon to come is the government's second. Its first budget came down following the discovery that the deficit was more serious than it had been led to believe. On the eve of the second budget, the economy is better and so is the forecast.

Bear in mind (as the government keeps saying), everyone is against the deficit and everyone is for removing it; the rest is detail. The minister of finance has said nothing is sacred, that he will even raise taxes if he must. (Which suggests he probably will, in support of the treasury myth of "equal sacrifice"—a food tax for the poor, a luxury tax for the rich.) Still, we all should bear in mind that no one stands in the way of the minister and, on budget day, no one will.

Because the minister has nothing to fear from Parliament, he has even less to fear from the voiceless in the land, or from parties-of-one, like myself. After all, he has "consulted" and heard a good deal of advice, most of it from people comfortable with his priorities and supportive of his purpose.

My own view, not widely held in approved circles of opinion, is that the minister's priority suffers from his excess of zeal, that the best way to reduce the deficit is slowly, and by growing the economy (the strongest among the G-7), by strengthening Canada's sense of nationhood, and by reforming the tax system by collecting taxes. Finally, any government whose first priorities exclude addressing the nation's cultural needs, providing for the health of its people and for the improved education of its young, is unworthy of its charge and, if Liberal, of its name.

Jean Charest, Communist

MARCH 11, 1994

A twenty-five-year-old veteran Ontario youth leader, who is an officer of the Progressive Conservative youth organization for the terminally adolescent, interrupted an otherwise peaceful political gathering in Toronto last week to complain that the speaker, Hon. Jean Charest, leader pro-tem of the federal Progressive Conservative Party, was saying Communist things, expressing Communist sentiments, generally sounding like a pinko, whacko Comm-symp.

Those who have since spoken with members of Charest's audience have failed to unearth anything having been said that could have triggered the reaction. It may be that any politician these days who speaks in a quiet voice and espouses moderate opinion—in view of all the wingnuts now in hyperactive practice, from Limbaugh to Zhirinovsky—*sounds* Communist. Someone, for example, might say that with so many empty houses out there, it seems a pity so many people are still sleeping on the sidewalks. Such sentiments might not lead to an arrest, but there would be complaints, nonetheless, about too many people who were not properly toilet-trained and are thus given to irresponsible, undisciplined thinking. My God —where would the money come from?

The gravest danger Canadians face today is from those who claim to know how Canadians feel about their lot. It is not true that most Canadians live in fear of the deficit, can't sleep nights for worrying about the deficit, and are willing to make personal sacrifices—such as giving up the school bus for their neighbour's children, or half their Canadian Tire money—if it would help reduce the deficit.

Put another way, there are probably as many Canadians who are *seriously* worried about the deficit as are worried about Jean Charest being a Communist. However many of them there are, you will likely be relieved to learn, most of them appear to reside in Ontario and are provincial Tories.

Nonetheless, there has been a relentless barrage of thundering editorials, burst of long-range artillery from the upper windows of board rooms, and heavy bombardment from the Business Council on National Issues, the Canadian Chamber of Commerce, and the *Financial Times*, along with continuous sniper fire from columnists manning the business pages. For an average Canadian pedestrian, the streets are no longer safe; better to stay home counting your money, if you have any, than risk being blown away by a six-inch shell aimed at the deficit.

The war on the deficit is not a Liberal war, or a Tory war, not even a Reform war. You will recall being told, at least eight times in your life so far, that "tourism is everyone's business." Well, the war on the deficit is everyone's war, whether you feel like fighting or not. Some of my best friends are deficit warriors; on the other hand, most of my friends think the whole thing is a crock. Is this because I run with the wrong crowd? Do you suppose some of them are Communists?

I don't know Charest's position on the deficit; he could not have been in Ottawa as long as he has without at least paying lip service. The Liberals, who appeared at one time to believe they could reduce the deficit by spending more money they didn't have, are now indistinguishable from the crowd they replaced. Paul Martin Jr. is every bit as serious a finance minister as Michael Wilson ever was (one can't say more than that for either of them) and Martin has spared no one—well, almost no one—from soldiering in his war against the deficit. Still, it's Wilson's War redux.

Even in Friday's paper, renewed action on the deficit-fighting front: this time, further reductions in Via Rail. You remember Via Rail? (It's a train—was a train.) This has allowed some surcease in the deficit fighters' war against its prime enemies: the unemployed, students, and the elderly who keep getting ill. It is a slow newsday when the deficit fighters do not overrun some position held by the jobless or terminate the scholarly careers of a few students. But war is heck, as General Sherman said, and since the budget deficit is even larger than the Liberals thought (they believed the Tory estimates, sillies), there is a need for a large body count among those idlers who are looking for work, not looking for work, or who have never looked for work.

At the same time last week, in the continuing war of nerves, the deficit fighters leaked word that they were thinking of downwardly adjusting pensions paid to seniors. After letting the old geezers sweat that out awhile, they further announced—heh, heh—they were just kidding. It was after that pregnant moment in the war that they went after Via Rail again.

South of the Border, Down Mexico Way

JANUARY 3, 1995

While we are all reeling from the news that Canada is in such bad shape, the minister of finance is *thinking* of raising taxes. We should think about Mexico. Things appear to be so critical, fiscally speaking, in Mexico that bailiffs from the International Monetary (are you standing at attention?) Fund have taken suites in Mexico City's better hotels so as to monitor the conduct of the Mexican government and, if deemed appropriate, take the country over and annex it to the New York office of Solomon Brothers.

No one could be blamed for believing Mexico is in a state of severe financial crisis, what with the peso falling and the trade deficit rising. But the real clue to the seriousness of the situation in Mexico is that Canada is sending money to help. In fact, we had already been sending money, sort of a tithe, to our new NAFTA partners. All in all, various countries and the banks—which are richer—have contributed either $18 billion or $28 billion (depending on how you look at it) in the form of credits, loans, and other forms of "international" assistance.

Canada's share in this is a modest $1.5 billion, we are told. Put me down as somewhat overjoyed to learn we can afford it. As C. D. Howe—the Liberal cabinet minister, not the think tank—once said, "What's a million?" Allowing for a generation of inflation, a billion Canadian dollars today is not a very significant sum. Still, that kind of money would go a long way towards sustaining Canada's hard-pressed cultural institutions about to be shredded (we have been warned) by the deficit warriors in Debt City.

But not to cavil. Isn't it nice to know, when some country's finances are in peril and the affluent nations and the international banks rally to help, that Canada is *there*? I mean, for a country proclaimed daily in our national newspapers, and out of the mouths of our politicians, as down and out, no longer able to afford its accustomed generous spirit, and—any day now—about to be impounded by the IMF, I ask: How come we get invited to those meetings?

As pleased and proud as we should be to know we're helping Mexico, we could have begged off. "We gave at the office," Paul Martin should have told them when he was called. Or, "Our cheque is in the mail. Sent by Canada Post, on Boxing Day."

There are, however, more important considerations in this $18 (or $28) billion Mexican bandaid. Whatever happened to today's ultimate wisdom? That which saith, "You can't solve a problem by throwing money at it." Why are we, and all those banks, throwing money at Mexico? Apparently, we're throwing money at the Mexican government because the world's senior politicians and wealthiest bank managers think it will help.

Caramba! But should we be throwing money at the Mexican government? There are alternatives: a year's subscription to the *Financial Post*; a planeload of editorial writers. Or both.

Further insight into Mexico's current crisis, if such it be, is found in my morning national newspaper. "The [Mexican] middle class and the wealthy," it is written, "have benefited from the market-oriented reforms of recent years, but working class wages still have not recovered to 1980 levels." Clearly, the Mexican problem—or part of it—must have to do with throwing money at the wrong working class.

The editorial writers we should send down there to enlighten the masses could remind them of the importance of keeping costs down and competitive spirits up, and thinking globally whilst journeying on the information highway, as Mexico hurtles towards the next millennium.

One can hardly emphasize enough the importance of downsizing, privatizing, and North American free trade—all the things Mexicans have recently concentrated upon and which richly contributed to the mess they are now in.

My morning paper concludes its Mexican news on a defiant note: "In the longer run, Mexican officials and analysts say the problems should blow over . . . As well, the peso's devaluation should lead to an export boom as Mexican products become cheaper in overseas markets."

In the longer run, of course, as British economist John Maynard Keynes once said, we'll all be dead. But we should not now fail to note the content of irony in all this business.

The fall of the peso has been accompanied by a backsliding Canadian dollar. Optimists in Mexico City see the devalued peso as an economic boom leading to improved exports. In Canada, the slumping dollar has already paid corporate dividends through increased earnings in U.S. trade, but the minister of finance sees it all through the glass darkly. The falling dollar reminds him of his need to raise taxes.

Meanwhile, as the G-7 nation with the most highly rated economy of the nineties, we continue to cry poor mouth. Even so, proud but poor, we have a billion and a half for the IMF crusade to save the peso in Mexico. But, the time may soon be at hand when someone in Debt City, or down at the *Daily Conglomerate News*, will warn us that Canada is in such bad shape we may have to ask Mexico for help.

But I Only Wanted to Renew My Subscription

JANUARY 13, 1995

The week's most intriguing news was to be informed, on Friday the 13th, that Canada had been noticed by the *Wall Street Journal*. In an editorial seething with moral outrage, the *Journal*—America's foremost financial publication—dumped on Canada, and its simple folk, proclaiming Canada had become "an honorary member of the Third World."

The *Journal* warned if things go on this way, Canada will have to call in the International (pause here for ruffles and flourishes) Monetary Fund to "stabilize" its falling currency. The *Journal's* editorial, written with a sort of balanced hysteria, cited as good news "the most impressive performance" of Ralph Klein, the premier of Alberta; it praised the plan of "the Ontario Conservative [*sic*] Party . . . to cut the top rate of income tax in the province," and gave New Brunswick a pat on the head because that province "abolished the school board bureaucracy and imposed tough workfare requirements." As for Saskatchewan, the *Journal* noted approvingly, it "has closed many marginal rural hospitals."

This in-depth overview of Canada was backlit by illuminations from the Fraser Institute, Canada's preeminent right-wing think tank, and by a former chief economist for the Royal Bank, and by Sherry Cooper, the present chief economist for Nesbitt Burns in Toronto. ("Canada has political uncertainty," Cooper informed the *Journal*, "[and] large budget deficits have created some nervousness.") The consensus among all seemed to support the *Journal's* thesis: Canada can't go on like this. No, it can't. It can't, can't, can't, that's all. Just can't.

On the day before the *Journal's* editorial board had its nervous breakdown over Canada, two of its inquiring reporters had written an article that, to give you an idea of its general tone, began by saying, "If you think the Mexican peso is America's only basket-case currency . . ."

You get the drift? The punch line in this Wall Street Journalese is also found in the original story: "To many economists," wrote the

Journal reporters, naming none of them, "the main issue is that Canadians have lived too high on the hog for too long."

It is not hard to understand why the *Wall Street Journal* would go ballistic thinking about Canada. Canada is ranked first among the nations of the world as enjoying the highest quality of life. Among the G-7, Canada's economy is ranked the most productive. Canada has its own publicly financed health care plan. Canada has strict gun control laws, allows gays in its military, and does not allow its elected politicians to take money under the table from so-called "political action committees" representing special interests. Canadians have a longer life expectancy and a lower infant mortality rate than do Americans.

America leads Canada comfortably in homicides, drive-by-shootings, arson, assault, battery, and homelessness. The most influential radio voice in America is that of Rush Limbaugh; in Canada, it is Peter Gzowski. The hottest political property in America is Newt Gingrich; in Canada, it's nobody.

Who can blame the *Wall Street Journal*—the certain trumpet and dutiful apologist for the New Right and the new American oligarchy —for its distemper? Are not Canadians an affront to all America stands for in today's competitive world? And is not Canada, its society and its values, the most egregious contradiction to the pious promulgations of the *Wall Street Journal*?

Canada, writes the *Journal*, gnashing its editorial teeth, "has now become an honorary member of the Third World in the unmanageability of its debt problem." Of course, membership in the Third World—in the view of the *Journal* and its admirers—has as its first criterion neither hunger, ignorance, nor disease—but debt. This, anyway, according to these bright, middle-aged old men who guard the ramparts of America's free enterprise at the *Journal*.

We should pity them, even while one of Canada's national dailies bows before the blinding light of their vision. "The Wall Street Journal warned yesterday," editorialized the *Globe and Mail*, breathing heavily, that Canada (like Mexico) is "flirting with the financial abyss." Holy Toledo, Robin: Is that a debt wall I see coming?

We might take another view of this Drastic Debt Scenario. Let us assume, to please the *Wall Street Journal* and its Canadian admirers, the worst happens. Who gets hurt? Well, the bondholders, of course, who will take a bath. Nearly all of them, we're told, are foreigners. Then, the Americans, for whom Canada is their most lucrative customer and trading partner. And then, still more Americans—those who own most of Canada's commerce, one way or another.

My question is: Why would all those smart acquisitive people stand idly by and watch the Canadian dollar fall, and the whole country hit the wall and tumble into a "financial abyss"? It seems like a lot of trouble to go to, just to support the assertion that America has the best gun laws in the world.

John Fund is Loosely Connected

JANUARY 27, 1995

The *Wall Street Journal* editorial that raised so much Canadian dander (including mine) was written by a man named John Fund. In his editorial, Fund nominated Canada as "an honorary member of the Third World," citing Canada's unsatisfactory (to him) efforts to manage its debt. The editorial came on the heels of a story on Canada written by two *Journal* reporters who had reported, among other things, that Canadians "have lived too high on the hog for too long."

The portrait of Canada as a country of high-livers awash in debt is being sedulously cultivated by right-wing organs in the United States and by minor league organ-grinders in the Great White North. As a generality, it is partly true. Canadians live longer and healthier lives than do Americans. It is an American opinion, shared by the *Wall Street Journal*, the insurance industry, and the private health care business, that we can't afford to do so much longer.

This month, editorial writer Fund has been the spokesman for the They-Can't-Do-That-Can-They? movement against Canada's suspect lifestyle. The CBC, another Canadian unprivatized freestanding insult to the disciples of Rush Limbaugh, invited Fund to discuss his editorial outlook on Canada with two or three Canadians, one of them a friend of Fund, and another, myself, who had never heard of him. Fund's friend was Eric Margolis, a columnist for the *Toronto Sun*; during the voice checks leading into the show, Fund, who was in

New York, and Margolis agreed to meet for lunch when the *Journal* editor was next in Toronto. It was from within this snug bed of camaraderie that I rounded upon Fund for his editorial, citing the "familiar" (American) ignorance and arrogance, the mistaken "facts," and the damage the editorial had done to Canada. Margolis, of course, dissented.

An enthusiastic Margolis, I recalled, had written an endorsement of Fund's piece in the *Toronto Sun* a week after it had appeared: "In a stinging editorial last week," Margolis informed his readers, "the *Wall Street Journal* wrote that Canada was broke and facing a major financial crisis . . . the *Journal* editorial was wrong on one key point. Canada's financial crisis is not coming. It began four months ago . . . [but] hasn't been noticed because it's developing slowly and largely out of sight."

Another thing developing slowly and out of sight was editorial writer Fund's knowledge of Canada. The *Toronto Star*'s Thomas Walkom had already tried—two days before the Margolis embrace of the *Journal* piece—to correct some of Fund's assertions about Canada. When Fund was challenged about his misstatements, he informed CBC viewers that he had got much of his information from Andrew Coyne, an editorial writer and columnist for the *Globe and Mail*.

Hearing about Fund's Canadian sources (which also included the Fraser Institute) reminded me that the *Globe* had reprinted Fund's editorial, the day after it had appeared in the *Journal*, under the compelling headline, "Bankrupt Canada." The *Globe* also reprinted the article written by the two reporters; it had appeared in the *Journal* the day before the editorial, under the heading, "Basket-case currency."

On the same day the *Globe* reprinted Fund's editorial, it published one of its own. Under the headline, "The message in the dollar," the *Globe* opined, "The forces weakening the Canadian dollar go beyond the fallout from the collapse of the Mexican peso." The *Globe* then switched to Fund's editorial: "Mexico isn't the only U.S. neighbour flirting with the financial abyss, the Wall Street Journal warned yesterday. Turn around and check out Canada, which has become an honourary member of the Third World . . ." and so on.

The *Journal* editorial did some damage to Canada in the world's exchange markets; certainly, no one in New York or Toronto would argue that it helped. More likely, it cost Canadians, and will continue to do so, in the eyes of currency speculators who, like wild birds, flutter at every shadow.

But it is interesting that this damage could be inflicted by one so uninformed on Canada as to be barely able to pronounce Saskatchewan, a province he appeared to have first heard of in the "Basket-case currency" story in his own paper. And while it is touching to know Fund consulted with the *Globe and Mail* before writing his Canadian *magnum opus*, it is a little discomforting we were not told of this intellectual-ideological nexus betwixt the editorial boards in New York and Toronto. Anyway, the warmed-over editorial in one of Canada's national newspapers, quoting the *Journal* quoting itself, merely serves to remind us what a small world it is after all. If only we knew.

The late Robert Tweedie, who was Lord Beaverbrook's man in New Brunswick, and myself were returning to our hotel following the Ezzard Charles-Rocky Marciano heavyweight championship fist fight held some years ago in New York. Our friendly cab driver asked Tweedie where he was from. Tweedie told him New Brunswick, Canada, adding, "I don't imagine you've ever heard of New Brunswick."

"Oh yeah," our driver said. "It's up there on the Saskatchewan frontier."

It would not surprise me to know he is now a senior editorial writer on the *Wall Street Journal*. I like to think of him joining Fund and Margolis for lunch next week in Toronto.

Confessions of an Unaffordable Canadian
JANUARY 31, 1995

On a bright, sharply crisp winter's morning a short while ago, I was standing outside the CBC's studios in Fredericton taking on deep draughts of cold fresh air. I was shortly to be secluded in a small, soundproofed room as one of a number of fellow citizens summoned by Peter Gzowski to answer the question, "Can we afford to be Canadians?" Who wouldn't take a deep breath?

We are being asked this question all the time these days, usually by those who are either snugly affluent or smugly powerful, or both. As it turns out, most of them are free traders who enjoy their own private medical plans and pensions, and who can play golf any time they like. They, and the Gingrich/Limbaugh Canadian wind-up think-alikes who serve them, press for answers from the nation's editorial pulpits and the endowed institutes of right-wing apologia.

The *Wall Street Journal* spoke for all of them. "To many economists," the *Journal* said, approvingly, "the main issue is that Canadians have lived too high on the hog for too long."

The affordability of remaining Canadian is a serious part of the question. It deserves serious thought and serious answers, which Canadians are getting daily in mind-reeling, gut-wrenching, teeth-aching detail from some of the world's most serious journalism. Canada leads the world in serious journalism and in journalists who take themselves seriously.

The affordability issue, as a result, tends to be overworked. The other issue is another and perhaps better question: What sort of Canadian *can* we afford to be? And what do critics, such as the *Journal*, mean by "Canadians [who have] lived too high on the hog?" What Canadians?

I may be a little sensitive about this because I suspect I'm one of them. I have lived beyond my means during several periods of my life. I could not have afforded university, but because I was a veteran I came directly out of the army and into university—three of them, all tuition free. Like most anyone else, I've had occasional visits to the doctor's office or the hospital—more recently, to get a new heart—and I have paid little if anything directly for services rendered.

There was a period when I earned what seemed a lot of money (to me at least), over half of which I returned to the government in taxes; the rest I spent. Many years ago, during my tycoon phase, I recall lunching at Winston's, in Toronto, with Barbara Amiel, among others. Barbara was going on over cocktails about paying taxes and how excessive the demands were, and I said I was happy to pay taxes because I thought, as a Canadian, I got a good return on my money. This silenced Barbara almost until we got to the petits fours.

Today, I am the recipient of the Canada Pension and Old Age Security, for which, in my halcyon days, I paid handsomely. The OAS, which I receive even though I feel eight years younger than Lloyd Axworthy, I take as consolation for all I've put up with and put out as a taxpayer for the past half-century. I realize this may sound self-serving and probably is.

I introduced such anecdotal material as evidence of a greater reality. Canada's social security system has long represented confirmation of a social contract between Canadians and their federal government. Most of that contract has been proposed, endorsed, and enacted in my lifetime and it has created a society until now determined to meet its responsibilities to its children, the aged, the unemployed, and those who are ill.

I believe these measures have defined the country. And not only because of what they provided, but because of the kind of society that flourished as a result. The Americans, quite rightly, have found us uninteresting, if scenic. But we have enjoyed an activist political agenda, a progressive political tradition, and a social culture of tolerance and compassion. Perhaps it was too good to last. What with our living too high on the hog, I mean.

But the question is really less about affordability and more about being Canadian. We would be naive not to understand what the critics, both here and abroad, mean by "unaffordable" Canadianism, which is precisely our medicare and pension programs, where "the big bucks" are. If we would agree only to privatize health care *and* the CBC, instant continental endorsement would be offered as to our solvency.

What Canada's critics seek is a new commercial contract to replace the social contract that has shaped us as a people. This is the question rephrased and the one Canadians need to answer. It is astonishing how many appear willing to reject the present social contract for any new model. Possibly, amidst the clamour of the argument over affordability, the majority has not yet seen the question whole.

Newt Gingrich, the $4.5 million author and titular head of yuppy conservatism, was quoting Peter Drucker the other day. Drucker, Congressman Gingrich was saying, believed in the need "to cultivate disagreement" before settling upon the great issues of the day. Drucker was right; so is Gingrich. The argument over "affordable Canadians" is far from over, but only in its early stage of cultivation.

David Slater's Mission Impossible

FEBRUARY 3, 1995

As to the busy week just past, where to begin? The Liberals brought their federal caucus to Toronto and put them on display before all of Canada's national newspapers and the TV networks. The caucus went on record as opposed to tax increases (the Canadian Press reported indications that the finance department had already nixed increased taxes on wealth as being "too complex and unfair"). The caucus was also resolutely for deficit reduction, deeply committed to "social reform," but not yet ready to trade human resources minister Lloyd Axworthy for a player to be named later.

The prime minister, as has become familiar, brought his own drummer to the meeting. He would not rule out possible tax increases and he pronounced social reform as continuing at the same breathless pace. "Social reform," he told the media after the meeting, "is as much a part of the equation as reforming our fiscal system." The prime minister's comments further strengthened widespread suspicion he is soft on the deficit, which, in the judgement of some, accounts for his high approval ratings in the public opinion polls.

Such insouciance did not escape the attention of the *Globe and Mail*, which inserted the next day, in its news coverage of the caucus meeting, the following weather advisory: ". . . interest rate increases have sent the cost of servicing the deficit soaring and foreign commentators, including the Wall Street Journal last month and again yesterday, have pressured Ottawa to confront the deficit."

One does not always find editorial comment tucked in the folds of news reporting, but then, one does not often see editorials about Canada in the *Wall Street Journal* twice in consecutive months. My own opinion on this phenomenon is that the *Journal* has a Canada fetish and its senior editors will soon be going to lunch dressed as Mounties. The other view of the appearance of a second editorial on Canada is that the *Journal* is still trying to recover from its first one.

The *Wall Street Journal*'s first hit on Canada was meant to teach Canadians their place and keep them in it. It impressed the hell out of the *Globe and Mail*, which had hailed it in an editorial of its own and, to begin with, had privately contributed to the *Journal*'s informed tone. Both papers agreed that Canada and Mexico were similarly racked by debt; any day now, visitors to Toronto would see begging Canadian children running the streets seeking alms from passing cars.

The *Journal*'s hysteria and hyperbole impressed one Canadian reader, David Slater, as "unwarranted and inflammatory" and "well below [the *Journal*'s] usual standards of judgement and integrity." But buttering up the *Journal* gets you nothing, as Slater learned, after having taken pains to write the editors in an effort to improve their general knowledge of Canada.

David Slater was formerly a ranking public servant in the Department of Finance, Ottawa, and for seven years a director, then chairman, of the Economic Council of Canada. Slater graduated from Queen's, going on to the University of Chicago for his M.A. and Ph.D. He had taught economics at Queen's and Stanford and been president of York University.

Trying to set things right—nothing you should try to do in the absence of witnesses—Slater wrote the *Journal*, in part: "You praise the government cutbacks in Saskatchewan and Alberta, but make no mention of the much larger cutbacks undertaken in federal government operations. You say Alberta's provincial debt has been cut by 80%; you must mean the current operating deficit which is a much smaller accomplishment . . . Your numbers for proposed reductions in the top personal rate of income tax in Ontario are for Ontario tax on top of the federal tax, not tax on income. Privatizing the Canadian National Railways and Canada Post would make trivial changes to Canada's debt position . . . Altogether this is a sloppy and misleading piece of work on your part."

Otherwise, one must assume, the *Journal* got everything right. Except, as Slater goes on to inform, its description of Canada's dollar as "a basket-case currency" like the Mexican peso: ". . . judged by the availability of credit and the interest differentials, Canadian government credits continue to rank among the world's best . . . A large part of Canada's external debt is denominated in Canadian dollars, not foreign currencies, and thus is not an immediate foreign exchange threat. Despite great difficulties from time to time, the Canadian government has never failed during this century to meet the interest and capital payments of its external debt. In proportion to its size, Canada has been one of the largest net lenders to the IMF since the end of the Second World War."

Slater wrote his letter and faxed it to the *Wall Street Journal* on January 13, the day after its editorial had appeared in New York and on the same day the *Globe* had republished it for its own readers, along with its own editorial drum roll on the page opposite. The *Journal* has not yet published Slater's letter, possibly on the grounds he knows too much. Anyway, the *Wall Street Journal* is under no obligation to inform its readers of the truth about Canada.

Failing an announcement that John Fund, the author of *WSJ* Editorial One, has been awarded a Pulitzer Prize for investigative reporting (Third World Division), I promise I shall write no more on this matter even though—let the record show—it has been as revealing to Canadians as it has been inconsequential.

I Did It My Way, Didn't We?

FEBRUARY 7, 1995

A letter to the editor in one of my morning papers encapsules the angst now devouring the innards of the neo-Canadian right: "Is it not time," the writer asks, "that we, who have spent years making a go of it on our own, carried the day and enlightened our politicians as to our willingness and the necessity to take these necessary tough measures . . . ?"

The "necessary tough measures" referred to are, of course, "the kind of changes Ralph Klein introduced to get Alberta back on its financial feet." (Whatever will we do when we don't have Ralph Klein to uplift us anymore?) Notwithstanding the quasi-legendary feats of Klein, what catches the eye in the rhetorical question above are the exalted words: "we, who have spent years making a go of it on our own."

We are not only a new nation of immigrants, but also a country of newly autonomous old Canadians. These latter are the folk who clearly have made it; not only that, they also have it made. But more impressive is the claim they did it on their own.

As fortunate citizens of one of the world's most advanced and prospering democracies, they remind one of former Texas Governor Ann Richards' description of scion-politician George Bush, that "he was born on third base and thought he'd hit a triple." People who hit triples the day they were born are common everywhere; in Canada, they usually arrive at third base later in life. On arrival, however, they are under the same delusion that they got there on their own.

These are the raw recruits Preston Manning is counting on to be his foot soldiers in tomorrow's "Tax Revolt." It is hard to say what Manning has in mind for the pending revolution—harder still when hearing him skate around the subject—but it appears to be an invitation to individual acts of heroic anarchy as well as offering opportunity for those Canadians who are self-made and auto-solvent to gather at mass rallies with their leader in locales other than Edmonton.

The concept of no-tax-increases-ever is American, born out of populism and wedded to oligarchical self-interest. The world's happiest and most successful revolution began in Boston Harbor as a protest against tax on tea, inspiring the revolutionary slogan "No taxation without representation." But even though the Reform Party and its leader seem to get most of their inspiration and ideas from next door, in the Great Republic, that doesn't mean the present Canadian tax system is not revolting and that Canadians who pay the most in taxes, in relative terms, have had the least say in preparing fiscal policy.

Many Canadians assume the present tax system is fair; since everyone complains, it seems likely. Still, Canadians should be cautious about signing on to a tax revolt with Manning when the tax tables are already loaded against them. For example, almost 50 percent of the tax revenues comes from personal income tax; only 6.7 percent comes from corporations. At the same time, in recent years, personal income tax has become less progressive with the tax rate on the wealthy reduced nearly to the rates for middle-income taxpayers.

It was interesting to see and hear from the president of the

Toronto Stock Exchange who appeared on CNN the other day, speaking to this month's hot topic in right-wing circles: "Is Canada just like Mexico or worse?" The TSE head man, Frederick Ketchen, ducked the question (as did everyone else except The Narrator), but he managed to appear grave and to say the next budget should contain more reductions in government spending "and no tax increases."

No surprise there. But it does reveal the essential banality of much of the advice being given the federal finance minister, Paul Martin, during this prolonged run-up to Budget Day. There is near unanimity that Canada has a debt problem and that fiscal measures are needed to reduce the deficit. After that, just about everyone the minister knows, hears from, talks to, and listens to, sounds like the president of the Toronto Stock Exchange.

Canadians are led to believe if Martin raises corporation taxes, which have nothing to do with taxes on small business, the sky will fall, investors will flee—perhaps to Mexico—while venture capital will wither away. Thus, the only way to reduce the deficit is to reduce spending, the details left to others.

As for raising taxes on those Canadians who have "made it" on their own, the plaint is that obliging them to pay a higher tax rate than those who haven't yet self-made themselves will discourage people from wanting to become rich or richer. Of this, there is scant empirical evidence other than in the case of those chronically on welfare, living on pittance, where argument has been forcefully made that only by cutting off their incomes altogether will they become successfully self-sufficient.

It is true that the federal government could further reduce its expenditures simply by ceasing to be a government at all. It has already become a cringing, sidling, shuffling apologist for our having a central government and frequently advertises its ambition to withdraw from any program, or ditch any policy, likely to cost money. The finance minister has the opportunity to become his own man here—in this new spirit of self-creation. He can take those "necessary tough measures" by obliging his friends and former patrons to pay their fair share of the cost of being Canadian. Out of equity will come solvency.

Moody Blues

FEBRUARY 17, 1995

According to Moody's Investors Service Inc., as breathlessly recounted on Friday by one of Canada's national daily newspapers, something is about to happen, or might happen, or is likely to happen, to Canada's "treasured triple-A credit rating on most of its debt."

For those who prefer bleak certainties to dire warnings, Moody's is not for you. Canada's credit rating is "in jeopardy," the newspaper headline informs. Downgrading is "probable," no matter what finance minister Paul Martin does in his forthcoming budget. Put another way, "a downgrade appears all but inevitable." A person identified as "a senior analyst for Canada" who toils anonymously at Moody's Investors Service Inc., in New York (gosh), is paraphrased as saying "even a strong federal budget could do little to ward off a downgrade." As it turns out, reading carefully, the "all but inevitable downgrade" is presently "under review for a possible downgrade." You get the picture.

According to a columnist found among the financial pages of the same newspaper, "There is now about a 70 percent chance that Moody's will downgrade Canadian government debt after it completes its review over the next couple of months." On the other hand, reading on, we are told, "Mr. Martin *may* be able to avoid the downgrade with his budget." This, however, contradicts all the drum-beating on page one, but by the time we get to page B2 in the financial section, matters only get worse as the story line diverges and dissolves into a new, enlarged premise: "Moody's officials yesterday made it clear that the review is more than just a prebudget watching brief on the federal debt. The entire country has coagulated into a giant debt clot that threatens to destabilize the whole economy."

Well, as for me, I think Canadians are being jerked around by non-news and manipulative editorializing (i.e., Canada is in worse shape than Mexico), Friday's adumbrations about Moody's "credit watch" being the most recent. When the "news" broke, the sparrows took flight; the Canadian dollar dropped, bond interest rose. As a result, speculators made money. Or lost it. But in Canada, the unwary and unwashed welcomed aboard another demon to join the IMF bogey, the spooks of higher interest rates, and the hobgoblins of higher taxes: Moody's Investors Service Inc. One reason for not taking a short position on Canada's future credit rating is that I have never known Moody's Investor Service Inc. to be right. Were they right about Mexico? Are they right about Britain? How about Spain? How do we know? On the other hand, I've never known Moody's to be wrong. The truth is, until my morning national daily brought it up, Moody's has never mattered, right or wrong, upgraded or downgraded, to me or anyone else I knew.

There must be a reason why Moody's has suddenly been introduced to Canadians through the front page of a national daily newspaper as some sort of Omnipotent Oracle. It's not that Canada has a giant coagulated debt clot, apparently discovered by a nuclear economist in a white coat over in Moody's busy laboratories. By carefully containing expenditure creep and by a judicious increase in selective taxes, plus an aspirin a day, the nation's coagulation could be remedially treated. Surely, Paul Martin could make a fist of that.

When the *Globe and Mail* published the *Wall Street Journal*'s ignoramus inventory of Canada's efforts to treat its deficit problems, comparing Canada's condition to Mexico's, the markets responded just as they did when Moody's began muttering aloud on the street last Friday. The federal finance minister has sounded aggrieved, saying Moody's conduct "surprised" him. Roy Romanow, the premier of Saskatchewan, who has done a better job knocking down his province's deficit than has Ralph Klein in Alberta, asked why Moody's was in such a rush.

We don't know and why should it matter? What is obvious is that some damage was done to Canada's financial interests and our politicians sounded injured but none sounded outraged. It should be noted, *inter alia*, that following the *Wall Street Journal*'s loud belch, the markets trembled but then recovered and the dollar strengthened. Once the *Journal* had retreated to its cave, Moody's then made its appearance among the pages of the *Globe*, giving further flight to the sparrows.

If Canadians are supposed to take this war of nerves seriously, they should first determine who their enemy is. For once, it can be said the enemy is not their politicians. It is, instead, this weird new economic system that has made us so vulnerable to the ignorance and indifference of total strangers, people without names or faces whose importance is heralded by the acronyms that precede them—NAFTA, IMF, and NYSE. These have in common great concentrations of wealth, unprincipled power, and arbitrary authority. Canadians do not get to vote for them; they only get to vote for those who will need to defer to them.

Accompanied by this mounting barrage of disembodied threats from abroad is the promise of relief if only Canadians will conduct themselves in approved multinational conglomerate fashion as sub-servient minority shareholders. Slash and burn; above all, do not tax. This is America's agenda, the world over. When one contemplates the range of interests represented by those now in mock fear and ter-ror over Canada's credit rating, it at least makes sense.

Everyone Knows Conrad Black, But Have You Met Maria Minna?

FEBRUARY 21, 1995

This just came in: A group of MPs has joined the Council of Canadians in warning the federal government against tampering with Canada's social programs in its forthcoming budget. Included were four Liberal MPs—Warren Allmand, first elected to the com-mons in 1965, and parliamentary newcomers Mark Assad, Wayne Easter, and Maria Minna.

In the Canadian Press story appearing in my morning newspaper, these protesting Liberals "wanted to show finance minister Paul Martin another side to the prebudget debate—not just demands for no new taxes and spending cuts." Canadian Press also issued a warn-ing of its own; the Liberals mentioned in the story, it reported, "have backgrounds as either social or labour activists."

It's all too true about this Liberal gang of four. Allmand is a noto-rious wet, a compassion freak, a Liberal in the bargain. CP quotes him saying Liberals should keep their election campaign promises—I mean, what sort of wingnut is this?—and reduce the deficit through "job creation, economic growth, trimming government waste and tax fairness."

As for the others, CP also has the goods on them. Mark Easter, it reports, "was once head of the National Farmers' Union." In any modern, civilized country, a guy like that would be locked up. As for Maria Minna, wait till you hear this. You thought you knew about Maria Minna? I'm quoting CP and not making it up:

"Ms. Minna once headed the Toronto United Way." And just to show what a United Way compassion creep Minna really is, listen to her fiscal views; they'll blow your mind.

"We're not overtaxed," she is quoted saying. "Companies of this country are not overtaxed. We seem to have bought into that kind of jargon and it's not true."

Well, I wouldn't blame anyone for wondering what the world is coming to. What with Allmand arguing Liberals should keep their promises, and Easter, who is just another trade unionist with hayseed in his ears, and Minna, an exposed United Way chair, all agreeing with him, a normal person could suffer a twinge of compassion for poor Paul Martin, the finance minister, except that's *outré* these days, so far as feeling twinges go.

According to Conrad Black, the chairperson of Hollinger Inc. and a lot else, "Despite the best efforts of the 'caring and compassionate' school of Canadian nationalism, the only believable rationale for a Canada separate from the United States has been the principle of a distinctive bi-cultural nationalism."

On the same day Canadian Press broke the story on Allmand, Minna, et al, my other morning paper published parts of a Black piece due to appear in next month's *Foreign Affairs* magazine. In the piece, Black repeats his earlier promulgation conveyed to Preston Manning several years ago, given the hypothesis of Québec separating from Canada. According to Manning, Black "felt that there could be worse fates than for English-speaking Canada to end up in the American orbit."

Updated in the March issue of *Foreign Affairs*, Black's hypothesis has become more sanguine: "The United States . . . would eventually embrace a fragmented Canada—either by satellization, partial absorption or outright fusion, whichever Canadians wished. As un-Canadian though this opinion might be now, no amount of spontaneous or orchestrated histrionics about compassion and the caring state would have much impact on the timetable, however enviable the perceived quality of life or keen the patriotic fervour . . ."

It's been a long time since people like Allmand and Wayne Easter have had to be explained simply because they announced themselves opposed to conventional wisdom. Black frames the Zeitgeist perfectly. "Canada has now reached the point," he writes, "where neither of its two distinctive missions—socialistic welfare statism and coddling Québec—is tenable."

It's a neat argument; heads I win, tails you lose. Win or lose the referendum, the country we knew is history. At the risk of sounding patriotic, I rather like the views of Maria Minna who, for all I know, may be as bright as Conrad Black. Many Canadians do seem to have bought into Black's kind of jargon.

Certainly, the Canadian people are presently undergoing a relentless media barrage of right-wing continental reaction fueled by many of the world's most voracious predatory interests.

The front page of my other morning paper (I forgot to say) features a photograph of two Reform Party MPs carrying mailbags allegedly containing "thousands of petitions against tax increases" for delivery to Paul Martin.

These are the pleadings of the gullible, eager to protect the tax tables from the principles of fairness, resolved to make secure the tax shelters of the rich and the swollen profits of the conglomerates. These are the witless who seek to prove Conrad Black right, to prove Canada is not only untenable but impossible. Those who disagree, of course, will need looking into.

Fan Mail

FEBRUARY 28, 1995

Dear Mr. and Mrs. Moody:

I thought I should write you there at your Investors Service Inc. office in New York to let you know from at least one Canadian how Mr. Martin made out with his budget up here. Ralph says I'm crazy to take to writing you, what with your being in the middle of a Canadian credit watch and all that, but I always say there's nothing like getting infor-mation from someone who has an ear to the ground and both feet too.

You would have been proud of Mr. Martin on budget night which was Monday. I know I was. The word up here among respectable people and the responsible press is that the budget should go a long way towards calming your concerns so far as we're concerned. Ralph says this should free you up to concentrate on Mexico which I know is your other big headache.

Many Canadians will welcome Mr. Martin's promise to reform the way the federal government transfers money to the provinces. From now on, he is giving them more authority and less money. This will be done by going forward and using a cooperative approach. For instance, Mr. Martin is replacing the CAP and EPF with CST. Ralph, who wasn't listening all that carefully, says that CST minus EPF and CAP equals LESS. But the provinces also get tax points. I don't see how it could be clearer than that, do you?

Of course, none of these things will happen until a year or two from now so, like I say to Ralph, he should keep his shirt on. It is like the new reform of the OAS, which Mr. Martin promises is only a beginning to his reform of both OAS and GIS in the interest of future generations who are so often overlooked in our busy world. Starting next year, OAS payments will be based on personal incomes this year. Actually, this is in place of paying OAS payments this year on your tax next year which only means you don't pay any tax, if there is one, this year but it's paid for you next year according to what you made last year. Many investment brokers of my acquaintance applaud this step.

I know you both will welcome the news that Mr. Martin did not raise taxes hardly at all. As he carefully explained, the tax rate for big corporations will be increased from 0.2 percent to 0.225 percent which should not drive anyone round the bend. He also raised corporation taxes by one point. Then there was a sixty-cent increase on a carton of smokes and a one-and-a-half-cent increase in the cost of a litre of gas. Apart from that, not very much of anything, although Ralph claims the reductions on the limits allowed for buying RRSPS is the same as a middle-class tax increase, but what does he know?

Besides, the new RRSP limits do not apply this year but next year, and the year after that, but by the next year after that they will be back to where they are this year. When you are doing your credit watch thing, I hope you keep in mind how careful we are planning everything up here. Nothing is being left to chance, including the CBC.

Even though it was praised by President Bill Clinton, the CBC does good work on very little money. In order to improve on the CBC, Mr. Martin is reducing its budget by 4 percent next year and 5 percent the next year and 6 percent the next. Everyone knows the government cares deeply about the CBC, but Mr. Martin wants the Canadian people to get ready now for the next recession and that includes Pamela Wallin and the others in the news. It's called tough love.

Ralph, who just brought me a nice cup of tea, says the budget reminds him of poisoning Canadians with arsenic just a drop at a time. After awhile, he says, we will all begin to glow in the dark and the end will be near.

What Ralph and a few others don't realize is that Mr. Martin's budget was carefully worked out in order to convince people like Investors Service Inc. that we are a serious country. It was only during the past ten years, when Mr. Mulroney was in, that things got out of hand. And can you just imagine how much worse it would be if that Kim Campbell person were in? But we're on the right track now and several nice editorials have already been published to that effect.

It's unfortunate about all those civil servants being let go but I know the *Wall Street Journal* will be pleased. Besides, just as soon as the deficit is reduced there will be jobs for all. Ralph keeps saying he's still waiting to pick up one of those five hundred thousand jobs Canada was supposed to get with Free Trade. The trouble with Ralph, you know, is he's not a Liberal and he tends to brood over losing his job on the railroad. All he likes to do is sit around the house reading the Red Book and cracking jokes. He's nearly ready for the Comedy Channel.

I hope you won't mind my writing you. It's just like you're part of our family now, sitting out there watching our credit. I would be happy to know how you feel about Mr. Martin's budget. He certainly tried hard enough.

I saw that nice Mr. Fund of the *Wall Street Journal* on the CTV network yesterday morning and he seemed more or less pleased with the budget although not as much as I would have liked, to be frank about it. But he can pronounce Saskatchewan now almost perfectly.

Maybe I should write him too. Please remember me and Ralph to all the good people at your place.

Very truly yours,

Radio Free Canada

FEBRUARY 28, 1995

Over these many weeks of the war games against the deficit, the public servants of the federal government have been the cannon fodder. Cutting the deficit by cutting down the public service is a win-win business for the politician.

For a decade now, various governments have been claiming important savings achieved by sacking civil servants. Finance minister Paul Martin has announced the firing of forty-five thousand *more* federal government employees over a period of the next three years. This impressive number has been translated into expenditure savings of more than $7 billion.

These forty-five thousand servants represent about 15 percent of the total number of government employees. It is not hard to be impressed by the budget's arithmetic: 15 percent fewer federal employees, $7 billion richer. The bargain of the millennium, you could say.

Did you hear the story about the guy visiting Ottawa walking through a government department? He sees this sign on the bulletin board; it reads: "Government employees will not look out the window during the morning hours. Otherwise, there will be nothing to do in the afternoon."

There were plenty of jokes like that around during the fifties. Anti-Ottawa jokes. Civil-service-bashing jokes. If you didn't hear them, you weren't listening. They were a part of our political culture.

Well, times change.

I'm not sure that sort of humour would get much of a rise out of audiences these days. It's not so funny anymore. I know some of those among the luckless forty-five thousand. Forty-five thousand— that's a hell of a lot of people.

Most of them are married, likely with kids. Many with a mortgage, with roots in their community, with friends, neighbours, and neighbours' kids.

I know—the world doesn't owe anyone a living. Downsizing, like space travel, is a phenomenon of our age.

But I'm not sure how the economics of this massive reduction is going to work out. I'm not sure about that $7 billion bargain. These people we're talking about—the forty-five thousand employees from agriculture, environment, national defence, transport, or whatever—what is to become of them?

Are there forty-five thousand jobs awaiting them? Doing what? Where? I watched Paul Martin on the TV. He was smiling. Why is that man smiling?

There are more questions. Who pays the social cost of government downsizing? Well, the foreseeable costs of dislocation, anxiety, stress, and pain are likely provincial. I was impressed by the finance minister's frequent references to fairness. As for the forty-five thousand people to be terminated, he promised "to be as fair as possible."

So, let's say you've had a job in Ottawa-Hull, in the Department of Transport, for the past ten years. You have a wife, two kids, one mortgage, and a car. Tomorrow, or next week, you're fired.

A woman in the government in Ottawa was talking about the work that lies ahead in this postbudget era. People will be working on plans to downsize their department, she said. It's like being asked to dig your own grave.

Firing forty-five thousand civil servants may make good business sense, but it doesn't make much sense as public policy. And at the inflated price of $7 billion—over three years—it's not a bargain either.

Told You So

MARCH 3, 1995

Two days after finance minister Paul Martin brought down his budget, announcing the separation of forty-five thousand civil servants from their jobs, the Agriculture Research Station in Fredericton terminated the careers of twenty-three of its employees.

One of these was Scott Rynax, a herdsman, who had worked at the station for seventeen years. Another was Mariet van Groenewould, a lab technician, who had been employed for fifteen years. Rynax and Groenewould are married. They have two children and a mortgage and slight prospects of future employment.

I recall the finance minister saying, the morning after his budget, when asked about the hard task of ending the careers of forty-five thousand public servants, that he meant to do it "as fairly as possible." I recall his precise words because I wrote them down. I also recall writing two weeks ago, after the public service purge had been promoted from rumour to fact, that the government had no plan on how to go about sacking that many people, but was acting in panic.

When I heard about Rynax and Groenewould, it reminded me of the wisdom of one of my mentors who used to say that while one could measure success or failure in politics, it was impossible to measure stupidity. You can often quantify success by assigning it some sort of number, which may not be precise but can give people an idea.

In Toronto last week, for example, Martin was telling a downtown crowd of businessmen at the Empire Club that an overnight poll revealed 69 percent of those polled thought his budget "was on the right track." Further expanding the minister's comfort zone was the revelation that 83 percent of those polled expected more budget cuts in the future. (Combining these two figures produces a hazardous nonsequitur and not much else, except an interesting insight into how finance ministers think.)

The problem with this latest poll is that it doesn't mean anything. Indeed, it is at least likely that 83 percent of those polled had no idea what was in the budget, much less what track it was on, but were inclined to speak well of it because it did not appear to touch their lives.

This would not be the case with lab technician Mariet van Groenewould and her herdsman husband and their family. What they now know about the budget is that nothing in the Liberal election campaign two years ago, or in the Liberal platform (the Red Book), or in the assurances of Paul Martin, as recently as a week ago, prepared them for the shock of their dismissal notices. But if their dismissal does indeed meet Paul Martin's criterion for being "as fair as possible," it could then be said we are very close to being able to quantify stupidity.

If the husband and wife can be seen as martyrs, the president of the Canadian Broadcasting Corporation emerges from the haze and smoke of Martin's slash and burn budget as a hero. When his minister, Michel Dupuy, betrayed him (and after the finance minister had reneged on his party's Red Book promise to restore block funding), Tony Manera resigned as president of the CBC.

The details, as distressing as they are, no longer matter. The government encountered, to its apparent astonishment, someone it could not dupe or manipulate or sweet-talk out of sticking to principle. It turned out Manera was unwilling to compromise his integrity in order to make Paul Martin feel better at the expense of the CBC. The government, to put this simply, lied to Manera, a man it grievously misjudged, and it is still lying in the effort to save face, though now it is lying to the country.

It is mildly diverting to watch the government thrashing about in this web of its own intransigence. It is also revealing. The truth is now apparent—and we must be grateful to Manera for exposing it—that the CBC does not have many friends in the Ottawa establishment or the regional elites, and fewer still in the national political community.

The media either resent the CBC, viewing it as a sheltered, indulged competitor, or despise it as an institution of influence with a life outside the hierarchy of the conglomerates and their shareholders.

The CBC has never been so vulnerable as it is today. While it has always lived with the hostility of its media competitors, it has generally had support elsewhere where it mattered—among the political parties and in Parliament. It is poignant to recall how much faith the corporation placed in the campaign promises of the Liberal Party clearly set forward in the last election. Indeed, embarrassing to recall how much faith Manera had placed in the assurances given him by the new government when he assumed the leadership of the corporation. Now betrayed, the corporation is without friends in Parliament these days, which may account for the otherwise inexplicably cavalier and bullying attitude of the government.

Meanwhile, Michel Dupuy rambles on about the CBC's mandate

and the need to redefine it—which only means to reduce it further. But the best way to begin defining the CBC would be to sack Dupuy and find a minister with backbone and some understanding of the importance to Canada of public broadcasting. Instead, since the CBC is merely the property of the Canadian people, minister Dupuy becomes a willing accomplice—if an inept and clumsy one—in this concerted effort to reduce the corporation's essential contribution to the defence of this country against the coming onslaught of the packagers, assimilators, synthesizers, and profiteers whose only country is their bottom line.

What's Continentalist and Drives Right?

MARCH 10, 1995

Now on stage at the little theatre on The Hill, the non-debate on Paul Martin's budget. Essentially a genteel discussion between Liberal Reformers and Reform Liberals, the root question to be determined is existentially challenging: If no one said anything, would it sound the same?

The truly important questions have already been answered by the minister of finance, the prime minister, and choirs of columnists, each quoting polls and showering their audiences in generalities to the general effect that, generally speaking, everyone is pleased with the budget because everyone wanted action on the deficit. No doubt about it, "everyone" has never had a better year.

Even though, generally speaking, everyone is happy about the budget and, as the finance minister has been saying, feels the government "is on the right track," not everyone agrees. This seems like a contradiction but can be explained. The reason the country has sounded so effusively single-minded about its politics is that a lot of people in the political process presently lack someone to speak for them and are not themselves being heard or listened to; they have become all but invisible.

People keep speaking of the seismic shift to the right; certainly both the dominant parties in Parliament—Liberal and Reform—

have positioned themselves to the right of centre. Not all Liberals who find themselves there are comfortable; but being on the "right" is more or less today's no-brainer. Where else is there?

There is nothing quite so intimidating as political fashion. As for neo-conservatism, the peer pressure is intense. The minister of finance, bearing one of liberalism's most distinguished titles—son of Paul Martin—dismissed forty years of his party's history with a throwaway sentence. The greatness in liberalism, he said, was in its ability to change with the times. Those who might still adhere to the liberalism of Martin Sr. may have failed to grasp the spirit of the times—lower budgets, leaner government, more for less.

It is unfashionable to disagree. The contagion has swept the North American continent; even the Mexicans bought into the package although with devastating consequences. Canadians have been more fortunate and can afford to indulge themselves in the lusts of the conglomerates, the illusions of shareholders, and the fantasies of the newly empowered. There is nothing like the comforts of belonging, whether your leader is Jean Chrétien, Preston Manning, or Newt Gingrich.

The Tories are out of it. The question for them is whether they will ever be in it and how soon. First of all, they need to remember their history. Where they have succeeded has been where they have identified themselves as progressive and followed the leadership of progressive men. When they have been successful, they have defined themselves; when they have failed, they have allowed themselves to be defined by others.

This may seem elementary but, in fact, the Tories who make up the federal party are in present danger of being co-opted and over-managed by Conservatives whose interests are primarily provincial and whose agenda has been prepared with objectives and scenarios of a peculiar kind. It is interesting to note, however, that among all those who agree the Liberal government "is on the right track," many also agree the Progressive Conservative Party should attempt to squeeze itself into the Liberal-Reform *entente cordiale* on the right. This is especially true of junior advisors in the media who are enchanted by the humour of Rush Limbaugh and beguiled by the wisdom of Jesse Helms.

Since the Tories are starting from the bottom of the polls, they start with all their options open to them. These include how they will define themselves and where they will seek their place in the political spectrum. Part of that decision involves consideration of whom they want to represent. It is easy, as well as stupid, to say a party should represent everyone; fair enough to say that governments may, but political parties should not even try.

Certainly, the Liberals have followed the course, and the Martin budget marks the emergence of a neo-liberalism driven by attitudes and interests once attributed to conservatism. Someone remarked that not only has the Liberal Party moved right of centre, but the centre itself has moved to the right, leaving the Conservatives in limbo.

Martin may believe neo-liberalism is merely the same old liberalism of his father's generation brought up to speed. This would suggest only a little pragmatic fine tuning, here and there. But it is more than that, if the budget be considered the precursor. As a political document, it reveals the new order as counter-federalist, continentalist, and callous in the bargain. The Tories could not have asked for a better opportunity to regroup their battered forces.

Wait Till Moody's Reads This!

MARCH 28, 1995

It has been about a month since the federal government brought down its budget. As a result, life has gone on pretty much as before. The market has been reasonably buoyant and the dollar stable. The posse of evil spirits hovering around the barn before the budget has vaporized. It's been a month now since anyone from Moody's Investors rode through here on a credit watch.

While one should be careful not to exude confidence, it does seem that the attentions of the Moody people, Standard & Poor, the *Wall Street Journal*, the World Bank, and the International Monetary Fund have been fixed elsewhere. Mexico, which the *Wall Street Journal* pointed out last January was in as bad a financial mess as Canada (according to ace *WSJ* analyst John Fund), has not responded to poultices and chicken soup applied by the forces of international capitalism.

Among the little differences between the Mexican and Canadian economies—both with "basket-case currencies," you will recall—is that inflation in Mexico has since risen by 95 percent, the former president of Mexico has been sent into exile, his brother has been arrested for conspiring in the murder of a political rival, and there is a continuous civil war in Chiapas. The embattled new government has introduced economic "reforms"—you guessed it: reduced spending, higher interest rates—designed to protect what is left of the share values held by foreign investors and the local oligarchy, while further depressing the poor and the fragile Mexican middle class.

So, it is altogether likely the eyes of the World Bank, the IMF, the *WSJ*, and Moody's Investors are on Mexico. The Americans have therefore pumped $14 billion in Yanqui dollars into the economy; billions more are available. (Canada had earlier sunk close to a couple of billion in the wreckage as a slight token of our esteem.) It is worth noting the futility of the combined efforts of these powerful world tinkerers and advisors, including the deployment of someone else's money. Things have only worsened.

There is, of course, a guilty little secret about Mexico's hapless condition. Mexico has never witnessed an honest election, never had a government that did not run on bribery and venality, and its political system has been routinely based upon the oppression of the poor, enforced by a lack of health care, adequate sanitation, and opportunities for education. Instead, the nation's resources, lands, and wealth —like its political institutions—are all owned by a governing, one-party oligarchy. Outsiders who do business in Mexico, particularly Americans and their corporations, pay their way through the pockets of the politicians. This was never a secret but only something unremembered. (I knew, and know to this day, some of the American CEOs who had lived in Mexico and paid their political dues.)

I mention this not only to refresh my own memory but your's. We should all stop and think about Dr. Martin's Miracle Budget of January 27, or thereabouts, and then what happened. In fact, nothing happened. The earth didn't move. One day Canadians were the quarry of the credit hounds and the money changers; the next day the heat was off. Turns out things were worse in Orange County, California.

I think there ought to be some among us who should feel a little used, maybe diddled is the word, by these people who have been telling Canadians we have been living too high on the hog and Judgement Day is nigh. A lot of them who play that game, it is fair to say, made money out of the fact that some of us blinked. It's that sort of business. But the truth is, the federal budget didn't change the nature of things—and for awhile it won't—and life went on and the speculators have passed on. (They began instead to knock down the U.S. dollar against the yen and the mark.)

But most Canadians may prefer to feel sheepish, for the moment. It is better than feeling taken, which they were. The frenzy and hysteria generated over the deficit effectively separated Canadians from their collective sense as citizens so they could dispassionately accept the sacking of forty-five thousand of their public servants, agree to the further traducement of their government's support of the national arts and of public broadcasting, and to the odious nickel-and-diming of the pensioned and the poor. But nothing of that now, but to come later—the way children are treated by parents who discipline by procrastination.

The little *Wall Street Journal*-Moody-Martin-Magic-Moment in Canada's fiscal history nicely relieved Canadians of their responsibility to their own social traditions. They swallowed whole the new heresy that liberal democracy has failed, has run its course of ruin, and Canadians are now to be the wiser and more contrite. It is no longer to be our society, but a new global one, nor our simple democracy, but a higher "complex" chain of international authority. If the welfare state is dead, the conglomerate state then survives, unambiguous in its purposes, devoted to its shareholders, opposed to either restraint, regulation, or tithe, and deathly opposed to liberal democracy.

Much of this continuing drama was played out in the last budget and during the weeks of orchestrated disinformation leading up to it. (Remember when there was "a 70 percent certainty" the dollar would be downgraded?) It is too soon to forget, but not too early to ask: Was it really that good a budget? So good that it would be forgotten by everyone except me, one month later?

Remember When We Called It "Ma Bell"?

APRIL 7, 1995

Bell Canada, everyone's favourite monopoly, holds the country's interest forever close to its corporate heart. Following established national trends, in which the Government of Canada has been a leader, Bell's president, John McLennan, announced last week that his company would be firing ten thousand of its employees over the next three years.

Sounding like both a patriot and a bean-counter, McLennan pointed out that Ma Bell had made $720 million in profits last year, but expects to make only $500 million next year. "If we don't change now," he said, "we'll let down both our customers and our country."

Also for the good of the country, the federal government is letting go forty-five thousand of its employees over the same three-year period. And according to the past president of the CBC, that corporation will have to jettison three or four thousand of its employees to achieve the cuts demanded by Canada's finance minister in his recent budget.

My question—likely a frivolous one to ask—is where in hell do all these people go who are being put out on the street? As clues to the answer, we do know there are more unemployed Canadians than we can count, even though fewer are on unemployment insurance. We also know more Canadians are now living in poverty and that the numbers of young people without jobs is a national scandal. The idea that sacking ten thousand people is an act of patriotism is also scandalous; a remarkable semantic turn for a Cape Breton boy like John McLennan.

Bell's parent company is BCE Inc., simply the most profitable enterprise in the whole country. Bell, which is the cash cow of BCE, intends to go to its regulators soon to ask approval to increase its rates to local phone users. Bell will siphon off some of its improved earnings to make its long distance rates cheaper compared to those of its competitors in that field. Down the road, Bell has plans to buy a television network or to start a new one. It will need both cash and credit, but basic to a healthy bottom line is its monopoly position in the domestic phone business.

We all have some idea what we owe Ma Bell; what does Ma Bell owe us? It's true, Bell gives good phone service. But we hardly suspected the company had a payroll swollen by ten thousand people it could do better without. It is not unlike the federal government's discovery of forty-five thousand surplus employees in its bureaucracy.

What becomes of all these people? What becomes of them while they work for Bell, or for the government or the CBC, or Harbourfront, waiting for the axe to fall?

And is it not true that, in this new age of global capitalism, no one has a job they could not lose tomorrow? Not because they are not performing well or doing useful work, but because of "market forces?" Or because of a leveraged buyout and the need to finance the deal by firing workers with the most seniority who earn the best wages? Or because all politicians have succumbed to the virus of timidity. Or because we have, in fact, lost all control of the management of our own affairs?

Choose one or all of them, but what has happened has been the shattering of our polity—in the plaintive words of the Streisand ballad, of "the way we were," the way we ordered our particular universe, and the way we saw and did things. In this present era of dislocation and social fragmentation, it has been necessary to change the meaning of words, so that "reform" now means destroy, and "renewal" means only obfuscation, just as stability means unpredictability, probability means chaos, and federalism means nothing.

"Downsizing" means death—the end of someone's dream or a life's plan. We have reached a peculiar state, not unlike some weird distortion of Marxism, in which everything is done by invisible hands, the commands relayed to the company cafeteria where assembled workers may view their future fate on TV screens or hear of it on the intercom. The torture of the language goes on; executives assigned to attending to those downsized and cast adrift are vice-presidents "for human resources." A related field, growing in the new ethos, is that of "stress counselling," which involves teaching employees how to breathe while waiting to be sacked.

This is becoming a toxic working environment for almost everyone. It is perhaps hard to say, exactly, what responsibility the governors of the present economic system should accept for casualties created by the ethics, or lack of them, of contemporary employer practices.

Ten years ago, on the eve of the Mulroney decade in Ottawa, I recall saying to a group of senior executives in a ranking Canadian corporation that I thought Canadians had acquired a restored faith and confidence in business and in businessmen (I know, but that's what I said), and it offered great opportunity to demonstrate how well the system could work and how many Canadians could be well served by its efficacy. Ah, well.

At almost the same time, Britain's Tory Prime Minister Edward Heath had described one of his constituents, whom he named, as "bearing the ugly, unacceptable face of capitalism." It is now the familiar look. Felix Rohatyn, one of Wall Street's more compelling figures, said the other day, "Economics is neither a science nor a religion." Only our politicians and senior corporate executives appear to believe it is both.

It is a useful view since, like any dogma, it resists all criticism and doesn't take questions. Still, it could be said—even if as an aside—that Canada, before this business cycle, was, in the phrase of social critic Robert Hughes, "a collective work of the imagination," and it worked. It now seems more like some sort of virtual reality creation, digitally enhanced, a vision become a bad dream. I think business and the businessmen have blown their opportunity.

PART II

Personals

Dire Prophecies

These are times that try men's souls; days when a man thinks about changing his will. "I have seen the future," a great twentieth-century philosopher has said, "and it sucks."

Someone else said, in my presence, that he'd heard the editorial board of one of Canada's national dailies was divided on the recommendation of its editor-in-chief that the paper endorse Preston Manning and his Reform Party in the pending Grand Assize.

Dear Sirs: Pray cancel my subscription, if I have one, forthwith.

On Peter Gzowski's *Morningside* last Friday, I heard a man from Alberta say that the trouble with Kim Campbell—one of them—was that she was not a westerner.

Dear Lord: Give me a break. Memo to myself: Find out where and how to subscribe to *Western Report*. Put in a rush order for cowboy boots. (Spurs?)

A dear friend told me last week that, should things go the way they appear to be going—a Prime Minister Jean Chrétien in a movie in b&w, co-starring Lucien Bouchard as Leader of Her Majesty's Loyal Opposition—she would be leaving the country and buying U.S. dollars. I advised her to remain calm, stay put, and wait for the country to leave her. Besides, I have it on the advice of a man who is in banking that history shows after every change of government in Ottawa—from one party majority to another—there follows an upward surge in the equity market of some ten months' duration. When was the last time a banker lied to you? Believe.

Also believe that we're watching a revolution for our time. It seems very likely Canadian politics will never again be the same; that being so, neither will Canada. It is far too early to quantify the differences, to say with reasonable certainty we will blunder through, as usual, or that the future will be even brighter and better because that's just the way it has always gone with us, the way God wants it.

Some twenty-five years ago, someone was talking about the urgent importance of political realignment in Canada and quoting John Wesley: "Are you persuaded that you see more clearly than me?

It is not unlikely that you may. Then treat me as you would desire to be treated yourself . . . Point me out a better way than I have known."

The quotation is of Wesley, the Methodist preacher, and the voice is that of Ernest Manning, Preston's daddy, who saw this day coming. Believe that too.

In 1967, Ernest Manning produced a thesis proclaiming "a better way"—political realignment. His essay was a call for a merger of Social Credit, Manning's party, and the Progressive Conservative Party. The first step proposed: "The enunciation of a commitment by the leaders and adherents of the Progressive Conservative Party of Canada to the reorientation of the party's philosophical foundations. This reorientation must effectively blend humanitarian concern with economic realism and freedom."

The result of the merger would be a new Social Conservative Party to be supported, Manning argued, by Tories, Socreds, some Liberals, and "that large group of concerned citizens who . . . have withdrawn from affiliation with any political party."

If none of the above could be worked out, if Manning's plea fell on deaf ears (which of course it did), the final page of his thesis proposed a "Consideration of One Remaining Alternative," which, Ernest wrote, "I hope will not be necessary."

"I do not believe," he concluded, "that the formation of an entirely new party is the best way to meet the serious national political needs of the present hour. Nevertheless . . . present national party leaders and federal politicians, especially those affiliated with the Progressive Conservative Party of Canada, should take cognizance of the following fact: if the Canadian political situation continues to degenerate, and if the cause of conservatism continues to suffer and decline, a wholly new political party committed to the social conservative position will find an ever increasing number of advocates and supporters among a concerned and aroused Canadian public."

That same year—1967, a vintage one for Canada—Ernest Manning received an honourary LL.D. from McGill, perhaps for political thought. Less prestigious (in eastern learned circles), but more salient, Dr. Manning's earliest academic degree came from the Calgary Prophetic Bible Institute. A quarter-century later, it can be said that Ernest knew something, that he had vision beyond the prairie horizon.

It may also be that Kim Campbell's cruel fate was to be pitted against the prophet's son at the moment in time when conditions and circumstances would conspire to expose the fateful contradictions in a political party with an antipodal name—Progressive Conservative—and when the universe would not be unfolding as it should, but as Preston Manning's old man said it would.

Of course, since we continue to live in a world of surprises, the son of the prophet may fail to fulfill the vision of the father. The House of Commons is not your everyday pulpit, its members not your ordinary devotees. And far easier to pass a camel through the eye of a needle than for one man to reform the place. Tories are born with strong legs and high arches; their forbears have known some long marches in a wilderness measured by decades. As for Preston, he has not been tested in the true crucible of Canadian politics, in a national capital that has repelled and reduced many a politician of promise and repute.

Frum Here to Eternity

MARCH 21, 1995

The other night, a young man telephoned to ask if I would be willing to engage in a debate—under the sponsorship of the Conservative Youth organization—with David Frum on the subject of "Whither the Progressive Conservatives—to the right or the left?"

Not to prolong the suspense, I declined.

It was said Frum was ready to debate "any time, anywhere." Against anyone. On a short list, I was flattered to know I was the first choice to oppose him. But not any more; the search committee has moved on in search of other foils for Frum. When we consider how many Tory Privy Councillors took early retirement in 1993, it is surely possible to find at least one willing to play the role of Red Tory.

It is interesting the young Ontario Tories believe there is something to debate in this right-left alternative. I had thought their minds were mostly made up; they agreed with Frum and Diane Francis, the *Financial Post* and the *Globe and Mail*, the *Wall Street Journal* and John Fund, the ace Mexico-Canada editorial writer and avid supporter of the New York Downtown Athletic Club working poor. What is also of interest is that few of these young people have much idea what they're talking about, or what Frum is writing about, since they know as little as he of the country, somewhat less of its history and of the realities of Canadian politics, which they have yet to visit.

This is not a protest against innocence; we all have to start somewhere. But the danger is that the young rush to fashion; readers of Frum may easily confuse his audacity with mere bravado. When he attacked Robert Stanfield as "squishy" on the subject of the deficit and for giving bad advice to Jean Charest, the Tory leader, he seemed to be stretching things a bit in order to sound authoritative. (Stanfield's blistering reply to the editor of the *Financial Post* curled the edges of the pages. Having devoted much of his public life to the subject of education, maybe Stanfield should debate Frum.)

The truth is, Frum is a political novice in these parts but he is a figure among a small swarm of cross-pollinators now working on both sides of the border, protegés of Newt and friends of Preston. The life of an intercontinental itinerant neo-conservative is not a hard one. Indeed, it can be a good life with happy landings easily available at one think tank or another while eating well on foundation money, and while exhorting the Gingrichian hordes to lurch, lunge, or plunge ever more to the right where none—save perhaps Francisco Franco—has gone before. Those who want the neo-conservative, Gingrich Republican revolutionary party to go further right are, by definition, thought to be brighter than the rest.

These young men have made a private virtue of their extremism and a growing profit from their excess. Still, it is only for now and only in America. What possibly could our young Canadian Tories learn from Frum? It is difficult to debate politics with an American theorist who is a Canadian neophyte, but it may be interesting—to students of American politics—to learn a month or so from now, as we near the end of the revolutionary regime's "first hundred days," what all went wrong.

It does seem clear that there are sober second thoughts in the

Senate—the U.S. Senate—about nearly all of the Contract with America. The revolutionary ardour is cooling; the louder the exhortations from the juniors, the more measured the protestations from their seniors. Parties are not managed out of the nurseries. Theorists have their uses, none of them to do with governing.

Before the young Ontario Tories consider whether they should tack to the right or to the left, they need to define their constituency. For whom will they speak? Obviously, many Tories in western Canada would like to try and win back the Reform vote. But the Reform Party is a regional party and it holds a lock on the votes of those in the West who want a reduced federalism.

But a reduced federalism—when and how much—is a stale argument. What many want, as the latest polls show, is a restored and strengthened Progressive Conservative presence in the federal Parliament. My hunch is that most Canadians favour the restoration of a basic two-party system, represented by national parties.

My advice to the young Ontario Tories is to invite David Frum over and have a nice day. But they belong to a generation that has been simply abandoned by government half-measures and timidity. The governments of Canada have squandered two generations and are now blissfully writing off a third. It has simply been a disgrace that the Government of Canada has been incapable of so ordering its affairs as to provide affordable post-graduate education, or adequate retraining or training for today's job market.

I would also build upon the scores of thousands who have been downsized, downgraded, or simply fired from jobs they had held for years by new management acting for new ownership, determined to get rid of their best people only to help finance their latest acquisition. Some day, some political party will not only insist upon a right to work law, but a right to stay at work.

Frum would plead the need for efficiency and economies in the competitive free world market. It's true, we are competing against slave labour and child labour and all forms of pitiless exploitation. But that is the ugly face of capitalism, so to speak. Canada's challenge is to maintain a decent, secure society and, if that can't be done and we need a Gingrich revolution to dull our collective social conscience, the *Wall Street Journal* will lead the way. It always has.

The Arts of Governance

OCTOBER 28, 1994

In the press of events, I had forgotten to observe the first anniversary of Jean Chrétien's tenure as prime minister. Anniversaries, even a first one, allow occasions for assessments, critiques, auguries, and the posting of grades. As to the latter, and as for me, the prime minister gets an A+ in Style 100, but in the more difficult first year course of Content, a straight C. The comment on his report card reads, "Popular with his classmates."

The prime minister is well liked and almost universally trusted. He has raised his act of Not Being Brian Mulroney to an art form. After the headaches of the Mulroney years, he becomes our aspirin-in-office. Something like three out of four Canadian adults are glad he is their prime minister, approve of the manner in which he holds the office, and are comfortable with his purposes and objectives, as much as they understand them.

There are two ways of explaining Chrétien's firm hold on the public confidence. First, he is less like Mulroney than anyone in present-day politics—in speech, manner, taste, and style. Second, he hasn't done anything.

He has not yet come down, in a contest between polarities, on one side or the other. The protagonists in public policy can fairly believe he is on their side, or is at least not on the other side. At the end of his first year in office, it can be remarked of him that he has decided nothing and disappointed no one.

Of course, when he cancelled the helicopter contract, he offended only the contractors, and when he cancelled the Pearson airport contract, he offended only a few Ontario Tories (and a few silent Liberal partners).

He has also given the appearance of being a man of his word. He did embark upon a sizable federal-municipal boondoggle devoted largely to fixing sewers, patching potholes, and making work, as he had promised. He went through the motions of trying to fix NAFTA more to his seeming satisfaction, which has allowed his supporters to claim he achieved "significant improvements" for the home side. And he was hell-bent not to reopen any effort to amend the constitution, nor even talk about it, a decision that flooded the nation with a rush of gratitude. Finally, he remained aloof from the Québec provincial election, at least for outward appearances, which displeased only separatists and the francophobes.

You could say all this is not bad for a first year in office, or you could say it is nothing to brag of, but you also must admit it's working. Mulroney's major problem, apart from his stylistic imperfections, was that he tried to do too much, that his cabinet suffered from what the civil servants called "agenda choke," and that he often pressed others too hard and pushed his own luck too far in order to get things done. Mulroney was an over-achiever; no one is likely to make the same accusation of Chrétien.

All the same, if the content be slight, the Chrétien style has been gratifyingly underwhelming. Everything the people wanted in their prime minister, after their prolonged paroxysm of rage, they now have in this palpably modest public man. Unlike Joe Clark, whose gait was awkward and chin too small, or Pierre Trudeau, who made a virtue of arrogance and insouciance, with expletives, or Mulroney, who suffered from speech-writers' hyperbole and an uncontrolled mellifluousness, Chrétien's imperfections and human failings have proved positively endearing.

He communicates better for not speaking well; between the diphthongs helplessly crushed by the gravel voice and the immutable tone of affability, his words are memorable largely for their failure to give serious offense or drive anyone to serious thought.

Most of what the prime minister has to say has to do with the projection of time and the postponement of decision. If there is something not presently under government review or study, it is only because no one has yet thought of it. When a Liberal MP, George Baker, made discovery of the fact that actual millionaires were drawing down unemployment insurance payments, the designated response minister—David Anderson at national revenue—was quick to say he knew all about that, of course, but more important, the matter was "being studied." A querulous man or woman might ask, "What's to study?"

He may well be simply the luckiest man to hold office in living memory, possibly in Canadian history. On the other hand, he has thus far made the most of both his inheritance, as an antidote to the past, and of his luck. After all, he has been a good politician for a good long time. And as Ben Hogan once said about golf being largely a matter of luck, he noticed the more he practised, the luckier he got.

Ethics Outbreak in Kleinburg

AUGUST 26, 1994

Many of those who worry most about ethics and morality in politics live in Alberta. Preston Manning lives in Alberta, the seat of the Reform movement that has swept like a prairie fire through Alberta and parts of British Columbia, Saskatchewan, and Simcoe Country, Ontario. Knowing this, it comes as a surprise to learn of an outbreak of dubious ethics in the provincial capital of Alberta, in the very office of Premier Ralph Klein.

Knowing how great a burden many Albertans bear trying to keep the rest of us on the right path, I often pray for them, as I did last night when I first heard about Premier Klein and his free-ranging advisors. It likely would not have happened had Preston Manning not been heavily engaged in good works elsewhere, since it is the sort of thing that goes wrong only when the righteous relax their vigil.

According to Edmonton sources, Klein has appointed eight college professors to help him keep his foot out of his mouth whenever he opens it to speak about the province of Québec. The chosen professors are learned in matters of law, political science, and history; their chairperson is Allan Tupper, a political science professor. Helping the premier keep both feet on the ground is sort of like an exercise in egocentric engineering, or counter-levitation, and could well prove futile, according to another of the professors. Political scientist Peter McCormick says the premier might harken to the advice of the professors and then say, "You pointy-heads are all wrong."

Unless they have been kept in the dark about this, I don't know how Albertans can sleep nights. It is true that the professors will not be paid for their services to the premier of Alberta. Nevertheless, there are enough questions about this something-for-nothing, or nothing-for-something, deal between the premier and the professors to give an ethicist enough work to produce real furrows.

The professors are employed by the taxpayers to instruct tuition-paying students in the law, history, and poliscience. They have not been hired and tenured to teach the premier of Alberta anything. Even if we assume they are working on the Klein portfolio on their own time, out of Professor Tupper's rumpus room, by what right or precedent does a politician have to seek and weigh their collective advice for free? If Ralph Klein were not the premier of Alberta, instead a Lethbridge lightning rod salesman and provincial MLA, could he also access the academy and help himself to a clutch of expert advisors from the fields of business administration, meteorology, and animal husbandry?

The salient feature of this arrangement is the attempt to improve the performance on the national stage of the premier of Alberta on the subject of Québec. This may be a consummation devoutly to be wished by admirers of Ralph Klein, or by those who cannot tolerate a little buffoonery mixed in with the overall seriousness of federal-provincial affairs. But it would be my opinion that Ralph Klein, unexpurgated and uninformed, might be a safer national political commodity than a Teflon-coated, professorially aimed intervenor on almost any topic, not least the subject of Québec. The trouble we will now have with the premier of Alberta is trying to figure out if that's Ralph Klein talking or Professor Tupper.

But to return to the basic difficulty: that of the taxpayers unwillingly financing the cost of advisors to a provincial premier, even though it costs nothing. *Especially* though it costs nothing. I take it as a given that the advice of the professors must be worth something—possibly as much as $150 an hour per professor, or a little less than it would cost to hire a plumber. Eight professors at $150 an hour, including tea breaks, comes to $1,200. Assuming Klein gets at least three hundred hours of advice from the lot of them during the year, that comes to $360,000 worth of waived instructional consulting fees. While any professor I know would kill for that kind of money, there is something else—no GST.

Not to be lost sight of is the fact that the professors are, in reality, employed as cranial cosmeticians, toiling to make the premier of Alberta sound smarter than he is. Clearly, this is a benefit bestowed upon a politician that need not be deemed free of tax. Under the federal elections act, as an instance, Klein's counsellors would have to have a value placed upon their advice, if given during a campaign for his re-election, and the amount reported as an election expense. Arguably, an alert department of revenue could assess Klein $360,000 as the value of services provided him by his academic beauticians.

The premier, who graduated from the Calgary Business College and ended up running the place, will know that in the real world—always one of his favourite spaces—there is no such thing as a free lunch; also in the real world, there is no such animal as a free professor. The taxpayers of Alberta, I dare say, have equipped their premier with enough advisors on Québec to fill half a building. These are all paid for; why not use them? Instead, they have people engaged by the premier who have authority without responsibility and who create obligations without invoices.

Labour's Love Lost

APRIL 19, 1994

Audrey McLaughlin, who has been the overlooked leader of the New Democratic Party since late 1989, finally found a way to get the attention of the media. She resigned on Monday, creating a blaze of news items, editorial perfunctories, and audio-visual ruffles. Her party, somewhat less than stricken by her decision to retire, promised to renew itself, a pledge that triggered a further effulgence of reportage. The NDP has not enjoyed so much attention since it won Ontario.

It is hard to know just what to say about McLaughlin's retirement other than to state the obvious; it really won't matter, one way or another, in the way the universe will unfold. Just between ourselves, I have found her an immensely forgettable politician, often, during turns on media panels discussing politics, groping for her name, in something the same way I have often struggled to remember Paul Martin Jr.'s face.

Remembering McLaughlin becomes the more difficult for lack of anecdote. What clings to the mind is a solitary interview with a CBC reporter, just after the Tory convention of 1993 that chose Kim Campbell as leader and, as a consequence, the next prime minister of Canada. The CBC question was: What advice would McLaughlin have, as another Ottawa political single, for Campbell and her future of long, lonely nights in the nation's capital? McLaughlin had no advice for the likes of Campbell; she was solely concerned, she said, about the long, lonely nights facing "unemployed single-parent mothers and their children."

Well, okay Audrey. And thanks for talking down to us.

This remorseless, and humourless, piety is not just McLaughlin's problem. It came with her membership card. Most of those who belong to the NDP simply believe they are nobler—of both mind and purpose—than the rest of us. And in fact, for many years, many Canadians liked to believe the party represented their better selves, practising politics as the good Lord Himself would have done, with every member a missionary. NDP (or CCF) national leaders— Coldwell, Douglas, Lewis—exuded public worthiness, goodness, and sound principle. It was not until Ed Broadbent came along, a man who could have run a pool hall as well as lead the NDP, that Canadians began to suspect the party might be a party like the others.

Perhaps where it went wrong flowed from McLaughlin's inability to let Broadbentism triumph. After all, the perception of the NDP as a party of unbending principle, commanded by leaders of vision who saw each sparrow fall, could not survive this decade's onslaught of pragmatism. This has been illustrated and annotated by the high visibility of Premiers Roy Romanow and Bob Rae—the one engulfed by agrarians, the other surrounded by the trade unions—who have dismayed their loyal followers when they did not merely disappoint them. Not to say that the Bob and Roy Show has been a political failure—something too early to tell—but it has been a public relations disaster in that it demolished forever the perception of the party as one that would never let either its principles or its supporters down, including those supporters who had never voted for it.

The federal party, however, has refused to yield to Broadbentism —to admit to the ultimate triumph of a non-ideological pragmatism. Although it was never comfortable with McLaughlin, even though she was virtuous to a fault, the party has been more ill at ease with the bruising confrontations with reality its members could observe taking place in Ontario. Besides, whatever people thought about McLaughlin, or about the doctrinal defaulters in the provinces, there is always the internal reality of the party's existence. It is, after all, the kept convenience of trade unions, notably those in Ontario.

It was Bob White himself—the ranking trade unionist in the country—who wondered aloud, not long ago, as to whether the trade unions should continue to underwrite the NDP, or whether it might make more sense to play the field or cut a deal with some other party or parties. The NDP, which has never failed to leap dutifully to its feet in Parliament whenever it sensed a threat to trade union interests, might also rethink its long association with generations of people like Bob White. In the end, where has it got either of them—the party or the union leadership?

Then there is the ultimate question: Who needs the NDP anyway, and why? The last leader may not have been everyone's cup of tea— clearly not mine—but the sorrowful irrelevance of everyone's favourite federal third party cannot fairly be claimed as her legacy. Louis St. Laurent once described them—the CCF-cum-NDPers—as "Liberals in a hurry." A boxed set of the collected speeches of Audrey McLaughlin to the person who first answers the question, "In a hurry where?"

Remembering Tonya

FEBRUARY 1, 1994

Day after day, ever since an assailant clubbed down Nancy Kerrigan in a hallway off a Detroit skating rink, the world has been closing in on Tonya Harding. Any hour now, some four weeks after the assault on one of America's premiere women skaters, media trackers are reporting "new developments" likely to lead to Harding being charged.

The media, however, have been saying something like that for some time. According to the ubiquitous polls, a majority of Americans already know Harding knew about the planned assault on

Kerrigan. A majority of Americans now judge Harding as unfit to represent the United States in the winter Olympics in Norway.

What Tonya did, or didn't, is the stuff of legend and song, part saga, part parable, needing only a strong closing, triumph or tragedy, to become the world's first musical comedy on ice—Evita of the silver blades. On the other hand, or foot, why a mere musical? Why not an opera?

One hears the media, as parabases, chanting to the audience, "There is no smoking gun." Law enforcement officials were saying yesterday, "She could have a lot of explanations." Perfect for an aria to end the second act: "She Could Have a Lot of Explanations!"

And what a cast! There is Kerrigan, the American princess, everyone's Homecoming Queen, a Just Say No Girl, good family, poor but honest; a "pretty little thing" who grew up and blossomed into serious possibilities, an athlete with bankable looks and skills to match.

The minor characters in this richly embroidered plot are from central casting: The obese bodyguard Eckardt, the zombie-like hitman and his accomplice who drove the getaway car, and Tonya Harding's sometime husband and hustling confidant, Jeff Gillooly, everyone's idea of the bad brother, chronic misfit, and neighbourhood nerd. As an observation from an earthbound couch-potato: "With friends like that . . ." The truth seemed to be either that Tonya Harding fell victim to the befuddled scheming of her "advisors" or that she commanded the operation and left its details to an incompetent clutch of knaves.

Consider the beauty and innocence of the victim—"Why me?" as she so audibly and poignantly asked on being struck down—and mark the awesomely unappealing nature of the crime itself. Then assign all these elements to a sporting endeavour celebrated for its purity of form, grace, and discipline. After that, introduce as apposite and—it soon becomes clear—also antagonist, Harding, and we have a drama with a world audience potential, along with a story line that could run to infinity, and into posterity as literature. Had it been another freestanding nut who attacked Kerrigan, minute editorials on the lives of endangered celebrities would surely have followed, but not for long. How is Monica Seles, anyway?

Instead, I find that Tonya Harding has gradually infiltrated my consciousness. I have her on my mind, almost full time. It may be I needed Tonya as antidote or counter irritant to that other women in the news, Lorena Bobbitt. For whatever reason, I identify with Tonya even though, it is necessary to say, I am not a skating buff; indeed, I do not even know how to skate.

And I haven't really followed the Tonya Harding story. If anything, it has followed me. While watching the news, about Bosnia or Middle East peace meetings, there, out of nowhere, would be Tonya, skating about the rink, working out in her black leotards, her long hair gathered in a ponytail. Round and round, the world has watched Tonya skate, day after day, week after week. Yesterday, or the day before, she fell.

Meanwhile, the media chorus was saying Gillooly would talk, had already talked, and he would implicate this distant, silent woman-child in the attack on Kerrigan: this woman with the wan, withdrawn face and vacant eyes, she of the thin, timid smile and the poor teeth, the girl with the single obsession and the twenty-year-old dream, this wraith of a champion whirling over the ice, expressionless, all her hidden furies vented in the routine of her exercise. Nothing in life has rewarded her that did not come from the surface upon which she performs; off-ice, there is only Gillooly, Eckardt, the FBI, the Oregon and Detroit police, bad polls, and the lure of a fast media buck, the quick trade-off of instant notoriety for a life's dream.

The last time I saw Tonya she was still skating, but the news is worsening. Gillooly is talking, they say. I have a problem with Tonya: I doubt that she's innocent. Now that she has invaded my dreams, this poor, driven, surrounded woman, I hope she will somehow go to Lillehammer, win the Olympic gold, and make a lot of money. I can't wait for the movie or the opera. Anyone have a problem with that?

Back to Being Brian

FEBRUARY 24, 1993

On the day Prime Minister Brian Mulroney met his party caucus to tell them he was resigning—which was Wednesday, February 24— Ottawa looked like Dead City. A woman I know who works in a government department said her office telephone rang only twice during the day and one of the calls was personal.

Politics and power are Ottawa's daily bread, its staff of life, the only serious game in town. So that after Ottawans had watched CTV's Craig Oliver, on the late news Tuesday night, mount an ingeniously speculative but convincing story proclaiming the prime minister's imminent retirement, the whole city went to bed resolved to rise the next morning and head for the nearest television screen. There would be no other business on Wednesday.

The CBC, sensing one of those moments in history for which its mandate was made, preempted *Fred Penner's Place*, *Under the Umbrella Tree*, and *Sesame Street* in order to bring viewers full details of this historic event. The coverage began on Newsworld with Don Newman interviewing a random assortment of Mulroney friends and advisors, along with veteran analysts and other all-sorts, until the baton was passed to Peter Mansbridge who looked as though he had just emerged from the shower.

There was a camera deployed at 24 Sussex Drive where closer Mulroney friends and advisors were seen departing in limos, while another camera positioned outside the government caucus room allowed an inquiring reporter to interview Tory MPs gathering at the scene. These interviews had a rare, amorphous quality about them since MPs were being pressed to agree their prime minister had betrayed them, or had let them down, by promising at the last caucus to stay and fight the next election, but was now going to abandon them. And how did they feel about that?

The trouble with this media spin on the Mulroney story was that most MPs had not been convinced by Mulroney at the last caucus that he was going to say on. One of them, the MP for Carleton-Charlotte, told me how he listened intently to the prime minister at that meeting—so intently he had "hung on every word"—and nowhere did he hear the prime minister say he was staying. Instead, he would say things like "we're going to win" and "we're going to stand together." What was missing was the first person singular—the "I" word—which is the prime minister's favourite pronoun and one he avoided in his speech to the caucus.

The caucus had nevertheless got the message, which was either that the prime minister had not made up his mind whether he was staying or going, and should not be hassled on the matter, or that he had decided to leave but was not yet ready to say so. Most of the Tory MPs I knew believed the latter. The caucus members also came away understanding their duty, which was to tell the media the prime minister was staying.

The story line that the prime minister had told his caucus he was staying had been reinforced by another news item, which informed that Hugh Segal, the prime minister's chief of staff, had chastised certain cabinet colleagues for appearing to be overanxious to begin their campaigns to succeed Mulroney without waiting for his signal. I could not find anyone who admitted to hearing from Segal anything remotely to do with that subject, so possibly the best to be said for the story was that it had been a controlled leak from the Prime Minister's Office, fashioned out of spun cotton and perhaps Segal's personal sense of propriety.

What is curious about all this—as became blatantly obvious on Wednesday—was that the media were unprepared for the prime minister's resignation, that they lulled themselves into a protracted period of denial and were, for some reason, determined to believe Mulroney would stay in place. When it seemed certain he was quitting, no one quite knew what to say.

The media were not alone. Unlike the resignation of Joe Clark the week previous, when everyone had seemed to have prepared statements handy for the occasion, the prime minister's announced departure brought a range of responses varying from Don Mazankowski's tearful breakdown during his caucus peroration, to comments that sounded more like admonition than tribute. It is not every day that both the media and the political community are so evidently lost for words; the silences on Wednesday were filled largely by garbled confusion. People were plainly having trouble finding out how they felt about the event they were witnessing.

When Peter Mansbridge asked former PEI premier Joe Ghiz, as "a longtime friend of Brian Mulroney," what he thought of the prime minister's departure, Ghiz was careful neither to confirm nor deny the "friendship." Instead, he said Mulroney had waited too long to quit, then launched into a tirade against free trade and the GST. It seemed clear this was not the sort of response Mansbridge was looking for, but Wednesday was proving to be that kind of day.

As proof, the CBC offered up a bouquet of provincial premiers all doing stand-ups on "how I feel about Mulroney resigning." Most of them spoke as though standing barefoot on broken glass; only New Brunswick's Frank McKenna was relaxed and ungrudging in his tribute. (No better method than this could be found for measuring the personal sense of political well-being felt by each of Canada's premiers. McKenna alone was secure enough to speak generously, even fulsomely, about Mulroney. The rest of them spoke behind barricades of caveats.)

As Wednesday's coverage progressed, the news of Mulroney's announced departure stimulated neither celebration nor remorse nor sorrow. The streets remained quiet. Most people stayed indoors and watched television, waiting for consensus to form, perhaps hoping to catch some message that conveyed true meaning and might improve their understanding. I cannot myself remember any event like this which carried with it so heavy a burden of ambivalence.

People who were in politics and government, or in the media, or in the hairdressing business, or members of the Gatineau Gentleman's Club, or the downtown Rideau Club, all had their own memories of Brian Mulroney and knew him (they would let you know) in a special way. But on Wednesday, apart from the uttering of leaden clichés that could as easily have been uttered to mark the retirement of Sir Charles Tupper, the Mulroney resignation was a story without a firm handle or a strong, guiding voice to it. (When I asked a man who was wandering about the house fixing the furnace what he thought of all this, he replied by making the sign of the cross before retreating to the basement.)

Soon after word reached the public of the prime minister's decision to retire, the Prime Minister's Office put out to the media a thirty-four-page document bearing the title, "Summary of Government Achievements, 1984–1993" which, sure enough, was what it turned out to be. I realize most journalists spurn this kind of handout as unworthy by definition. But it struck me as a more interesting read than anything else I'd heard or seen all day.

The style and presentation are intriguing. For example, expanding on the Mulroney government's achievements in "fostering change in the public service," the document cites "launching Public Service 2000, a comprehensive initiative to reform and renew the public service. The objective is to achieve a results-and-client-oriented culture, provide improved service to the public, streamline government operations, and encourage innovation . . ."

This is not the familiar "Blam! Zowie" style of PMO recountings of the government's achievements, but the work of unseen, knowing hands elsewhere. The accent is unmistakably High Twinkie: "Enacted the Lobbyists Registration Act to bring transparency to the activities of paid lobbyists. Individuals who engage in certain lobbying activities are now required to register so that the public, as well as those holding public office, can be aware of who the lobbyists are and on whose behalf they are acting."

No one in the PMO, or among its consultants, could write like that if they tried. No one in the PMO thinks like that either.

Who has written this recessional on the eight years of Brian Mulroney? If you guessed it must be a committee you would be right, since compiling government "achievements" is the stuff of committees, and only a committee could list thirty-four pages of government achievements (1984–93) without once cracking a smile, elbowing the Grits, or dropping in additives for flavour and colouring, like the odd adjective or two. But this was a committee struck in the Privy Council Office, though the Chief Pamphleteer and Senior Editor was likely the prime minister himself.

By Wednesday afternoon, "Government Achievements" became the most widely circulated and unread handout in a town that lives by the handout. Still, it seemed a curious gesture, even a little old fashioned, this austere, bloodless recounting of the works of Tory governments under Mulroney. It was, however, the way the prime minister preferred to be remembered; he had put it out there, for the record, just in case anyone had the time to look it over.

Of course there was too much going on, including a cameo appearance by Maude Barlow who told someone on the CBC she was mounting a campaign to ensure a Liberal-NDP coalition government after the next election. Canadians who share in that dream should hope the Tories choose Michael Wilson as their next leader, she said.

By this time, the prime minister had already held a news conference, which left only one event in the day of any magnitude: Mansbridge's interview with Mulroney on *Prime Time News*. When the encounter with Mansbridge took place, Mulroney had on the armour of righteousness, which also meant he was armed with statistics and "bullets" to put down any guff. The two men sat facing each other in what looked like the parlour of the PMO, a side table holding a small vase of flowers in the background. Both had had a long day and both looked it, drawn and grey and locked at the knees, body language that expressed both deference and hostility.

One-on-one interviews with the media, or anyone else, are, for Mulroney, an unnatural act. He is not comfortable being asked what he thinks, or means, or what he intends to do. Because it is not natural for him, his interviews tend to become theatrical and the politician gets buried in the role of the actor. He will carry in his head rehearsed responses to the more offensive questions he may be asked, which usually serves to create a suspenseful tension so that even the answers to soft questions sound stiff and guarded.

People who work for him soon become familiar with his skill in deflecting messages by distracting the messenger. People who imagine their moments with him will allow them to ventilate their problem-centred agendas are often disappointed; the prime minister as often has his own agenda, which may be gossip, or protracted musing, or something else of greater interest to him. It would not be an easy thing for a messenger to go to the prime minister and tell him to lighten up in his interview with Peter Mansbridge, since the meeting may be entirely taken up by a discussion of his efforts to save Newfoundland's offshore oil industry. This is all part, as someone put it, of Mulroney's "unique management style." It is a way of keeping unpleasant thoughts and negative ideas at a distance. If the prime minister needs that sort of intelligence, he can always get it by reading the papers.

Or by being interviewed by Mansbridge. When asked to explain his chronic unpopularity, Mulroney has his answer ready. He was once, he says, the most popular politician in the history of Canada; he was twice elected with overwhelming consecutive majorities, which set another record for electoral victories. But it was only when he had to make hard decisions—about free trade and the GST—that he became unpopular. Doing the right thing, he was saying, makes you unpopular, and the more right you are, the more unpopular you become.

This is entirely likely, yet there is more to it than that. The prime minister's unpopularity had become systemic; it could not be treated by changing the medicine from the right thing to the pleasing thing, even if that were possible. But a good part of the reason for his unpopularity can be found in his revealing answer to Mansbridge's question. The trouble is that he appears to have an answer for everything, and this answer is especially clever and self-serving: Dear God, why can't people be allowed to dislike their prime minister? Have we all forgotten Mackenzie King?

Besides, Mulroney's answer took away from his triumph. He had, after all, simply confounded his critics, so many of whom would not believe him capable of objectivity, of any willingness to let go, to confront the irreversible nature of his unpopularity, and to discharge the most fundamental of all responsibilities for a party leader, which is to depart with grace and in good time. And he had outwitted his political adversaries, leaving them without room for manoeuvre. Indeed, his triumph had been simply stunning, which is why there was so much difficulty for so many in capturing the moment, and with trying to remember all those years of Mulroney and finding context for it.

Nine years, or ten (counting from his beginnings as the Conservative Party's leader), is a long time in the life of a politician, or anyone else, for that matter. Mulroney's years do not yield easily to summary. Certainly the subject needs time for perspective; likely distance would help too. The most obscure view of the prime minister is the one taken close-up in Ottawa.

So far, among the muted, ambivalent, and strenuously balanced summaries of Mulroney's career to appear in the editorial pages, the most appealing to readers at 24 Sussex Drive (and myself) thus far has come from the *New York Times*. "Regardless of who wins the next election," the *Times* editorialized on Thursday, "he has launched his nation in a promising new direction." The *Times* also insightfully commented, "Some Canadians say he is too friendly with Washington, but that's only one of his problems."

True enough. Mulroney's manifestly cordial relations with President Reagan and the subsequent even closer bonding with President Bush cost him, and it was more than just "one of his problems." A more devious and subtle man (which he was supposed to be) would have introduced some geopolitical space, however illusory, as antidote to the centrifugal forces driving the continental economies together. Mulroney preferred personal diplomacy with family picnics. The moral, for those who succeed him, is that Canadians want a good neighbour policy but they do not want anyone to be seen enjoying it.

Remembering Brian Mulroney, I go back to the student at Saint Francis Xavier, seeming all elbows and knees, who everyone said was terribly bright with a pleasing personality and thoroughly bilingual. He was all of these, at least, and in the 1960 Nova Scotia election campaign, he did missionary work for me among the Liberal priests in Antigonish and Inverness Counties.

Three years later, arriving late at night at Québec City for Carnival, my wife and I found Brian quietly weeping in a dark corner of the airport. He had just lost his father and was waiting for his flight to take him home to Baie-Comeau, and we waited with him and saw him off. A year later, while in Montréal, we found him in hospital, looking older than his years, painfully thin and terribly vulnerable. There was about him, in those days, a vulnerability that compelled people to enlist in his cause, to encourage him and believe in him.

Not long after that, after he had passed his English bar exams and become a promising young lawyer, we had a family dinner on top of Place Ville Marie and afterwards went with him to a crowded, noisy pub in old Montréal where the evening progressed with Mulroney standing on a chair, stein in hand, leading the crowd in song. It was hard not to be charmed by his irrepressible high spirits—after all, everyone else was—and for a long time one of the attractions of going to Montréal was in seeing Brian for a drink, or a meal, and long, lively, animated conversation. He was, everyone agreed, a joy to be with.

Of course it did not last like this, but there remained enough of the essential Mulroney—the boy in the man—even as he began to acquire *gravitas*, became a Royal Commissioner, and later even someone who flew in his own jet. Along the way, he had lost out to Clark in his impulsive first run for the Tory leadership. The next time we met in Québec City, thirteen years after finding him in tears at the airport, he was choking with rage because his friends—some of whom had gathered for a dinner to honour Bob Stanfield—had supported Clark or otherwise let him down. After dinner, we walked for an hour in the cold, dark streets while I listened to his endless lament and vainly tried to console him. Some of those he would never forgive have since served as ministers in his government.

When he became prime minister, he brought his own entourage and with it a dangerous aura of self-indulgence. But there was much to be said for the argument that he had made it largely on his own, with the fine-honed skills of a conciliator and the familiar persuasiveness and personal charm. But the kid who used to be in the man had been largely suppressed. Royal jelly comes with age, as does a wardrobe of impeccable tailoring and studied casualness. It was hard for many who knew him to believe this prime ministerial model was real; only the truest of sycophants did not worry about the disappearance of the real Mulroney. But a number of people came to the despairing conclusion that they had gained a prime minister and lost someone they had known.

Ambition is a spur, but also a drug; it changes personality. This is not meant as psychoanalysis, but as a political statement. Politics does things to people, both those who achieve power and those who, in a phrase often heard during Mulroney's years, "sleep at the foot of the bed" of the powerful. Mulroney and Pearson may have had in common the fact that they were each used more than they were served by some of the people around them.

One morning before cabinet business, the prime minister was talking to his colleagues about lobbyists. One of them—known to all present and whom he named—had recently called him at home. He had stepped from the shower to take the call, and the lobbyist-friend proceeded to put in a word for one of his clients (this was before there was a lobbying bill). Having done so, he then told him what a great job the government was doing and said goodbye. "I thought," the prime minister said, feigning hurt, "he'd called to wish me a happy birthday."

Everyone laughed.

One should not, I suppose, discount the importance of being Prime Minister of Canada. For as long as history, there have been people who have wanted to become prime minister even though, it becomes increasingly clear, being prime minister is a bruising, overrated and misunderstood occupation, one that invites ingratitude and inspires mistrust. Otherwise, it's a life.

There are other important things to be, including becoming once again the original Brian Mulroney. It is truly not important how Mulroney is rated by his contemporaries—really, who in hell knows enough to make that judgement today?

But I do know Mulroney is not the inflated, marbled caricature he has become in the media and public eye. His cronies may weep to see him go and the public may be transported to various stages of ecstatic bliss. And I am unabashedly with the public because nine years of Prime Minister Mulroney is enough. But decades more are left for the restoration of the one we first knew and loved before he became, for a time, the most popular politician in the history of Canada.

Waiting for Chrétien

MARCH 2, 1986

So, Little Nell is no longer with us, and Lord knows where the Match Girl went, and it's still hard for some to contemplate a world without Elvis. But let's try to comfort one another in our present sorrow; after all, Jean Chrétien has only gone on leave of absence. He hasn't gone far and I'll bet my fleece-lined parka he hasn't gone forever. Looked at on the cheerful side, Jean Chrétien has gone away to make a little money and, maybe, to write another speech.

Think upon those who jumped or fell from the pinnacle of power, yet lived to scramble back again. Churchill comes to mind, retired to Chartwell to become a bricklayer; de Gaulle, brooding at his country estate between regencies; Richard Nixon, even, who abandoned politics for corporate law. What about John Turner, who bolted the Trudeau cabinet and went into voluntary exile, taking a corner table at Winston's?

The record shows that Churchill returned to save the Free World, De Gaulle came back to save France a second time, while Nixon reversed his field to become president of the United States and invent investigative journalism. As for Turner, after ten years of studious retirement from politics, he emerged to become prime minister for ninety days.

There is no commandment in the theology of politics that says, "Thou shalt not quit." Indeed, there is an abundance of empirical evidence that suggests the best way for the ambitious to achieve high office is to know when to lay low. It doesn't always work, of course. Robert Winters, George Hees, and Davie Fulton all took early retirement, going off to improve their fortunes or tilt at other windmills while awaiting their opportunity. It seemed clear none of them missed life in Ottawa, but none missed the next leadership convention either. For a decade, Paul Hellyer never missed a leadership convention of either major party.

Banking the fires of a burning ambition is hard to do when you're spending most of your waking hours in the company of a leader whose talents are conspicuously lacking when compared to your own. The life of the Crown Prince in politics can be unbearable, inviting severe depression, gout, and damage to the liver. Turner found it so; it should not surprise you that Chrétien feels the same. If anyone understands Chrétien's decision, it would be Turner.

Heirs apparent to the leadership of political parties tend to grow old before their time if they spend it in the House of Commons. Length of service and prolonged experience cut no ice with convention delegates; in fact, these factors are more likely to repel them. Politicians who put their political careers in mothballs, or otherwise mask their interest, have better convention prospects than do those who relentlessly serve and ply their trade in Ottawa. If it were otherwise, Paul Martin would have swept Pierre Trudeau off the convention floor; Davie Fulton would have routed Robert Stanfield; John Crosbie would have buried Brian Mulroney. The present prime minister was the most pristine candidate in history, having never run for anything except the leadership of his party. There appears to be a message here: The less you're seen in the midst of things, the more you're noticed when there's an opening at the top.

Chrétien got the message. If Turner prospers in his role, Chrétien will not have his opportunity. If Turner falters, then the longer Chrétien stays away, the more he will be missed. Meanwhile, the role of heir apparent, as Turner would know, is more enjoyable when spent profitably and in the company of one's own choosing. Imagine the pleasures and palaces in a new life spent without André Ouellet.

Mr. Chrétien's Whispering Campaign
for Human Rights

NOVEMBER 6, 1994

No one should be surprised how little memory there is of the prime minister raising the issue of human rights with China's Premier Li Peng. A foreign ministry spokesman for the Chinese government denied the matter had been discussed "either in the large meeting or in the private meeting."

The premier of Nova Scotia, one of the Gang of Nine who accompanied the prime minister on the trade mission to China, said the human rights issue was "not raised in our meeting." (Later, Premier Savage recanted. He said, while removing bamboo slivers from under his fingernails, "I checked my notes and I made a simple honest mistake.") It is now unanimous among the Canadian delegation that the prime minister raised the matter of human rights with Premier Li. Sort of.

It was surely naive of anyone to think the prime minister was about to risk a very nice trade junket by needling the Chinese about their wretched treatment of some of their own citizens. They are not amenable to our opinions and sensibilities and would much rather talk about the possibility of buying one or two Candu nuclear reactors. And so would we. As to how best we can foster trading relations with this potential consumer colossus, the answer is any way they would like.

If the Chinese were to announce that they proposed to shoot those now being held following the demonstrations at Tiananmen Square at a rate of one per day, the response of the world's principal trading nations would be interesting if not entirely principled. The ambivalence and procrastination would be exceeded only by the anxiety induced by the prospect of lost sales. But of course, the Chinese would not behave so abominably. Torture and imprisonment and slave labour, yes. The prime minister and his entourage grant them that. But no more than that. And we reserve the right to raise the subject of human rights in whatever roundabout way we wish, if at all. We do not expect them to be responsive since they have a good idea of just how we feel about the subject. They know fervour and genuine concern and commitment when they hear it; they didn't hear it from us.

The prime minister has the same view of China as that of the American Congress. Whatever else they are, the Chinese represent a market of more than a billion consumers and growing. Canada's China policy is rooted in the first principle of affordability: Can we afford *not* to develop positive, friendly, constructive relations with a nation offering so promising a market for Canadian goods? In the rush of the world trading nations to do business with the Chinese, what is Canada supposed to do? Become the moral missionary for the G-7? Who then would sell the reactors?

The American Congress has twice, since the Tiananmen riots, extended the benefits of most favoured trading nation to the Chinese, much to the relief of Presidents George Bush and Bill Clinton. The Parliament of Canada, in its own way, will approve of the prime minister's visit and the results. After all, everybody got something, except the prisoners and the repressed.

Robert Kennedy, as idealistic a public man as could be found in this century, once warned of the need for realism in politics. To ignore reality, he said, risked becoming sentimental, which would mean crying a lot. I once repeated Kennedy's words to a full hall of Queen's University students and felt a shudder of protest run through an audience that clearly preferred sentiment to an often bleak reality. I wonder how they feel today about Jean Chrétien's mission to China. Do they weep?

The reality is that the subject of human rights—and our probative concerns, having seen the riots on television—was not raised by the prime minister in any substantive, direct manner. Indeed, mentioned, if at all, *en passant*, in such a way as to convince Dr. Savage, on first recollection, as to not having been mentioned at all. The further reality is that this suits most Canadians, including most editorial boards whose members would, on any other day, hound a prime minister to his grave for appointing a party hack as wharfinger. And it suits our new theology, which is the religion of the Bottom Line.

It would be quite unfair to expect anything more from the prime minister than the tangential mutterings he devoted to a topic hardly anyone back home deeply cared about. Instead, there were the signings of commercial agreements worth more than $1 billion and there is more to come. The nuclear reactor sales, if consummated, will save an entire industry. Besides looking ahead, nothing so improves the civil conduct of nations so much as free trade, as the prime minister is sure to remind us. In the Great Hall of the People, strike up the band and let freedom ring.

Man of the Year Found in Halifax Hotel

JUNE 20, 1995

This will not be about the G-7. Promise. It was interesting, in watching the coverage, how often CNN television reported the site of the meetings simply as "Nova Scotia." A good enough description since Halifax, as a dateline, would be insufficient for many American viewers and, besides, according to one visiting journalist, Halifax was only Akron, with sea water.

But the G-7 gathering served to remind me of the prime minister. I don't know about the rest of you, but I need to be reminded from time to time since I cannot think of any prime minister since King who so infrequently occupies my thoughts. My head has more time for Bill Clinton these days, or Boris Yeltsin. Then, last week, there stood Jean Chrétien, the host at Halifax, posing between Clinton and Helmut Kohl in the photo, and I said to myself, "Gee, there he is." It was almost like an Elvis sighting.

You may have noticed Clinton is now totally grey; Yeltsin has become more flushed and bloated, while John Major looks—well—desiccated (as would any of the others had they that avenging woman constantly on their case, spouting memoirs). Meanwhile, Chrétien has not aged a day since taking office.

Were we to rewrite the constitution and re-allocate the various powers, it might be wise to give politics to the provinces. As it is, without amendment, the only serious politics in Canada today is provincial.

The reason politics is still a serious business in the provinces is because that is where serious matters of governance are now domiciled. In the emergent style of pass-it-on federalism —"if you can't privatize it, give it to the provinces"—the challenge to government is how to make indolence look like work. The angst of federal ministers in today's cabinet is the result of seeking career satisfaction in doing little and planning to do less.

It is a period of history in which this prime minister was born to serve. No prime minister in our history has ever been held so entirely and agreeably blameless. Whatever the difficulties, they are mostly provincial, and when not, they are global. On arrival in Halifax last week for the summit, the prime minister was pressed to justify the conduct of his Nova Scotia minister, David Dingwall, who had arranged the transfer of $34 million in federal highways appropriations away from improving a part of the Trans-Canada Highway known as "Death Valley," to improving a road (and himself) in his own riding in Cape Breton. (Even the citizens of Glace Bay, near-by, would protest.)

The prime minister's reply to media inquiries was to say the subject was a provincial matter, a statement that was partly—about 26.8 percent—true. It was enough to get by under today's conditions in a market where most politicians are discounted on sight. When facing the usual bleak summary of the day's non-achievements of the G-7 at Halifax, the prime minister remained exuberant, in his familiarly dogged way, insisting "we got a lot of business done."

That was, maybe, 14.3 percent true. But such partial scores yield their own magic. Those who supported Allan Rock's gun control bill admired the prime minister for his unflagging support of both the bill and his minister, and his unyielding firmness with caucus waverers. Those who opposed the bill were vociferous in their hostility to Rock, and relentless in their pressure on Liberal MPs, but no one took on Chrétien.

It is agreed: Chrétien continues to appeal to Canadians because he is not his predecessor, Brian Mulroney; but the relevance of all that is surely declining. Also as plain is the fact that, for most of the electorate, Chrétien has no obvious or palatable alternative. Certainly not Preston Manning; obviously not Lucien Bouchard. The prime minister, then, competes every day against himself; it should be hard to lose in that sort of contest.

But the Mulroney part of this excogitation could be stretched further to suggest he was, or may have been, the last of the Canadian prime ministers who would be given serious work to do, barring future wars or other disasters. John Diefenbaker, Lester Pearson, and Pierre Trudeau were each enormously busy men at the job of being prime minister. Each professed a personal vision as broad as their agenda was long. Whatever else, no one could suggest they were not men of purpose.

Mulroney governed in that tradition, enjoying successive popular mandates greater than any of his predecessors. What now seems apparent is that he did whatever was left to do, and the cumulative works of all of them have left a country exhausted of purpose, limited in vision, and convinced it is broke. Enter Jean Chrétien, not in the least yesterday's man, as some of us had said, but very much the man of the hour, of the year, of the decade, and perhaps beyond. Not a man for all seasons, but easily sufficient for this one.

Profile in Courage, Ottawa Style

FEBRUARY 10, 1995

The minister of national defence—an oxymoron dressed in a suit—now has two more videos on his hands. One of them, the third in a series of "Airborne Hits of the Nineties," was filmed after the regiment had been reportedly tidied up. The video, on a scale of one-to-ten in shock value, was not much better than a four.

The newest hit video, however, features an all-navy cast from the HMS *Yukon*. It confirms persistent rumours that it is not only elite paratroopers who still remain at the anal stage of life, but sailors too.

For defence minister David Collenette, this latest release, rated PG-13, invites speculation as to when he will resign. It would be no less than reinforcement of the sound ministerial principle he established in resolving the Airborne video crisis: The best way to solve a problem is to remove it.

I realize how impolite it seems to make light of matters others in the journalism trade are obliged to take seriously. Surely, however, it is becoming difficult to keep a straight face amidst all this posturing and buck-passing and amidst the debris of the minister's policy of a simplistic, massive retaliation against anything coming before him that is not clean-shaven, properly dressed, and polite. It is because of his cut-and-run, dismissive style that he now finds himself so soon running out of scapegoats.

It might keep the wolves from drawing nearer to his sleigh if the minister now threw a few generals over the side, or an admiral or two. But in the end, there may be one more video from some other military formation and the sleigh will grind to a halt. The minister will then have the terminal option of firing himself.

What George Bernard Shaw said about youth still holds: It is a pity it is wasted on young people. The rites of passage of exuberant young men, in particular, invariably involve acts of self-abasement and the complete abnegation of the manner in which they have been raised.

As, for example, the rites of spring, depicted annually from the beaches of Florida, observed in fraternity initiations, graduations, and—lest we forget—office parties, not to mention the newest fashions of flesh-piercings and brandings. The fact that rites of the military seem somewhat off-the-latrine-wall should not mislead even a novice politician into the belief that the armed forces have somehow become the exclusive refuge for demented young men. The minister's response has been to forbid practices of which he disapproves (quoting military rules and regulations that, in reality, forbid everything).

The military has a discipline problem. Has anyone checked the average Canadian family? Or the Liberal caucus? More important, the military has a morale problem. When nursemaid Alice told Christopher Robin "a soldier's life is terrible hard," she could have been speaking of the downsized Canadian military now that the enemy is the deficit: obliged to do more, put more of its people more often at risk, and be paid less for it.

The Canadian soldier is paid as little as $21,100 a year. When someone asked if that were not a tad light (military pay is frozen for all ranks), a spokesman for the minister replied, "a lot of Canadians are paid less." But a lot of Canadians are not asked to go to Bosnia, or dig up land mines in Cambodia, or be belittled by David Collenette's director of communications.

Is Prayer on the Wayne?

JANUARY 20, 1995

Elsie Wayne is the only Progressive Conservative member of the federal Parliament east of Sherbrooke, Québec and, for that matter, west of Sherbrooke. Wayne represents the electors of Saint John, the loyalist city of New Brunswick, in the province of Premier Frank McKenna, who is the Robin Hood of regional disparity.

While McKenna is snatching whole payrolls from the indolent and wealthy—such as British Columbia and Ontario—and relocating them in Sherwood Forest, New Brunswick, Wayne is conducting a drive to restore the Lord's Prayer to the House of Commons. Wayne's drive so far has recorded twenty thousand names of those who have signed a petition calling upon "the House of Commons to close the Parliamentary prayer with 'Through Jesus Christ our Lord. Amen,' and reinstate the Lord's Prayer at the conclusion of the opening prayer."

As a child of the manse, raised in the belief in the efficacy of prayer, I will march in any parade demonstrating in favour of praying for our members of Parliament, especially those in the House of Commons, and more particularly, the minister of finance and Lloyd Axworthy. Even though I don't think there is a hope in hell all the prayers will be answered, allowing as how not all those who pray will be beseeching the same result. Yet there is value of a sort for supplicants in admitting some temporal matters are well beyond them—among these, praying for wisdom for our parliamentarians, something parliamentarians themselves have been doing since 1867, with limited success.

In the Book of Common Prayer, Anglicans find prayers prepared for their political leaders. In my more callow years, I found it difficult to join the congregation in offering up humble petitions for Liberals I considered beyond salvation. However, as a latter-day ecumenicist, and allowing for the severity of my country's present condition, assuming the *Wall Street Journal* has the scoop on all this, by all means let us pray.

It is not yet clear to me, however, that a recital of the Lord's Prayer is essential to the order of business of the House of Commons. Nor should it be necessary, in the public interest, that honourable members conclude by praying, "Through Jesus Christ our Lord. Amen." And I doubt very much that Wayne's petition will persuade her colleagues in the House to change the revised prayer, which makes reference to God but not His Son.

This is not confirmation of the triumph of Satan (in a recent by-election) nor of a new majority in the House committed to godlessness. It's only the fact that—how to put this?—not every member of the House is a Christian. And not all of the constituents of honourable members are Christian. Since the House of Commons represents all Canadians, of whom some are Christians and others are not, the true religion of politics and government is secularism. No one needs to be a Christian to be a politician. And vice versa.

It is well within the mandate of a bishop of the clergy to aver, in the course of his prayer at Elsie Wayne's "first annual prayer breakfast" (according to my morning paper), that those present were committed to Jesus and there was "no other name in which we can be saved." That's okay, as spoken by a professed Christian, but one might wonder how it resonates among those not of the faith, who are Jews, or Muslim, or heathens, and who are also Wayne's constituents or parliamentary colleagues.

It was the Americans who took pains to draw the line in their constitution to forever separate the church from the state. As Canadians, typically, we have managed to do the same thing without talking about it. But today, the American right—inspired by its congressional bishopric in Washington—lists school prayer well ahead of debt reduction among its priorities. Not too far behind the issue of compulsory time-out to pray in America's schools are other issues on the right-wing agenda including text book censorship and, in the eloquent words of House Speaker Newt Gingrich's recently deposed official historian, a more full and fair presentation of the viewpoints of the Nazis and the Ku Klux Klan in the contentious issues of their day. These, and the banishment of Big Bird and the Public Broadcasting Service from American television, march in the vanguard of the foremost purposes of the new order.

The romance of the right with religiosity does not need any endorsement or blessing from us, much less emulation. While it is impressive that twenty thousand petitioners in and about Saint John have signed on to Wayne's crusade to put Jesus back in the prayers of her parliamentary companions, I like to believe that goodly number better represents the powers of Wayne's persuasiveness than it does the merits of her case.

Still, no one who wants to pray should be denied the opportunity. Those who want to pray Wayne's way are free to do so, silently or aloud—wherever a few are gathered, the Good Book says—but they might wish to do so out of hearing of those who prefer to pray their own way. Isn't that what our country is all about—so far?

Thanks, But No Thanks

APRIL 25, 1995

The Tories, having found themselves a leader, need now to find their party. Despite the high-toned, haughty advice of some, the road to political recovery is not through Preston Manning's backyard in Calgary. To rediscover their identity as a national party, the Tories need to decide who their constituents are, for whom they speak, and what they represent.

It is entertaining, in an otherwise bleakly cynical prospectus, to read recent criticism of Jean Charest, the new Tory leader, as being "calculating," having expressed his opinion the budget cuts were too severe. Whereas, following on, the Reform Party is proclaimed "the conscience of Parliament," so burdened with scruple its members dare not eat in the parliamentary restaurant, and whose heart is so pure it would happily sacrifice universal health care to cut the deficit.

But the Reform Party is not the conscience of Parliament; indeed, this may be the first Parliament we've known to be without one. What the Reform Party does represent in today's politics is the guarantor of a Liberal majority. (One of the secrets of Jean Chrétien's popularity is Preston Manning.) So long as the Reform Party serves as the government-in-waiting in Ottawa, the wait will remain interminable. Why is that so hard to understand?

This is not to suggest the prime minister is without redeeming qualities; he has many of them. One of them is to be lucky, to enjoy a Parliament without serious opposition, one without a true alternative government-in-waiting.

Still, it is breathtaking to read criticism of the Tory leader as "calculating," followed by advice that the Tories and the Reformists must either merge or form an alliance of convenience, the one party running where it is strong while the weaker party stands aside. This works, we are told, "in many other democracies."

How wonderful. It is true that trade-offs and deals are routinely cut where the parties are nearly all marginalized by the narrowness of their own dogma, so that the weak or venal men—invariably they are men—may enjoy some taste of power in incoherent coalitions. The proposal that the Progressive Conservative Party of Canada do the same is insulting. But not nearly so as the inference that most Tories would be happy wearing Reformist clothes and upholding Reformist policy.

But let us imagine how the deal—a merger, let us say—would work. For the brief time he might survive, Charest would serve as Manning's senior Québec advisor, next to God. The party policy, of course, would be as already cast in tablets, handed down from the Calgary head office: (1) the deficit, (2) the deficit, and (3) the deficit. The policy, as writ, guarantees lost deposits to Reform/Con candidates from the western borders of Québec to the eastern shores of Labrador; never before so great a moral victory for a party of conscience.

Apparently, everyone has forgotten that the political party that won the last election—the Liberals—talked the least about the deficit. The Reform Party, on the other hand, was irrepressible on the subject, as were the Tories. There is, however, no evidence to suggest the issue interested the voters.

The Tories need to recall their folly, which was to engage themselves—and worse, their new leader—in a bidding war with the Reformists as to who could cut the deficit more and faster. All of it, of course, was written on the wind. No one can now remember who said what about the deficit—albeit much of it desperate foolishness worked up by amateurs—or that the Liberals wisely said as little as possible.

But Kim Campbell, the Tory prime minister of the moment, did say—once—that some of the items filed under The Sacred Trust might have to be revisited in search of savings, an observation that seemed to induce media hysteria laced with frenzy.

Once let loose among the actuaries and the editors of the business press, upon a dark and uncertain terrain where her ignorance of proper answers was exceeded only by the superficiality of the questions, Campbell clearly failed to measure up.

But tomorrow is another day and another leader. There is some evidence of public interest in, and latent support for, a reconstituted Tory party. As for a constituency, the new Tories should look to the millions of Canadians who now feel shut out of national politics, unrepresented by either the party in power or by the Reformists to the right. These potential supporters include those who continue to be outraged by the government's hapless inability to retain workers jettisoned by corporate greed or to improve job opportunities for despairing young Canadians.

And it includes those Canadians who are nationalists in spirit and who look with alarm at the continuing erosion of their cultural and political institutions. In a media world fixated by the new accents of continentalism and internationalism, and the globaloney about unfettered free markets, there is urgent need for a distinctly Canadian voice and defined Canadian interest.

Finally, the more one learns about the tax system in the upper levels of corporate enterprise, the less equitable the system appears, and the more apparent it becomes that the middle class is being propagandized even while being victimized and slowly destroyed. The solutions to these problems are all political and are the proper work of the political parties. But nothing will get done, or even underway, until some party—dare one hope the Tories?—reforms the obscene methods of party campaign financing so that our political and parliamentary institutions are at long last in the hands of those who truly represent the Canadian people.

Why a Steamroller to Crush a Gnat?

JUNE 1985

Probably the best thing to do with Ernst Zundel would be to repatriate him or send him off to the next country of his choice. He has indicated a preference for South Africa and there is always Libya. Anyway, we have our own ample quota of home-grown nuts and we are less in need of imports.

Alden Nowlan, the late, much-missed Canadian poet, professed to the profound belief that the world was flat. He was a shameless promoter of the Flat Earth Society, a pamphleteer in the bargain, but such views were considered tolerably harmless—the Flat Earth constituency was never large, since 1492—though the cartographers might have been offended.

Zundel's heresy is considerably more grandiose and deeply offensive and it extends to the limits of society's tolerance for eccentrics. Still, we get into trouble with show trials, such as Zundel's was certain to become, because in the zealous attempt to prosecute a fool for his beliefs, we make fools of ourselves.

We prosecute a man, under a dubious section of the Criminal Code, for saying there was no Holocaust, an opinion deemed "likely to cause injury or mischief to a public interest." Were this so, nothing could have better served mischief to the public interest than the trial itself. Zundel was right: For forty thousand dollars in legal fees, he got a million dollars worth of advertising for his opinions. At least that much.

But if, on the other hand, it does no harm to promote Zundel's views through the media, providing them the notoriety of national exposure, where was the danger to public interest, to begin with, rising out of the personal exertions of an obscure pamphleteer?

What is most offensive in all this is the implication that Zundel's opinions regarding the Holocaust might, if not confronted in a court of law, somehow find currency among the Canadian general public. Either believe that, or conclude that politicians, by seizing upon the Criminal Code, summoned a steamroller to crush a gnat in order to impress their constituents of their intolerance of one man's unredemptive ignorance.

In the end, it is hard to believe anyone was made any wiser, including Zundel and his few pitiful supporters. If there are any surviving doubts, they could only be as to the motives of those who thought bringing Zundel to trial satisfied any interest other than their own.

Anyone who truly believes Canadians need protecting from the fevered mongerings of every crackpot in their midst is doomed to an eternal life of trivial pursuits. The Zundel example will not drive the authors of such opinions underground; it is more likely to inspire imitators to more vehement expression. And to paraphrase Andy Warhol, every crackpot in Canada will become a celebrity for a month.

Not to say that anti-Semitism and other vital poisons of racism are a trivial matter. But there is no evidence, in this country, of our belonging to a society so susceptible to intolerance that it cannot withstand the publication of outrageous opinion. Part of the satisfaction, for the racist, is in knowing his views are offensive to majority opinion. How much more satisfying to know they are also considered harmful to the public interest.

There are those who believe the Holocaust to be the figment of an enormous conspiracy. They are not many and most are either neo-Fascists or neo-illiterates. But others, who know the truth, are not beyond lending their own version to it.

Last January 27 marked the fortieth anniversary of the "liberation" of Auschwitz, the most infamous of the Nazi concentration camps, by forces of the Soviet Union. The anniversary at Auschwitz was observed with the laying of wreaths, a return by a remaining few of the camp's survivors, and by a torchlight parade (joined by Lech Walesa) in remembrance of those put to death there.

Journalist Hella Pick, writing in the *Manchester Guardian*, reported on the Russian commemoration: "This week Soviet media marked the anniversary by praising the courage of countless Soviet prisoners of war who had been among the dead at Auschwitz. But although the Soviet media noted that nationals of twenty-four countries had suffered in the camp, they made no mention of the fact that Jews had been the principal target of Hitler's holocaust."

Ironically enough, Zundel's revanchist views would be allowed in the Soviet Union since they do not challenge established opinion. It would be better that his views, or those like his, were tolerated here for the opposite reason. The truth, after all, is secure in a free society because no one is compelled to subscribe to it.

Me and Mr. Parizeau

MARCH 1991

For a man of nearly perfect certitude, the economic theorist and the politician fused in a common enterprise, the monetary question—which troubled Lévesque—has not been entirely resolved. Could Québec become independent while its monetary policy was made in Ottawa, its currency in Winnipeg? Ventilating these questions, the most vexing of all for Parizeau, takes one into the higher altitudes of banking and commerce, into thinner air. Could a ground-level observer, looking up, see entrails of doubt?

"Technically speaking," Parizeau says, "it's not all that difficult to answer the question. However, every time you mention—in any society—money, all kinds of emotions flow in all directions. I've never been particularly emotional about these things. It doesn't prevent me from speaking; it never did. There's no doubt, as far as Québec is concerned, a distinct currency has been in the past—less today, much less today—considered something extremely dangerous, something that would move all kinds of people to make emotional statements: 'We'll go down the drain . . .' "

Since then, these emotions have been tempered by experience. The monetary policy conducted by the Bank of Canada in 1981, and the policy conducted by the bank last year, have been—"and I'm not the only one to say so"—contrary to the interests of the Canadian and Québec economies.

"That should never happen," says Parizeau. "And therefore, I'm faced here in Québec by two groups of people—no, by two reactions—and from week to week they're never quite the same. [There are] those who say it would be more comforting if we had the same Canadian currency, but does that mean we'll have the same monetary policy? And I say, well, you can't have it both ways. If it's the same currency, it's the same monetary policy. It's how our system works.

Our banking system and our financial system is so structured that you can't have one monetary policy on one side of the country and another monetary policy on the other."

But regardless of monetary policy, I ask Parizeau, you can have more than one fiscal policy?

"Oh yes," Parizeau says, enjoying the opening. "Canada is proof of that." For example, when the Bank of Canada tightened the monetary screws, largely because of inflationary pressures in southern Ontario, the fiscal policy of the Ontario government headed in the opposite direction.

Then, returning to the major question: "Some people would be more comfortable. But on the other hand, dammit, will we have to sit still for those monetary policies such as we opposed in 1981? No. Enough. Of course, a lot of people in Québec are ambivalent about this. While they consider that comforting, they are much less afraid than they were ten years ago."

Parizeau says there are now spokesmen for Québec's business community who are saying, 'If we need to have a Québec currency, we'll have it.'

"Ten years ago, the issue was never discussed in these terms," he says. "In English Canada these days, I hear all kinds of reactions about this question: 'Who are these guys in Québec who think we're going to have the same currency? That's pie in the sky. We'll never accept that.' "

Indeed, we are all hearing these things. Canada's currency has become our karma, a comfort to its own ambivalence. And to the karmic force of the money supply, add some good, old-fashioned Anglo-Saxon common sense, which yields our strategy: Since Canadians would refuse to share their currency with an independent Québec, what would Québec do for money?

"The problem with that, you know," Parizeau said, "is eventually one has to go back to techniques. Even for when there is a Québec currency, Québecers become the proud owners of a quarter of the [Canadian] money supply. There is no way, in our financial system, that the Bank of Canada could reduce the money supply in one area. If they wanted to reduce the money supply, they have to do it throughout the country and Canadians would find themselves with a floating debt—thank God for each and every dollar—a floating debt of a hundred billion dollars in Québec. And when you start looking at simply the technicalities of this, well, you do just about what I do these days: I say, look, we'll have to look at a common currency.

"Everyone is very sentimental and emotional about these things. Let us pray after a few months it will pass. Eventually the technicians will have to handle the issue. I just leave you—I always repeat the same thing—with one thought: When Ireland left the United Kingdom in 1923, in a very difficult atmosphere, the pound sterling remained the common currency for twenty years. Money talks. Actually, I would think everyone will realize that. Technically speaking, it is much better to have a common currency."

Was it too craven of me, at that moment, to agree? I imagined myself driving from New Brunswick through Québec to, perish the thought, Ottawa. Should I stay overnight in Québec, would not the common currency be a convenience? A convenience for anyone doing business in Québec?

"What you raise here is something different," Parizeau says, to my surprise, since it had not been my intention to change the subject. "A lot of people in English Canada, at the present time, are saying about economic association: 'No way, no way. They won't have their cake and eat it too.'

"A lot of what they're talking about, in terms of economic association, isn't really connected to having your cake and eating it too. Transportation, for instance—water, the St. Lawrence Seaway, railways, roads. There are all sorts of arguments with respect to transportation. If Canada came to be divided in two parts, do we keep the present arrangements or do we change them? The first country that would raise these questions would not be Québec. It would be Canada. In a number of such areas, the idea is not Québec asking for something, hoping to get it, and Canada saying, 'Well, let me think about.' It isn't that way at all."

People have asked me, on returning from Québec, the question, "Okay, but did you like him?" In the way it is possible with an adversary, yes; I found a lot in him to respect. I also see him as a more formidable adversary than Lévesque, who came close enough to separating the country.

In an encounter I once had with Lévesque, off camera in a television studio, he appeared to be angry, which made whatever he said sound scolding. In a way, he seemed arrogant, but also unsure of himself. He lacked Parizeau's serenity, perhaps because he was not at peace with himself.

"Our great weakness," Lévesque once said, "and the source of nearly all the others, is economic. In my opinion, that is the Number One problem." It may also have been the Number One problem of his leadership.

He could not make a reasoned argument for his case. Instead, he would be scornful of the argument against it. He would say, "I pity those who, in the name of artificial and misguided concern for the individual and for human values, which they feel [Québec] would be unable to respect, unless properly hemmed in, superciliously isolate themselves from the errors as well as the collective achievements of French Canada. This kind of attitude is what withers men most. It is a caricature of individualism."

It is not difficult to decide which of these two champions of their cause would be the more persuasive. Since "the main argument against sovereignty" will be over economics, Parizeau brings to the debate both credentials and credibility, along with considerable political experience. He is also unlikely to be distracted by sentiment or by a Cassandra chorus from English Canada.

At the close of our conversations, as we stood at the door, I told him many English Canadians, who have been ardently devoted to Québec for so long, and militantly sensitive and responsive to Québec's interest, are now fearful—should things turn out wrong for them or right for him—that both would lose in the end. Before turning away to his desk, Parizeau said, "Lévesque used to worry about that."

PART III

Somewhat Uplifting

O Canada: Could You Hum a Few Bars?

JUNE 30, 1995

It should be an easy task to write a Canada Day eulogy, some vaulting paean of praise and celebration, something to stir the blood, quicken the pulse, and lift the spirits. What this country probably needs is a poet laureate. The British always keep one on hand and the Americans produce one for their presidential inaugurations.

God knows we must have enough poets; they are almost as plentiful as painters. The lack of a poet laureate in Canada may be a budget matter, what with the enormous deficit and all. Since our government can't afford any longer to buy Canadian art, it is unlikely it could afford a poet laureate, even if we had one.

Still, it should be easy to write some inspiring prose, if only blank verse, on the birthday of the greatest country in the world. Perhaps you noticed, as you read those praiseworthy words about Canada, your own slight, involuntary flinch. Not so much a flinch, but more like a twitch, a sudden compulsive jerk of the shoulder, accompanied by a grimace, as though from a spasm of pain.

For 127 years—or is it 128?—Canadians have been fiercely proud of their country but reluctant to let it show. They have frequently been told by scolds of one sort or another that they do not know enough of their own history. It is also often said we are a country without heroes. The sparsity of heroes may be attributed to our paucity of history, which might explain why Canadians do not talk about themselves much. A man named Herman Finer once wrote, "Happy nations have no history." He was an American.

We do of course have a history. But it is not a rivetting narrative, unless you are particularly drawn to explorers and bachelor politicians, and the telling of it defines us as rather benign, somewhat noble, and quite forgiving. Happily, Canadians have never suffered under the spell of tyrants, indulged in the slaughter of innocents, nor committed calculated acts of genocide. Compared to other nations of the world, Canada's history, if not utterly happy, could at least be pronounced satisfactory and suitable for our own children.

A further word about heroes: It is not so much we do not have them, it's only that we appear not to have settled upon who they are. One of the striking differences between sightseeing in a European city and in a Canadian city, is that European cities are crowded with statues of their national heroes. In Fredericton, the capital city of New Brunswick, where this Canada Day eulogy is being composed, there are only two statues around that I know of; one is of Lord Beaverbrook, who was born in Ontario and became famous in England, and the other is of Robert Burns, the Scottish poet.

None of this tentativeness need dampen our spirit of celebration. In my humble (of course) opinion, Canada is simply the greatest country in the world in which to live, work, raise children, and become a grandfather. That we are not a nation like any other makes comparisons too often strained. What can one say about a 127-year-old country, going on 128, that did not have its own national flag until sometime in the 1960s?

On the eve of Canada Day, listening to the CBC, we heard Joey Slinger singing Canada's national anthem; he made a poor fist of it. But Slinger is everyman in Canada; everyone knows the tune, hardly anyone knows the words. In America, everyone knows the words to the "Star Spangled Banner" but you have to be a coloratura soprano to sing it. In Canada, when people are upset, they boo their national anthem; in America, they burn their flag. (There is a bill before the U.S. Congress that would make flag-burning unconstitutional.)

You see where we're headed with this eulogy. Whenever Canadians begin singing the praises of their country, they end up talking about America. It may not be possible to define Canada without describing America and how it looks to us. Still, the reason Canadians get uncomfortable when they hear someone say Canada is the greatest country in the world is that it sounds American. This has always made it difficult for us to express our satisfaction or acknowledge our good fortune on being Canadian without sounding holier-than-thou, even though we are.

We have got this far in praise of Canada without mentioning the scenery. One ought to have credentials as a poet, or lyricist, at least a novelist, to do justice to how Canada looks. Canadians cheerfully take the scenery as a given; it's what goes with it that they enjoy. People walk around with memories of Canada in their heads that they don't talk about, but will hang on to all their lives.

Twenty-six years ago, I went fishing for bass on a lake in northern Manitoba, and we took the morning catch to shore where the guides cooked it over a wood fire and served it up with baked beans and cranberry sauce and we dined on the huge, flat rocks at the water's edge drinking strong coffee cut with tinned milk, sitting afterwards in the afternoon sun and smoking cigars.

When people come to visit where I live, which is along a great watershed of lakes and rivers, they always ask about the fishing, especially if they are from America. Have I been fishing lately? Where do I fish mostly? For what?

The truth is I don't fish anymore, though I feel awkward telling people so since I don't like to disappoint their definition of me. When I was a boy, I often used to rise early, walk three miles to a brook, cut an alder for a pole, put a worm on a hook, and catch trout. I'd clean the fish, take it to my grandmother's and she would roll it in flour, put it in a frying pan and I would eat fresh brook trout for breakfast.

Many of us love this country even on the day after Canada Day because of all we carry around in our heads about living in the greatest country in the world. Most of it is our secret and more awaits our discovery. For all anyone knows, the best of being a Canadian is yet to come.

Besides, I Knew Her Mother

AUGUST 23, 1994

The Queen has completed her visit to Canada, which took her from Halifax to the Northwest Territories. Like many Canadians, I suspect, I have not been an avid follower of her tour, being distracted by events of greater immediacy. But had the royal itinerary brought Her Majesty anywhere close to Jemseg, New Brunswick, I would have gathered up my grandchildren and found them space along her route of passage.

A correspondent for one of my morning papers who covered the royal visit (in a manner my grandmother would have described as "smart-alecky") referred to Elizabeth II as "the British Queen of Canada." On reading that, I tried to sort out its meaning. Does it mean, "the British Queen" who is Queen of Canada? Or does it mean, the queen of Canada "who is British?" Is it more like saying, "the British Queen of Wales?" Or like saying, "the Canadian Queen of New Zealand?"

And what is so strange, or amusing—since I suspect it is seen to be so—about a woman whose husband is Greek, and whose father was the King, and who is now the Queen of Canada? As our children say, "You have a problem with that?"

In a world swarming with multiculturalists, amidst an emergent ethos, encouraged by the *Wall Street Journal*, proclaiming a new commerce that knows no border—why can't a monarch come from just any old place? Anyway, is the trouble with "the British Queen of Canada" that she is born British, and not born Canadian? Or that she lives in London? London, England, that is?

For many years now, argument has been made that for Canadians to have a proper monarch, she or he should be Canadian-born, bred, and resident. To achieve this, either the Queen would have to give birth to a child while visiting Ottawa (or Hamilton or wherever), then leave it behind to become Canada's reigning monarch and to seed our very own royal family. Otherwise, Canadians would have to invent a royal family, perhaps through the facilities of Lotto-Canada, or by allowing the choice to be made unilaterally by some scrupulously detached and unconflicted body, such as the National Association of Canadian Newspaper Publishers; or maybe by striking a Royal Commission.

But in the Canadian way, reason is restored when it is explained that the Queen of England, as she is often described, is really only the Queen of the Commonwealth, which used to be British but no longer is. This is also to mollify those who imagined the presence of British royalty a constant inspiration to separatist sentiment in Québec, as well as provocative to Roman Catholics or latter-day Lutherans, among others, who are not entirely comfortable bending the knee to a "Defender of the Faith" who is, among much else, the First Anglican.

Of course, the Queen is the Queen of Canada, and there is no other. Her father, who was the King of Canada, was King, emperor, and Defender of the Faith; further, the Canadian monarch's agent in Canada once truly represented the monarch, being the likes of Viscount Monck or the Earl of Minto or Lord Byng of Vimy. All governors general posted to Rideau Hall once came from Great Britain. Not until 1952 was a Canadian appointed to the post, the first home-brew GG being Vincent Massey, whose family was in trade. The next may be a hockey player.

The Canadian monarchy has been whatever various of Canada's governments wished it to be. Canadians now have an anthem of their own, with flag to match, while royal visitors come and go under the managed care of Canadian keepers. Possibly the only truly generous contribution ever made by a Canadian government to the perpetuation of the monarchy was during the St. Laurent years, when the decision was taken to remove the royal (Canadian) coat-of-arms from mail boxes, thus liberating the royal family from all responsibility for the post office. (At the time, this act was mistakenly seen by monarchists as but further encroachment on the Crown by republican activists.)

It is remarkable the monarchy has survived in Canada after so many years of tinkering, tampering, and running down the institution. Each generation has produced its own quota of the intellectually precocious and ideologically daring who have taken a run at this anomalous Canadian institution.

The point to be made is that the Queen is our monarch, and likely she and her successors will be all that will be available in that line of work. Our ruler only does what we say. And only says what we ask be said, and goes where we tell her to go. Whatever the problem with the monarchy, it is really a problem we have with ourselves; we cannot make up our minds about it. But for all those who don't want the Queen (and nothing personal in that), there are easily as many who don't want a president, and even more who certainly would not want one if they knew who it would be.

Would it be a woman? A man? French? English? Other? Religion? Would we have a Triple-E president or an appointed one? Would the president have real powers, such as those of dissolution, or be kept around purely for ceremonial and social purposes? Would the president retire at sixty-five? On a pension? How many presidents and ex-presidents could we afford to keep at one time?

As you can readily see, I have given more thought to this subject than most and I have reached my own conclusion. God save the Queen.

The Passing Parade

AUGUST 12, 1994

On a splendid summer's Thursday in August, a touch of September in the air, I drove over to the Combat Training Centre at Canadian Forces Base Gagetown (which adjoins the town of Oromocto) to attend the Officer Graduation Parade, an occasion that sounds better in translation: "Cérémonies de fin de cours de la formation d'officier."

Thursday's parade produced something of a bumper crop of second lieutenants—three hundred and two of them—some of whom will serve in community-based militia units. About 60 percent of the graduates, however, soon will be, or have been, serving in United Nations peacekeeping missions around the world. The commanding officer of the Combat Training Centre describes his command as a "Land Force Centre of Excellence" charged with training "professional combat soldiers and leaders." From where I watched, they looked the part.

These young men and women (I counted three women in the march-past) "will be taking Canada's reputation" with them as they serve abroad in Croatia, Bosnia, Herzegovina, Mozambique, and Rwanda, said Maj. Gen. Robert Gaudreau, speaking at the ceremonies. He told the graduates they would soon be wearing the UN blue beret in a country where they would represent "one of the few who cares about human life, the elimination of pain and suffering, and the establishment of real peace."

A number of the graduates on Thursday rose through the ranks to become junior officers. Gaudreau, who joined the army as a signalman in 1961, was another, and his service record annotates his progression towards the senior officer he has become.

Within a year of enlistment, Gaudreau was selected for officer training. After being commissioned, he was posted to the Royal Twenty-second—the "Van Doos"—as a platoon commander, later intelligence officer, transport officer, the company second-in-command, at postings at Valcartier, Québec, Lahr, and Cyprus. He spent a year at Army Staff College, Kingston, returning to Cyprus as operations officer and company commander. He made major in 1974, became commanding officer of One Commando Airborne Regiment, serving a third hitch in Cyprus. From there, onward and upward still. Some of those graduating in Thursday's ceremonies will enjoy parallel careers.

"You are entering interesting times," Gaudreau told the army's newest officers. "On the other hand, the battle for the budget dollar is ongoing and never-ending. Don't worry about that. You can't control it in any event. Your seniors will do the worrying for you. In operational terms, it is an unstable world out there. There are going to be more Somalias and Bosnias in our future, and you and the soldiers you lead have to be ready . . . Take your new skills, your enthusiasm, your hopes and apply them in leading the best soldiers in the world."

I don't know what the graduates and officer cadets made of Gaudreau as they listened, standing at ease under a blazing sun leavened by a brisk northwesterly blowing off the Saint John River. In truth, this was a good day, a merciful day, to be standing on parade with the cooling winds and the speeches brief. It was during the Invocation by the two padres, representing two religions and both official languages, that the corps sustained its only casualties; I watched two cadets, fallen to the ground somewhere in the rear ranks, being helped to a nearby ambulance.

On this date, fifty years ago, and within the memory of at least some of the invited guests, the Canadian First Army had hurled itself against the German enemy near Falaise in Normandy and been turned back. Three days later, they tried again to reach Falaise—this was Operation Tractable—but when they lit yellow flares to show their position (as planned), they were bombed by Allied aircraft who saw the flares as target indicators. Thirteen men were killed and fifty-three injured. Six days later, August 17, the Canadians finally captured Falaise, closing the iron ring on two German divisions and opening the way to Caen.

Such ceremonies as a graduation parade for young officers of the land force (which is to say, not only the infantry but armour, field artillery, and air defence artillery), give oxygen to memory and reflection. The army is rightly a deeply conservative institution: Half the nation's history is of its making and falls under its care and custody. The old men who return to witness these parades are heavy with their battle honours and they clank like mounted cavalry as they walk. One meets people at these sorts of function one otherwise rarely sees, the sort of random crowd one might encounter in a hotel lobby, after the fire alarm has sounded. But some of those present had fought in the Falaise gap and are among the few who know exactly where they were fifty years ago, to this day.

They are comfortable in this familiar environment, even if it is the new army, and at home with these young officers. Perhaps they feel a twinge of envy. The comradeship, while unspoken, is profound. The experience all know and hold in common is the apprenticeship in the art and practice of soldiering. What they know, they know no one else knows.

They have learned the traditions of regiments, the many histories of war and peace, of hardship, fear, and misadventure, and the redemptive value of courage and tenacity. And they know their politicians who, through all history, have willingly sold them cheap as parts and pawns of national strategies. As they did yesterday, today, and will tomorrow. When I said to Dick Dillon, honourary Colonel of the Royal Canadian Regiment, that the graduates looked like very good soldiers, he said, "They always do." Then he said, "They're a hell of a lot smarter than we ever were." They will need to be.

Why Aren't We in Haiti?

AUGUST 2, 1994

Bosnian Serb snipers began their week well. On Monday, they shot two women and a dog. In a related development, Serbian President Slobodan Milosevic proved unable, or unwilling, to prevail upon the

Bosnian Serbs to accept the peace plan proposed by American, Russian, and several European governments. The shooting continues.

Meanwhile, the United Nations has voted to approve an American invasion of Haiti, should it be deemed necessary, in order to depose the military junta that had earlier deposed the democratically elected president, Jean-Bertrand Aristide. It interests me that the UN would be so eagerly compliant (the Chinese abstained) when there has been such great reluctance to threaten military action against the intransigent Serbs.

The troubles created by Bosnian Serbs, Croatian Serbs, and Serbian Serbs, flow from the end of the Cold War and out of the resurgence of Balkan nationalism. We have long since become accustomed to the barbarian excesses; there is a broad consensus which holds that however brutal and inhumane the Bosnian conflict has become, the price of military intervention is still too high.

Obviously, many feel differently about the Haitians who, in the popular opinion, can't fight a lick. But the problem is not that of defeating the Haitian army, which appears to be mostly made up of colonels; the problem is how long it would take afterwards to restore public order, neuter the police and military, declare victory, and get out.

The Americans, simply the most versatile and potent military force in the world, have an understandable abhorrence of becoming involved in long wars, a lesson painfully learned in Vietnam. These days, no one wants any part of a war that might go on too long, result in unacceptable casualty rates, or end in ambiguity. And, of course, no one wants to begin a war in which virtue is not an ally.

Haiti would seem to be ideal as a site ripe for American armed intervention. The conflict would likely be brief, the casualties "light" (a military euphemism), and victory certain. As for being virtuous, a U.S. invasion of Haiti reeks of *noblesse oblige*: powerful invaders come to rout the tyrannical forces of an illegitimate regime. Should anyone be taking a poll, put me down as a supporter of relieving the sufferings of the Haitian people by the force best able to do the job.

Indeed, while a dove at heart, I have been on record as a belligerent, supporting military intervention in Haiti, since last May. It is hard to understand why there has been so much heel-dragging and tacking about in the Greater Antilles. The Haitian people, held captive at gunpoint by a repressive band of thugs, can only be rescued by a superior military force. So, why not? Of course, the last time the American military came to Haiti, it remained for nearly twenty years, but even that precedent does not deter my resolve. After all, it may require an American presence to restore and expand the Haitian tourist industry, which, as I read in the financial press, could alone work wonders for a backward economy.

Unlike the Bosnian Serbs and that ilk, something can be done about the plight of the Haitians. While there is contrary opinion—mostly that of Republicans—there is something positively appealing about watching a helpless and impoverished people being rid of a gang of murderous thieves. Diplomats, understandably, shun sentiment and walk wide of morality, save when it serves the interests of their clients. For those of us who think in more simple, uncomplicated terms—even about the world that surrounds us—there will be something deeply satisfying about seeing the liberation of an innocent and helpless people, if and when it comes, and however unseemly and unknowing the rescue may be.

As for the fratricidal wars in the former Yugoslavia, greater restraint and patience are required. Thus far, nothing has worked; neither moral indignation, threats, fitful, feeble attempts at retaliation, nor economic sanctions (also employed against the Haitians) have made any difference. The difficulty many have is that so much of our common history as Europeans intersects (in old Yugoslavia) and it is hard to despise those whom only recently, as history runs, you have admired. As well, revenge and reciprocal savagery seem understandable, however regrettable, to students familiar with past events.

But the example of Haiti becomes the great teacher in understanding today's world politics. The reason the Americans, French, and British are not in Bosnia fighting to stop the fighting is only the frightful cost of it, which, plainly, no democratic government could bear. Still, because nothing can be done about Bosnia does not mean something cannot be done about Haiti. American power has its uses; these are not many, but few. The rescue of five million helpless people should be one of them.

A Neighbourly Interest in Bosnia

DECEMBER 6, 1994

I was pleased to have confirmed, by a dispatch in my morning paper, that we still have military forces in Bosnia, serving as peacekeepers even while being held captive by the Bosnian Serbs. The prime minister (our's), speaking utterly in character, has said Canada will review its Bosnian peacekeeping role next month. So there.

But not to be misunderstood: I am not pleased to have Canadian forces, whose families live down the road from me, pinned down in a United Nations "safe haven" in Bosnia. It is only the difficulty of not knowing for certain that they are there since, were it not for the CBC, which might be out of touch with the latest developments in wartorn ex-Yugoslavia, one could only gather from the coverage by CNN, the Associated Press, and other serious media sources that no one is in Bosnia except the Brits and a few Bangladeshis.

In fact, what I have learned though American channels of information, is that the Bosnian Serb forces are risking a crushing retaliatory blow at any moment from American aircraft, to be unleashed by NATO. Speaker-elect of the U.S. House of Representatives, Newt Gingrich, who also ducked active service in Vietnam, has called for "massive air strikes" against the recalcitrant Serbs. This, of course, would add immeasurably to the risks to the safety and well-being of our eight hundred soldiers on the ground, including those being detained. But as I have pointed out, I know the Canadians are there, you know, we all know, even the British appear to know, but it remains a secret to the American people.

To borrow from Norman Mailer: "Why are we in Bosnia?" Hearing the new rage of the right wing, Representative Gingrich's call for an American-imposed, air-to-ground, bloodletting in Bosnia reminds one of the winning strategy once proposed by U.S. Air Force Chief of Staff General Curtis LeMay for making peace in Vietnam. "Bomb them into the Stone Age," the general counselled.

The prime minister is right to review his options and he could do worse than to review his review; the recent parliamentary committee on defence policy recommends downsizing everything except our commitments. We have eight hundred of our own people now in Bosnia, which is eight hundred more than have the Americans. Yet it is they who are fidgeting over Bosnia, blaming the British and the French for lacking the stomach for a ground war against the Serbs, and threatening to intervene with air strikes unilaterally or by holding NATO by the throat. They are a curious people, the Americans, but more dangerous to themselves and their neighbours now that they are led by such mystagogues as Speaker Gingrich and the new chair of the Senate Foreign Relations Committee, the reactionary Jesse Helms.

Certainly, if we listen to the new nabobs to the south, Bosnia is no longer a United Nations' matter but a NATO one. The distinction should not be lost on anyone for, while the United Nations is not under the command of the American military, NATO clearly is. And while Canada accepted the leadership of the United States throughout the Cold War, and indeed longer than that, what needs reviewing is how far—and in what cause—Canada is prepared to serve in a post-Cold War alliance under the uncertain leadership of a republic in which—think about it—people like Jesse Helms will have profound influence.

As to why we are in Bosnia, or anywhere else in that wretched territory, we arrived under good auspices to help contain the slaughter through peaceful interdiction and to help people survive the threat of starvation and the hostile elements. Our people there have saved countless lives and not without casualties in the result. No one ever said peacekeeping would be a bloodless business, but Canadians, though not without flaw or fault, have been in the business from the start and are as good or better at it than anyone else in the world.

But we are not in Bosnia at the behest of NATO, another club in which we hold membership. And if Bosnia becomes a NATO matter, we should get out since Canada should not put forces in a place like Bosnia under the command of the American military. We did, of course, consent to serve in the Gulf under American command, but there is no oil in Bosnia and George Bush, the president of that day, had no need to share power with mastodons like Gingrich and Helms.

It is hard to tell, in policy matters affecting Canada's external relations, how much the Canadian people care about the shifting tides, and the rising of some political forces and the ebbing of others. While it represents something less than the approved polling sample, a surprising number of people have volunteered the comment that the fact that Canada's presence in Bosnia is totally ignored by the American media is either annoying, aggravating, or maddening—any one will do.

Further, it has not gone unnoticed that the next speaker of the House—a man two heartbeats removed from the presidency—has been publicly recommending a military course of action in Bosnia that would needlessly endanger Canadian lives, just as though there were no Canadians there. At least, none to speak of.

The End of Baseball, Almost

AUGUST 19, 1994

Bill Veeck, the strategist who introduced the midget pinch-hitter to baseball and was the first team owner to go without a necktie, called the game "an island of surety in a changing world." Bart Giamatti, who chose to become president of the National League rather than president of Yale University, described big league baseball players as "temporary custodians of the public trust."

The custodians are on strike and, while the world is doubtless changing, the island of surety is clouded with uncertainty. There are no boys of summer at play, there are no games; the season may be over. Neither Veeck nor Giamatti lived to see the day. But while this is not the first strike baseball has seen, it looks like it may become the longest.

Several millions of baseball fans, for whom the game provides a vital daily fix, confront the void. Nothing on the tube but gunfire and geopolitics; no box scores, league standings, or stats; no defeats, no wins. Puts one in mind of the old, irascible football coach, Woody Hays, who once postulated, "Without winners there wouldn't be any goddamned civilization." It's that serious.

The Expos, to give you an idea, were possibly the best team in baseball. We may never know how good, but they had the most wins and fewest losses when the lights went out. The Expos may end up an asterisk: (*the best team in baseball in the year there was no season).

Meanwhile, relief is not in sight. Those who have followed baseball for a half century and more are ill prepared for the contingency of a life without baseball. The sports pages read like something out of the *Labour Gazette*. The television networks, booked solid with international arm wrestling and mixed volleyball, have reduced a meaningful four-syllable word like desperation to a bleak acronym— CFL.

On Tuesday, cable television sports were solely represented by a cigarette company sponsoring tennis. Acute withdrawal sufferers with dishes could watch arena football; last week's shut-ins in traction could access Dream Team II basketball. The Sports Network, gamers to the end, has scheduled three more Canadian Football League contests, the first to be played Saturday between the Toronto Argos and the Baltimore Whatchamacallems. (You didn't know?)

None of the above will suffice. The black hole left by the disappearance of baseball cannot be filled by horseshoes or mud-wrestling, even when the latter is sponsored by the NFL working out of Mexico City. Baseball is a semi-occupation even for those who have never played it; witness the number of women seated in the bleachers today or last week. Everyone is saying what a great year it was for baseball, how close the pennant races were, how many individual records were being challenged. For once, everyone is right.

Don't get me wrong: I can live without baseball, but it will take time to adjust. After all, it's only a game, though part of the rhythm of daily life. When baseball suddenly shuts down, it's like a death in the family. A favourite uncle, sort of. When it's shut down, it's not like you can go out and pick up another game, anymore than you can go out to a find another favourite uncle.

Still, complaining is not for me. There can be life without baseball, just as there is life without politics. But as much as politics is also a game, it doesn't have a season, much less a World Series, and I had already given up the Québec provincial election for the western division race in the National League. It seemed silly to me, watching the media trying to demonize Jacques Parizeau (who may be too bright for provincial politics). I think the guy is a born deputy minister of finance who will never learn to hit the curve.

What with separatists Parizeau and Lucien Bouchard, and Don Fehr, he of the players' union, and Richard Ravitch of the baseball owners' committee, we have two matched pairs of serious comedians the likes of whom have been unseen on any stage since Rosencrantz and Guildenstern. So wake me up when it's over, people will say of the Québec election and the baseball strike.

Good advice, but no man can sleep forever. Last Thursday, I played eighteen holes of golf, striking the ball a recorded 130 times while losing four balls to the provincial Department of Forestry and Natural Resources. Everyone—well, almost everyone witness to this event—says I could have a future in this game. I dread to think of it.

While four-putting the final hole, I recalled the sombre words of that illustrious side-winder, Dan Quisenberry: "I've seen the future," he said, "and it's much like the past, only longer." Then again, during the brief players' strike back in 1981, you may remember Bart Giamatti's adjuration to the strikers. "Resume your dignity," he told them. And they did.

A Change of Heart

FALL 1993

It was in the shortening days of early winter last year, with the darkness gathering at the windows at Northwood, my home in the country sixty kilometres from Fredericton, and Michael, my second son, was saying, "You know, some of your family think you should tell us a few things, just in case something goes wrong and you aren't around to tell us."

"Like what?" I asked.

"Well, for example, where would you like to be buried? In Woodstock?" (I had been born in Woodstock, New Brunswick. My parents are buried there.)

"No," I told him, "not in Woodstock. Not anywhere, really. I would like to be cremated and have my ashes scattered over Queens County from an airplane."

The conversation struck me as lugubrious; I had made no plans for my demise even though it was, I had been advised, coming to be imminent. Three years earlier, when I was sixty-nine, an Ottawa cardiologist had told me I might have as little as two years to live. A year after that, when converting a paid-up life insurance policy to an annuity, the actuaries had put my life expectancy at five years, at the outside.

The cause of death would be congestive heart failure, having to do with the irreversible deterioration of the heart muscle and the filling of the lungs with fluid—a sort of death by drowning. I had become familiar with the symptoms that produced episodes when the lungs would fill with fluid so that breathing became very near impossible.

In medical terms, the condition is called cardiomyopathy—I had it written down on a piece of paper that I carried around with me in the event that the need arose to put a name to my complaint. I do not mean to dwell on this. After all, dying is a common experience, another of the bodily functions with which all humanity becomes, in time, familiar (save those, I suppose, who die suddenly) and one we don't much talk about or want to know more about. In the expanding shelves of "how to" literature, there have been few popular works written on "how to die." (I exclude here recent works on suicide.)

Still, knowing one is going to die, and soon, and from what cause, does not—as has been said about hanging—concentrate the mind. Not mine, anyway. But it does foreclose the future and it is surprising to find how much less there is to think about when the future is not a live consideration. Nor does the past mean much, being also beyond reach. Instead, in Norman Mailer's phrase, one lives "in that airless no man's land of the perpetual present." Today is all there is; while tomorrow may be possible, anything beyond is shrouded in doubt and uncertainty.

Not a whole lot can be said for a quality of life ruled by declining energies and increasing debilitation. But, the mind informs, there is still a life when morning brings confirmation of yet another day in the "perpetual present." So many "todays" having already come and gone that, after I had arrived in Ottawa and moved into the Château

Laurier (on April Fools' Day) for what I would call "the vigil"—which meant waiting for the new heart to replace my failing one—I came to assume I would tough it out in my hotel room for all the todays unto September, though I knew, in more reflective moments, there was not likely that much life left in me.

But at least I was not entirely without prospects, since I had been accepted as a candidate for a heart transplant. As a result, I had become wedded to a regimen of sorts: a measured existence with increasingly arduous and shorter walks on Major's Hill Park behind the hotel, a spartan diet, no hard liquor, little wine, and fewer beverages (I had become nearly addicted to Diet Coke). With the exception of family and a few close friends, I was engaged in a practised deception as to my condition and my purpose for being in Ottawa, both of which I simply left to surmise. It was, anyway, too conjectural—too iffy—to talk about. "How are you?" I would be asked, and I would say, "Fine." Isn't that how it always goes?

It was also difficult to think about; the metaphysics were complicated. I disciplined myself not to be my own doctor and tried to give short shrift to insubordinate thought. Such as the raw ambivalence of my state, which was that of waiting for someone else to die in order that I should live. As the days and weeks passed, with optimism tempered by caution learned from the doctors who spoke increasingly of the need for luck in these matters, I stubbornly refused to yield to pessimism. Although I did once say, during a visit with the doctors, that if I were still in the Château Laurier standing by, come October, I was checking out and flying to Portugal. One of them laughed and said, "If that happens, get two tickets and I'll go with you." Another said, "Make it three."

So, later on, I wondered: Why were we laughing? Because we all knew I would never see October? Even in May, I tried not to think about June.

One evening, joined by a friend in my hotel bedroom, our conversation became overwhelmed by the roar of a cavalcade of motorcycles passing under the window, coming out of the city market and turning onto Sussex Drive before rocketing up Colonel By Drive. As their racket faded in the distance, my friend said softly, "I hope no one will ever know what I'm thinking."

"I know what you're thinking," I told her. (Bikers are believed, with some truth, to be among the more likely heart donors.) "They ride by here every night."

I was fifteen when my father died. We were living in California. He was a very young man, not yet forty years of age. He died at Oakland's Peralta Hospital late one night, after I had been summoned to his bedside and stood before him listening to his terrible breathing. He suddenly reached out and seized me in his arms, holding me fiercely close to him for a long moment. After I left my father, I went down to the darkened hospital lobby, which was empty, and stretched out on a couch and shut my eyes. Later, someone entered the lobby and I heard a male voice asking the receptionist, "What is that kid doing over there?"

"His father is dying upstairs."

Many years later, a nurse called Northwood one evening from the nursing home to tell me she did not think my mother would last the night; she was dying of old age and—I also thought—of an understandable impatience with her life. I left immediately to drive to Harvey Station, some one hundred kilometres away. When I arrived, Mother was dead.

I went to her room, held her hand and kissed her forehead, which was cold. The nurse wept a little and closed my mother's gaping mouth. I remember feeling sorrow and relief.

During my vigil at the Château Laurier, I worked fitfully on contingency plans in the event of my death. I consulted my lawyer about various tinkerings with my will. I thought about special bequests, and about how my death could be made gentler, or less traumatic, for my own fifteen-year-old son. As the weeks wore on, my son and I saw less of each other, largely by choice, since we both found his visits difficult. Neither of us was of an age or condition where we were comfortable with small talk. I remembered myself at fifteen and being where he was. Besides, he was in the midst of exams. After my father died in early September, I left school and, because the family was moving back to Canada, I did not return to the classroom until after Christmas. But as often as I thought about this, as often I tried not to think about it. I never did do anything about my will and I did not find any way to make my death easier to bear for my youngest child. It seemed to me that the simplest and best plan would be to stay alive, until the heart came.

It seemed also wise not to over-doctor myself: to be constantly checking my breathing, which I felt anyway with each shallow breath, or monitoring my energy levels, which ranged from adequate in the morning to negligible by late afternoon. I learned to keep company with those who truly shared my optimistic view of things, or those who knew nothing about my condition. As much as possible, I immersed myself in the company of the unshakably confident or the blissfully ignorant, the best of companions for a vigil allowing for such a disparate result.

One antidote to depression or to introspection could be found in an ordinary routine that measures out the passing hours and becomes, through faithful adherence, quite endearing. Each day could be made eventful, even if comprised of daily rounds of medication; a ten-minute walk; visiting the newsstand to acquire the *New York Times*; five o'clock tea in the parlour of the Gold Floor; the *Wall Street Journal* and the *Ottawa Citizen* sports pages at breakfast; cold poached salmon on room service along with MacNeil/Lehrer, followed by televised Blue Jays baseball, followed by the news and then the scores from all over; thence to picking up Conor Cruise O'Brien on Edmund Burke, or Vaclav Havel's *Summer Meditations*, or Fannie Flagg's *Fried Green Tomatoes at the Whistle Stop Café* (all of them as yet unfinished); then finally the darkness and silence of the hotel and night sounds from the street outside—sporadic traffic and the occasional exultant shouts of youth out on the town—times when the mind became vulnerable to the insurgency of an unfamiliar anxiety. But there was a pill for that, if necessary, and occasionally it was.

Sometimes, in the darkness, I would begin to imagine the surgical procedure; how they would go about removing one's heart and replacing it with another. This remained a mystery to me though I knew, from routine self-examination, there could be no easy way to reach into the chest to retrieve a heart and insert another. It seemed likely, thinking further, that they would need to saw their way down through the chest, separating the rib cage, much as one would gut a fish. But I could not be sure where the opening would begin or where it might end. At any rate, the patient would be spread-eagled in some fashion, the rib cage sprung open to allow the surgeon, or surgeons, to do their work. When I had asked what the odds were on the success of a transplant operation, I was told they were about seventy in one hundred, though someone else put them at sixty-five in one hundred. Even money would have been good enough for me.

What I needed to know most, though, and believed I did know, was that I was under the care of the most competent and skilled surgical team in the field anywhere in the world. This was good enough for me—so I would tell myself when questions arose in the night—and likely the less I knew of the details, the better off in the long run. Anyway, should I be fortunate enough, I would learn first-hand how, exactly, the surgeon reaches the heart and replaces it.

After several weeks of my sojourn at the Château, friends started to ask, "Aren't you bored?" Of course I was. But because mine was such a unique personal experience—something between hibernation and house arrest—I learned to live off my own intellectual fat. And the vigil was not without discovery of a certain kind: how large the wasteland of television had become, for one. I resumed for a time my occasional review of the TV evangelicals, an endeavour demanding tolerance and true benevolence, not unlike that of God Himself.

Because I had consigned myself to a hotel room for an indefinite time, something hard to explain in a few words, I enjoyed life in a curious sort of limbo. Telephone calls, which were usually screened, were erratic and unpredictable but interesting; normal patterns of communication and regular contact with familiars became part of the past. Each day brought its own surprise: one morning a call from Premier Frank McKenna; another day the voice of an old friend confined to a military hospital across town; calls from a cheerful new voice, who was Christine, assistant to Senator Norm Atkins (my brother-in-law), usually about my attenuated social life that involved occasional lunches with mystery guests downstairs, or confirming whether Atkins would be available to watch the game; or from distant children, keeping in touch.

Six weeks and two days into the vigil, my first wife, Linda, arrived, having driven from Toronto. We had finished dinner and Linda, being the stronger, pushed the room service table out into the hall. I was looking forward to the baseball game; the Giants (my favourite team) would be playing the Reds on TSN. I had some difficulty changing into my night attire when, with one shoe off and awaiting enough breath to attempt removing the other, the phone rang.

The voice said, "This is Christine."

"Oh hi," I said, "Thank you for getting my mail to me."

"No," the voice said, "this is Christine Struthers from the Heart Institute."

"Oh," I said, "I'm sorry."

"We have a heart for you," Christine Struthers said. She told me not to hurry. "But come as soon as you can."

Linda, who had been out of the room talking to the staff, had returned to overhear the conversation. After hanging up, I remember saying to her, "It's crunch time." Then, she remembers, I began to change into a clean white shirt.

PART IV

News and Reviews

Winnie Was a Red Tory Too

I realize not everyone is on vacation, at the cottage or visiting relatives; neither am I. But for reasons that may have more to do with the duration of the American professional football season, which is my preferred recreational drug, I read more books during the summer months than at any other time of the year.

Summer reading includes rereading. Every summer, I reread all or part of Winston Churchill's second volume of his World War II memoirs, *Their Finest Hour*. The book is nothing more than the story of the crucial struggle for the survival of Western civilization, as told by the twentieth century's greatest political leader.

I have been something of a Churchill student over the years and have, I believe, most of his written works and a fairly representative collection of all that has been written about him. My eldest son recently sent me Martin Gilbert's *In Search of Churchill*, published this year in paperback. For a Churchill buff, it proves a joy. Mr. Gilbert, who became the great man's biographer, producing six volumes and a seventh general work, is easily the world's ranking authority on the subject.

Talking about Churchill the other day, someone remarked that the British Bulldog had American Indian blood in him. I was sure this was wrong, but apparently I was. According to Gilbert, and one-time U.S. Secretary of the Interior Stewart Udall, Churchill's mother was descended from "a full-blood Iroquois," making Sir Winston "1/16 degree Indian."

Many things many of us thought we knew about Churchill, we don't. For example, he never said, apropos of Gen. Charles de Gaulle, "the greatest cross I have to bear is the cross of Lorraine." (It was said by Gen. Sir Edward Spears, Churchill's liaison officer with de Gaulle.)

And if Nancy Astor said to Churchill that, were she his wife, she would put poison in his coffee, he did not say that, were he her husband, he would drink it.

On Churchill's return to the Admiralty as First Lord in 1940, a signal did not go out to the fleet: "Winston is back." An actor (Norman Shelley) did not read Churchill's broadcast speech on June 18, 1940, pretending his voice was Churchill's. And Sir Winston did not define the traditions of the Royal Navy as "rum, sodomy and the lash!" Finally, it is simply not true that British intelligence either knew or informed Churchill in advance of the German bombing of Coventry; Gilbert provides the convincing details.

Churchill was a Conservative, after his father, then a Liberal, then again a Conservative. "Anyone can rat once," he once said, "but I ratted twice." He was, throughout his political career, a Red Tory.

Before the turn of the century, Churchill was calling himself "a Tory Democrat." At the end of World War I, as secretary of state for war, he wrote the prime minister, David Lloyd George: "I hope you will endeavour to gather together all forces of strength and influence in this country and lead them along the paths of science and organization to the rescue of the weak and poor. That is the main conception I have of the victory government."

During the bitterness of the General Strike, Churchill told the coal miners' leaders, "I sympathize with you in your task." He supported their demand for a minimum wage, while the owners wanted to reduce their wages. Prime Minister Stanley Baldwin, however, refused to support his minister, not for the last time.

Churchill was nearly alone in his support of a Jewish homeland in Palestine. He introduced the first government premiums for widows and orphans. As early as 1910, he held radically progressive views towards crime and punishment: "A calm and dispassionate recognition of the rights of the accused against the state, and . . . a constant heart-searching by all charged with the duty of punishment, a desire and eagerness to rehabilitate all those who have paid their dues in the hard coinage of punishment, tireless efforts towards the discovery of curative and regenerative processes . . . these are the symbols which in the treatment of crime and criminals mark and measure the stored-up strength of a nation."

On his twenty-fifth birthday, Churchill wrote an American friend, Bourke Cochran: "Capitalism in the form of trusts has reached a pitch of power which the old economists never contemplated and which excites my most lively terror. Merchant princes are all very well, but if I have anything to say about it, their kingdom should not be of this world. The new century will witness great war for the existence of the individual.

"Up to a certain point, combination has brought us nothing but good: But we seemed to have reached a period when it threatens nothing but evil."

These days, on the breathless heights of Tory cant, Churchill would be (likely is) scorned as a wet "squishy" and a covert socialist. But then, true blue, deep-eyed conservatives never liked him. They preferred a Calvin Coolidge, a Stanley Baldwin or a Preston Manning, along with a few bright young things to speak well of their ordinariness. With the right leaders and the proper promotional entourage, you could either run the world or be run by it, and never know the difference.

And I Couldn't Put It Down . . .

NOVEMBER 18, 1992

I'm sorry to say I have still not read reporter Stevie Cameron's bestselling, muckraking book about low life in Ottawa during the recent Tory administration. I have, nevertheless, reviewed the book in this space, as they say, and debated its merits relentlessly with the author and others on the national television network of the CBC.

Critics of my criticisms of Cameron's book, *On the Take*, complain I have not read it. Fair enough. But my position on the book is the same as my attitude towards that well-known Bedouin delicacy comprised of sheep's eyeballs smothered in buzzard gravy. I have never cared for it though, truth to tell, not so much as a spoonful has ever passed my lips.

Willfulness has not prevented my being apprised of the contents of the Cameron *oeuvre*; for example, her reporting that Don Mazankowski, the deputy prime minister *de jour*, and powerhouse lobbyist Frank Moores, once the premier of Newfoundland, had roomed together in Ottawa. I asked Cameron, during our joint TV appearance, why this struck her as worthy of mention.

Her answer was to the effect that it goes to show how close—to the point of cohabitation—lived those with power and those in the access and influence business during the Mulroney Years. When I then pointed out that, in fact, Mazankowski and Moores had never roomed together in Ottawa (or anywhere else), Cameron seemed startled. It was, she said, something she had been told. At this juncture of the author's discomfort and my modest satisfaction, the host of the show intervened to ask, "What difference does it make?"

That is a very good question; it may be indeed a question for our times. It speaks to a new culture yeasting feverishly in journalism today. It is one of the old-fashioned virtues of our society that it is the right of anyone to express outrageous opinion, to say anything, however unpopular, untrue, or unjustified. What the public is supposed to know is that, with respect to the opinion being aired, it enjoys its distinction as a matter of free expression. With regard to the facts, if any, ventured to support this opinion, the public should also know that the facts don't matter. Not anymore. People are now free to give their opinions and equally free to invent their facts.

Since this is plainly true, we must now spend much of our lives preparing addenda, adding footnotes, demanding withdrawals, and filling protestations with editors. Or we can go with the flow, comforting ourselves with today's good question that never needs answering: "What difference does it make?"

Thus, one can read Cameron's book or the *Toronto Star* or the New Testament with the same blithe assurance that some of the details are not necessarily so and not to be believed, much less taken seriously. True or not, it doesn't make any difference anyway. One could, for the sake of convenience, take it all down in one great, consensual gulp.

Flying to Toronto last week, I was given a copy of the *Financial Post* to speed my flight. After casting my eyes upon the quotations on the Vancouver Stock Exchange, searching for bargains, I then turned to the op-ed page in search of ideological and intellectual inspiration. I found a piece written by David Bercuson that addressed yet another urgent question; in his own words, thus: "Have the Tories learned anything at all from their thrashing in October 1993?" Thus enticed, not to say enthralled, I found I could not put Bercuson down.

His question I deemed a rhetorical one, to be answered in the negative. "Since the late 1960s," Bercuson wrote, "the Tories pursued a

Québec strategy that was essentially based on wooing Québec ultra-nationalists into Tory ranks while ignoring true Québec federal-ists . . . The strategy was launched by Robert Stanfield, who gave his blessing to the Tory adaptation of the 'two-nations' policy prior to the 1968 federal election and who worked closely with such people as the current PQ minister . . . Richard Le Hir, to make the Tories acceptable to the ultra-nationalists."

As one entitled to speak with some authority on Tory policy under the leadership of Stanfield, in 1968 and after, I can say Stanfield's blessing was never given to a "two-nations" policy that the party never adopted in 1968 or at any other time during Stanfield's tenure. As for Stanfield working "closely with such people as Richard Le Hir," to the best of my knowledge Stanfield had never heard of Le Hir. (Stanfield is presently out of the country, but asking former members of his staff draws the same blank response: "Who?")

Bercuson goes on to say this: "Québec strategy"—originated by Stanfield—"was central to the near-total destruction of the Conservative Party." That is his opinion; nothing of it, however, is supported by the facts.

So, what does it matter? Bercuson is entitled to his opinion. Right? The *Financial Post* is entitled to publish it. Okay? But there is one fact to ponder in all this: Bercuson is not your average, everyday, opinionated columnist. He is, it says here, "dean of the faculty of graduate studies, University of Calgary."

I suppose that doesn't matter either, but it does make one wonder if anyone studies history at the Calgary university. Maybe they all take journalism.

What's a Four Letter Word for America? B-e-s-t

MARCH 14, 1995

Larry King, the talk show impressario, was talking to Pat Buchanan, the neo-conservative Republican pit bull, and Buchanan was duti-fully making his appearance worth King's time by announcing he would announce next week he was running for the Republican presidential nomination. Politicians who appear on King's show are expected to announce something; Allan Specter, another incipient Republican presidential candidate, will appear tonight, or tomorrow night—or maybe already has—to announce his candidacy.

After Buchanan announced when he would be announcing, King "opened the phone lines," inviting viewers to call in their questions. One caller asked Buchanan how come all the G-7 nations except the United States had universal health care. Buchanan's answer was in two parts: First, America had the best health care system in the world; second, it had always interested him that so many Canadians went to Cleveland to have heart surgery.

I am reminded we are at yet another advent to the rutting season in American politics, and we shall be seeing as many as a dozen Republicans who aspire to the presidency, or at least to the windfall benefits of subsidized self-promotion, butting heads, pawing the turf, and baying at the moon. Canadians have the choice as to how much of this frenzy of nature they wish to endure.

It is possible, by taking the axe to the television, to avoid eye contact with any of the proceedings, including all the lying and posturing and the everyday onslaught upon the finer senses. Still, there is something compelling about being repelled in the comfort of one's own home, which may explain in part the astonishing ratings for such political porn stars as Howard Stern and Arianna Huffington.

I favour a policy of detached engagement; after all, it shouldn't matter who becomes the Republican candidate for president of the United States since any of them will be—on being elected—nudged and shoved about by Republican majorities in both houses (assuming neither of these are reversed by the voters). But there are good reasons to pay attention and listen up since neo-conservatism is now continental, and though its canons and articulations have largely been American, it has already made substantial inroads in Canada.

Otherwise, to put the matter in the most obvious light, Preston Manning would not be in Washington supping with Newt Gingrich, billed by the CBC as "the second most powerful politician in America." Otherwise, federal and provincial budget deficits would not have become the single issue of Canadian politics. Otherwise, the Parliament of Canada would not now be dominated by a governing party of chartered accountants and an opposition party of bookkeepers.

The North American revival of the politics of reaction has produced a new generation of young fogies whose precocity knows neither borders nor boundaries. They are on parade in this month's issue of *Harper's* magazine, notable among them Bill Kristol, former chief of staff to Dan Quayle; Frank Luntz, a Gingrich advisor and pollster; Ralph Reed, the director of the Christian Coalition; and David Frum, author, columnist, commentator, former *Wall Street Journal* edit page editor and Canadian.

These guys are serious; if the politics of reaction has a future, they will plot it. The moderator asks Frum what cuts the Republicans should immediately make to get the deficit down. Frum says "[it] will take a little time" to get rid of welfare, Medicaid, and Medicare. But right away, cut the rural Electrification Administration; all programs to promote research on fuel efficiency; the Small Business Administration; export promotion; advanced-technology projects; the commercial space program; a lot of the Department of Transportation's demonstration projects; and all farm subsidies.

"Farm subsidies," Frum says, "are indefensible . . . pure political pork." He would also cut all student loans.

Reed, the Christian Coalition fellow, volunteers to cut the Legal Services Corporation, which provides legal aid to the poor, along with the National Endowment for the Humanities and the National Endowment for the Arts.

Kristol points out, "You cannot, in practice, have a federal guarantee that people won't starve . . . My preference is not to have federal entitlement programs but to send them all down to the states, let the states experiment much more, and have private charities take care of people."

Reed is inspired to add, "We live in a country with the most generous people in the entire world . . . People want to return to nongovernmental solutions to poverty. We've got to challenge the churches, the synagogues, and the families to dig deeper and do more." (Returning, soon, to a church near you, another Republican miracle: *trickle-down charity*.)

What is eerie about all this is its resemblance to the mindset of Paul Martin's federal budget, including the proposal to "send all the entitlement programs down to the states"—in this case, the provinces.

"What I hope to see," concludes Frum, "is a government whose social-welfare functions are essentially confined to insuring people against the catastrophic risks of ordinary life—catastrophic illness, short periods of unemployment, indigence." That's not too far from the latest thoughts of Jean Chrétien, not to mention Pat Buchanan.

I Don't Know You, But the Face Is Familiar

MARCH 24, 1995

I have always thought March among the more forgettable months of any year. This March is no exception, except for the fact I have had a ferocious virus of some sort which, I am told, is making its way everywhere. Enough for me that I have it, in the grasp of my own personal viral vicissitude.

One of the events I missed, while indisposed, was a private dinner held at Queen's Park by the Lieutenant Governor of Ontario, Henry N. R. Jackman, in honour of His Excellency, the Governor General of Canada and Her Excellency, Diana Fowler LeBlanc. Were it not for my virus, I would have been there since I had not encountered Romeo LeBlanc since his becoming the Queen's First Minister and, in fact, had not seen him since we flew back to our native New Brunswick together after the leadership convention in 1984, where the Liberals had chosen John Turner. Besides, as an additional attraction to His Honour's dinner, male guests were allowed to wear business suits.

During my confinement with the dread plague, there was a total news blackout; no radio, no television, no newspapers. Instead, whenever I was awake, I read Doris Kearns Goodwin's book—*No Ordinary Time*—which is about the lives and activities of Franklin and Eleanor Roosevelt during the Second World War. It filled the silences nicely.

Reading *No Ordinary Time* reminded me of one of the great common currents running throughout our modern history (if not all of it): the consistently obstructive and reactionary role of the political right who were, in Roosevelt's time, the America First adherents, the admirers of fascism, those who opposed "government" in either organization, planning, or in the provision of equal shares and fair prices for civilians.

Big Business in America at first refused to join the war effort until it had wrung from the government its guaranteed share of the profits of war. It refused to stop making passenger cars even while the lack of armoured vehicles for defence was a national scandal, and, like the army, it balked at hiring Negroes.

An Army War College report, published in 1925, declared "the American Negro has not progressed as far as other sub species of the human family . . . The cranial cavity of the Negro is smaller than whites . . . He cannot control himself in fear of danger. He is a rank coward in the dark." This document governed manpower policy in America to the end of the war.

It really was not until the Vietnam war, when so few of the children of white families were willing to fight, that it was discovered the American Negro was no more, no less afraid of danger or the dark.

Times change. The old fools give way to new generations of fools. Where there was once the Klan, there is now the Clown, such as the Reverend Pat Robertson, his disciple, Ralph Reed, and a growing gaggle of Republican Party chaplains. These politicians-at-prayer are of immense value to the neo-conservative scenario for the new America. Robertson has long been a major prophet who has seen the enemies of the new America, among them the Jews.

Anti-Semitism may grow, Robertson writes, because American Christians will not tolerate "cosmopolitan, liberal, secular Jews" who insist upon "unrestricted freedom for smut and pornography and the murder of the unborn." This seems a departure from the more familiar refrains about school prayers and family values. But Robertson insists that "the part Jewish intellectuals and media activists have played in the assault on Christianity may very possibly prove to be a grave mistake." After all, "the liberal, wealthy Jews voted for democratic candidates Carter, Mondale, and Dukakis, not Reagan and Bush."

This is all sickeningly familiar to anyone who has read the comments coming out of Europe in pre-Nazi Europe, opinions voiced by the same bland, angelic, slightly florid and inflated faces, spoken in the same earnest, scholarly tenor, crisp with sincerity. What many knew at the time they spoke was how approvingly their words fell upon the ears of the rich and the powerful. I mention this only as a curiosity, realizing how many may have forgotten or never knew.

I am curious about these new-breed reformers and their flashing smiles, lacquered hair and mannered speech. Can they explain the roles of people like Robertson in the party? While they advise and poll for Pat for President, are they serious? Are Jewish intellectuals a danger to Ralph Reed's Christians?

And I'm sorry I missed the dinner in Toronto. There are more toy Tory admirers of the American right within a half-mile radius of the Four Seasons Hotel than in the whole of my own Queen's County. I had hoped afterwards to catch sight of a few of them and, if I had the chance to speak to them, tell them how sorry I was to know of their loss.

Nuggets from Neo-Con Country

JUNE 16, 1995

I have been reading *Saturday Night*, the magazine. Once a Canadian institution, *Saturday Night* is now Conrad Black's new world foothold, written and edited for those who can find solace in Calvin Klein two-page spreads and are keen to keep abreast of Canadian right-wing chic (". . . if you squeeze twenty years and a lake of beer from Ralph Klein you'll get something that looks a lot like Jean Charest.").

Saturday Night offers the political post-adolescent a spiritual home while providing political intelligence you won't find anywhere else. For example, both Ralph Klein and Mike Harris "flirted" with becoming members of the Reform Party; when young Tories are asked "what they want in policy, most of them recite chapter and verse from the Reform Party handbook." These are nuggets penned from the magazine's neo-conservative mainstream "editor at large," Kenneth Whyte. There are more.

In a piece on ex-Albertan author Nancy Huston, one reads the comment of a Québec journalist who wrote, "a bit cryptically, 'If Nancy Huston did not exist . . . Preston Manning would have to invent her.' " I can handle that, just barely, but not the next sentence which reads, "Preston was too busy inventing a political system that runs along the cheerful, bag-lunch lines of a high-school student council, and the task of invention fell to Huston herself."

You may ask, "What is this about?" Good question.

There is good reading in *Saturday Night*; the June issue produces extraordinary verse by John B. Lee and bonus pieces from former editor Robert Fulford and from Mordecai Richler. So, what's wrong with *Saturday Night*?

Well, I can't remember the magazine when it's tonal voice was snide. Today's *Saturday Night* has acquired a *faux* injured editorial tone, and when it is not looking for ways of making Preston Manning seem endearing and inevitable, it is on the prowl for hurts and slights, some invented or imagined. To bring this off, it shamelessly plays the regional card: the familiar, paranoid them-versus-us.

It just might stir up folks in Alberta to know "a small group of eastern Ontario Tories" had asked Tory headquarters "for permission to invite" Premier Ralph Klein to speak at the party's April general meeting. "Permission was declined." According to *Saturday Night*, "the mention of Klein's name—synonymous in some circles with 'dump Charest'—was spice enough to choke convention planners."

Good grief.

But this is the present voice of *Saturday Night*. And it's making stuff up. Nobody at national Tory headquarters (eight paid staff, receptionist included) could remember being pressed to invite Klein to speak (he was invited as an ex-officio delegate to attend), and of the seventeen hundred Tories who did attend, no one expressed surprise or regret on not having heard from him. According to *Saturday Night*, the "eastern Ontario Tories" invited Klein to speak anyway—to whom was not clear—but "Alberta's government-slashing premier" declined. As, of course, would any politician old enough to own a razor.

I remember reading *Saturday Night* when it was *Toronto Saturday Night*. The magazine was part of my introduction to Canada. It later went through a troubled patch when acquired briefly by a mining magnate (I have forgotten the details), but the magazine developed a stubborn will to survive and has maintained throughout the years an authentic Canadian voice. Its opinions, when it had any, were rooted in a sympathetic understanding and awareness of the country and its institutions. No longer.

But I remain an unabashed member of the *Toronto Saturday Night* generation. As a young Liberal, studying at the London School of Economics, I recall coming upon the writings of Herbert Spencer who, along with Huxley and Darwin, founded the theory of evolution, best expressed in the cliché "survival of the fittest." Spencer went on to write that "mankind is bound to improve," and to invent sociology. I went on to doubt Spencer and become a conservative.

Reading the June 1995 issue of *Saturday Night*, I am the more convinced Spencer's optimism about mankind (and magazines) was excessive and, based upon subsequent empirical evidence, entirely unsupported by facts. As proof, there is *Saturday Night*'s yuppy philippic delivered against Canadians of my generation. (Proclaimed on the magazine's cover thusly: "Sorry seniors, the party's over. Get back to work!") The author, clearly young beyond his years, launches his piece with the following rivetting riposte: "Canadians enjoy retirement, and why not? Most retirees are having the time of their lives: long, lazy summers at the cottage, gambling jaunts to Vegas in the winter, golf all year long."

Such are the thoughts of a spokesperson for a generation of Canadians whose most serious responsibility in life for at least the first twenty years of it had been to show up for dinner. They are written of a generation raised during an honest-to-god Depression when most of its members actually knew people who were poor, who fought a real war (from start to finish) against a real enemy, a generation that neither bitched about its past nor whined about its future. In our time, not even Republicans did that.

So, What Became of
the *Buffalo Courier-Express*?

MAY 7, 1994

Wolfville, Nova Scotia: Word reached here this weekend that the *Globe and Mail*, one of Canada's national newspapers, has appointed as its publisher and chief executive officer a fifty-two-year-old American from White Plains, New York. The *Globe* made the announcement in an abbreviated statement on its front page, followed by a more detailed one in the Report on Business section inside the paper. The news appeared in the Saturday issue, the day of the week preferred by media manipulators within the federal government when releasing bad news. Likely a coincidence, I told myself.

It is Canadian law that foreigners may not own Canadian media properties, such as newspapers. There is no law, however, that would prohibit a daily newspaper being edited and published by the night staff of the *New York Times*. The *New Yorker* magazine, for example, is presided over by Tina Brown, who is British. Similarly, the *Globe* will be run by an American. The elevation of Tina Brown to the top of the pole at the *New Yorker* did not particularly disturb me, as a subscriber; under her, the magazine publishes more articles about London and there has been a huge increase in the publication of four-letter words, much of which I attributed to the canons of contemporary sophistication. But what do I know about stuff like that?

Anyway, there is no law to say the chief executive of a daily Canadian newspaper cannot be an American or a Brit or even an Australian. While ownership has nationality in Canadian publishing, journalism itself is sublimely stateless. And while the supply of underpaid, overworked *Canadian* reporters and editors appears limitless, there is an apparently serious shortage of top-drawer Canadian candidates for the jobs at the top. This is how the *Globe* saw it, when searching for a new publisher.

"We set out to hire the best person available to run a newspaper like ours," Roy Megarry, the past publisher of the *Globe* is quoted as saying. "The nationality issue was not nearly as important as getting the better man [*sic*] for the job."

I don't know why, but this somehow reminds me of George Bush explaining his nomination of Clarence Thomas. Still, what Megarry says, stripped of prolix, is that there was no Canadian both "available" and good enough to be the publisher of the *Globe and Mail*.

As for the nationality thing, the new publisher and CEO, who is Roger Parkinson, is quoted saying, "I'm not sure that nationality is all that relevant to what we're about here."

Well, yes and no. Isn't the *Globe*, self-proclaimed, Canada's national newspaper? And isn't that relevant to what it's about? To be fair to Parkinson, he is quoted as saying, "I have a lot to learn about the *Globe and Mail* and about Canada." On the other hand, this new boss of Canada's other national daily is preceded by a forty-eight-trombone resumé: Dartmouth College and Harvard; the *Washington Post*, *Newsweek* magazine, the *Buffalo Courier-Express*, and the *Minneapolis Star-Tribune*; also, a tour in Vietnam as a "briefing officer."

Parkinson says of the *Globe*, "It's a very good paper—the best in Canada—and, like any newspaper, it can be better." Not to be picky, and aware how uneasiness often inspires hyperbole, it is not apparent from our briefing notes how the new publisher judged his new paper "the best" in a country in which he barely qualifies as a landed immigrant. Has he read the *Brandon Sun*? How long has he been reading the *Globe*?

There will be, about this latest development in national journalism, a lot of rowing about with muffled oars. Politicians, apart from their private mirth, will be taking novocaine. The business community will, of course, welcome the Parkinson appointment as an important step towards converting the *Globe* into a northern edition of the *Wall Street Journal*, with accommodating theology. Journalists will say it doesn't matter; of course it doesn't matter to them since newspapering is a business these days—maybe forever more—and it is their bad luck to be in a business managed by bean-counters. As to the lack of response to this news from the *Globe*, Canadians are excessively polite, forbearing, and generally adaptable to changes brought by world trends and other phenomena, such as Coca Cola. A national modesty has been a vital staple in our survival kit, warding off evil spirits and dangers from a world of predators.

Still, there must be limits and we must be reaching them. There must come a time and an occurrence up with which we will not put, and that time may be near at hand. Two years ago, alarmed by the sales increase of competing Cott's beverages, the head office of Coca Cola fired its entire Canadian management team and shipped in reinforcements from the U.S. Canadian shareholders seemed temporarily mollified, consoled by the national superstition that Canadians would naturally know less about selling pop than would the inventors of the real thing.

Soon thereafter, an American was placed at the head of Air Canada, an appointment greeted by those shareholders bright enough to recognize that no one could know more about flying than the descendants of Wilbur and Orville Wright. Then a coin salesman from California bought a major piece of the Toronto Argonaut football team, living unhappily ever after.

What has been established from all this is that nothing is sacred. Why not an American to run the troubled CBC? Have we not tried everything else? Americans are here today wanting to run our railroads. Why not let them? While the American Constitution insists that its presidents be American-born, our highest offices are more accessible. In Canada, anyone can be prime minister, as witness recent examples. And anyone can publish Canada's national newspaper, provided the one chosen is "the best person available." Canadians, no longer content to be hewers of wood and drawers of water, cannot expect to find much room at the top in the new world order. But in-between is not bad, while it lasts.

Collenette's No Eisenhower, But He Has More Staff

JULY 19, 1994

Someone kindly sent me the "premiere edition" of a publication out of Ottawa, *Parliamentary Names & Numbers*. It is a treasure.

PN & N provides lists of MPs, Senators, agencies, House and Senate committees, and "selected Tier I lobbyists." With telephone numbers. It also lists the support staffs of MPs and ministers. Awesome.

When I was still young enough to be impressed by Ottawa but old enough to know better, most members of Parliament had a staff of one; she would be the secretary-receptionist. Cabinet ministers had considerable departmental staff, lodged elsewhere, but their staff on the Hill was thin on the ground, usually the ubiquitous secretary and perhaps a runner, messenger, gofer. Their "policy advisors," if any, were in the Press Gallery.

Thumbing through *PN & N* reminds me how times do change. Roy MacLaren, minister of International Trade, has a personal staff of ten: a press secretary, a chief of staff, a legislative assistant, a scheduling assistant, one senior policy assistant, a caucus liaison person, plus "Hill assistants" and "riding assistants"—two each.

David Collenette, minister of National Defence and Veterans Affairs, has one more staff member than MacLaren. Collenette's eleven-person staff is also configured differently. Instead of a press secretary, there is a director of communications. While MacLaren has one senior policy assistant, Collenette has two senior advisors, and Collenette doesn't have a caucus liaison person but has a special projects advisor.

All ministers and members of the House have constituency offices where their "riding assistants" are stationed. Most objective observers agree riding offices are a good thing. They allow members of the House to keep in touch with their constituents and vice versa. Constituents may telephone or visit the MP's riding office.

Constituents of Nova Scotia Liberal MP Harry Verran have the luxury of three riding offices to choose from, in Yarmouth, Digby, and Middleton, all in the riding of South West Nova. Having three offices may be deemed a requisite for a riding of that size. Still, it's no match in size for the riding of Nunatsiaq, which begins north of the Manitoba border and extends into the Arctic to include Santa Claus's workshop. Liberal MP Jack Anawak serves his widely dispersed constituents out of one riding office, with one riding assistant and two telephones.

No one really knows what, or how much, goes on in the riding offices of members of Parliament. But like the baseball diamond built in the Iowa cornfield in W. P. Kinsella's short story, don't worry—"you build it and they'll come"—a constituency office attracts a crowd just by being there. In South West Nova, visiting one or two of Harry Verran's constituency offices may be something folks do as a private treat, something they promise the children, like a trip to the Dairy Delight.

You would not expect to see your MP sitting in the riding office, other than on some weekends. But the MP's office represents the member's presence. This serves to silence those who used to complain, having voted to send an MP to represent them in Ottawa, that they never saw her or him again, either in the Queen Hotel lobby or at the counter in the Imperial Café or chasing ambulances.

So, the riding office has come to our town or neighbourhood because of popular demand. Some offices are staffed by one assistant, others have two. Preston Manning, the advertised archbishop of affordable populism, has three riding assistants on his staff. The Reform Party leader also has a chief of staff, an executive assistant, a legislative assistant, an administrative assistant, and a press secretary. This is a fair-sized personal staff for a member of Parliament who has no designated parliamentary function. It is hard to argue, of course, that Manning is not a special person; he is almost the leader of the opposition. On the other hand, he has more staff than anyone else in the House who also has no status, other than almost.

Anyway, it is difficult to imagine what all these ministerial aides— their so-called exempt staff—do. On the face of it, most of them are very young and also very energetic. But what does a special assistant specialize in? What is Collenette's special projects advisor doing these days?

We are looking at a Parliament whose majority supports a government cheerfully firing, downsizing, and terminating everyone who casts a shadow before its personnel review committees. Has Parliament ever reviewed itself? Don't all these assistants cost money, even to house and wire them to their ministers?

The prime minister, God bless him, went to Europe a fortnight ago. He took with him six—a half-dozen—of his top advisors, analysts, writers, and arrangers. They went with the PM to the ceremonies marking the fiftieth anniversary of D-day. Jean Chrétien had more personal staff at his side than General Eisenhower had, fifty years ago, when he launched the Allied invasion of Europe.

Sell Your Dollars, Buy the Escudo and Punt

APRIL 21, 1995

In my morning paper, which today is the international edition of the *Miami Herald*, Trudy Rubin, editorial writer for the *Philadelphia Inquirer*, laments the decline of the American dollar. Her lament will sound familiar to Canadian ears; we have heard all this so often most of us can sing the words to music.

"Don't tell me," Rubin writes, "America can continue to play its accustomed role [in the world] when jokesters now refer to the dollars as 'the peso of the North.' "

"We continue to run huge budget and trade deficits that are financed by borrowing from abroad," she goes on to say, in words familiar to all Canadians. "Investors and central banks overseas hold so many dollars that they simply don't want any more. But our deficits keep pushing billions of dollars into the hands of foreign lenders or exporters every month."

To paraphrase the *Wall Street Journal*: "You think the Mexican peso is in trouble? Take a look at the U.S. dollar!" Zowie, Mr. Fund, how long has this been going on?

Among twenty-one of the world's more active currencies, during the period January 3, 1994 to April 4, 1995, the U.S. dollar declined in value against nineteen of them, including the Portuguese escudo, the Irish punt, and the Danish krone. But the biggest hits on the dollar have come from Austrian, Dutch, German, Belgian, Japanese, Swiss, and Finnish currencies, in ascending order.

Among the twenty-one currencies listed, against only two has the U.S. dollar improved, over the past fifteen months. One of these is, of course, the Mexican peso, which has declined in value by more than 111 percent against the U.S. dollar, while the Canadian dollar has lost 5.88 percent since January 1994. The redemptive feature in the lowly estate of our dollar is that Canada enjoys a whopping trade surplus with the United States.

Anyway, I understand Trudy Rubin's concern even though I do not share it. The skidding U.S. dollar, she maintains, gets no respect and "will make it harder for America to influence international trade policy . . . [and] make it more expensive to keep or send U.S. troops to foreign hot spots."

As I said, some diminution of American influence in trade or "foreign hot spots" may not be altogether a bad thing. Certainly, so long as Jesse Helms, a right-wing hero from the Carolinas to Canada, chairs the Senate Foreign Relations Committee, prospects for a coherent American foreign policy are dim. We speak of a man who cannot distinguish between the president of India and the president of Pakistan (those people all look alike, don't they?) and whose most recent pronunciamento held a promise to invade Cuba. The senator is also opposed to gays in the military (or anywhere else), and is not yet resigned to the result of the recent war between the states.

But who cares, really, about the U.S. dollar? We have been endlessly hectored to respect the workings of the free market economy, the idea being that no one should try to do anything to it except those who are exquisitely qualified. So all can witness, with ideological equanimity, the falling U.S. dollar, a persistent trade imbalance, massive problems of poverty and joblessness and escalating criminal violence, high interest rates, record corporate profits, astronomical executive salaries and benefits, a soaring stock market, rising dividends, and Republican reactionaries ruling the Congress. Relax; it is the Lord's will.

On Friday, stock values on Wall Street reached record highs. International Business Machines Corporation announced first quarter earnings of $1.3 billion—an increase of almost 300 percent, producing a record per share dividend. IBM credits these high earnings from "product sales and its service businesses," but over the past three years, IBM, AT&T, GM, GTE and Sears Roebuck have been on a downsizing binge that has resulted, altogether, in 324,650 employees losing their jobs. Part of this quarter's dividends is the gift of the downsized victims.

But not everyone has been downsized, even though it is a jungle out there. Over the same three years of the combined big corporate job killing binge, the president and Chief Executive Mouse at Walt Disney earned $215,911,000 in salary, bonus, and stock options. According to Richard J. Barnet, writing in *The Nation*, "more than 40 percent of corporations doing business in the United States with assets of $250 million or more 'either paid no income taxes or less than $100,000' " (information from the General Accounting Office). And while in the 1950s, Barnet reports, corporations in the U.S. paid 23 percent of all federal income taxes, the figure was down to 9.2 percent by 1991.

In my other morning paper (the *New York Times*), an editorial laments the unsurprising revelation that the rich in America are getting richer and the poor are getting poorer at a faster rate than anywhere else in the western world. Since the 1980s, the *Times* avers, "three-quarters of the income gains . . . and 100 percent of the increased wealth went to the top 20 percent of families. The richest 1 percent of households control about 40 percent of the nation's wealth—twice as much as the figure in Britain, which has the greatest inequality in Western Europe." Move over Duke, the Yanks are coming.

Elsewhere in the *Times*, on a related subject, we read from an earlier editorial, "It should not be surprising that the Republican majority in Congress, almost totally beholden to big business, is quietly trying to wreck the health and safety achievements that have been painstakingly developed over several decades."

As we all know, there are many voices in Canada—in the political parties, in the media, and in fashionable urban circles—who envy and admire the New Reactionary Right in America. It is simply astonishing how many Canadian parliamentarians are in awe of this southern blight. It is pitiful and sad to know how many admirers include young Tories or, to be fair about it, simply young anythings.

Condos on the Floes

MAY 7, 1993

Joe Gould, a Harvard man who during the Dirty Thirties enjoyed the distinction of being New York City's leading Bohemian philosopher and panhandler, developed a fine disdain for statistics as a result, he said, of reading the financial sections of daily newspapers. In one of his public lectures on the subject, Gould claimed that after extensive reading of the financial pages he could conclusively prove "the eating of tomatoes by railroad engineers was responsible for 53 percent of the train wrecks in the United States during the last seven years."

Unhappily, very few people these days share Gould's skepticism about statistics. Indeed, the majority of those who are citizens of the world's leading industrial nation are driven by numbers, including the most recent compilations from the public opinion polls. It has come to pass that neither social discourse nor public debate is possible without buttressing speech by numbers. Children whose parents used to quote the wisdom of elders now cite Decima, Gallup, Reid, or CROP; otherwise, they would be speaking from experience, which is now universally resented where it is not despised.

Last month, Statistics Canada—national mother of all numbers— reported that, by the year 2036, the percentage of Canadians sixty- five years of age or older will have increased to 23.2 percent. According to Ivan Fellegi, the Statscan chief, these alarming num- bers are made more so as a result of "a much lower fertility schedule" practised by today's generation of baby-boomers. Fellegi goes on to say that last year, for the first time, the Québec Pension Plan paid out more than it took in, which represents "one of the first signs of how the aging population is affecting the economic life of the country."

I'm not sure, frankly, if any of this is true or merely the sly work of Statscan, as a government mouthpiece, to spread terror among the population by carpet bombing them with all this statistical shrapnel. To begin with, the argument that the future of Canada (and its pen- sion programs) is imperilled by the reluctance of baby-boomers to breed is a nonstarter: If the boomers can't make out, we can always import immigrants who can.

But even assuming Fellegi is giving it to us straight, which is to say that by 2036, one out of every four Canadians will be an old-age pen- sioner, what do we do about it now? We could, of course, haul half our old folks up to the Canadian Arctic and set them loose on ice floes, resulting in huge savings to the national debt. Or we could send half our medical doctors to Texas so as to reduce the life expectancy of the Canadian population, again resulting in huge improvements to the peace of mind of finance minister Don Mazankowski and his successors.

While there are possible solutions that I'm sure neither the gov- ernment nor Statistics Canada would have us shrink from, there may be a third way we should look at the problems raised by Fellegi's numbers, the same tiresome problems raised by hand-wringing editorial writers and candidates seeking the Tory Party leadership: debt, deficits, the economy, and the lack of competitive fervour in the likes of you and me.

Taking a leaf from the works of Joe Gould, we should look for clues to solutions to these—um—worrisome and growing problems by reading the financial pages of the daily newspapers. After all, Gould, who claimed to have translated many of Longfellow's poems into sea gull, should not stand as the only deep thinker to probe the financial pages for something other than stock market quotations.

For instance, a recent study in the *Wall Street Journal* informed that half of America's corporate chief executive officers drew down salaries of $1 million or more. Given the condition of the American economy, argument can be made that at least 50 percent of that country's CEOs are overpaid. American financial pages, just like our own, are littered with complaint and exhortation about the need to be more competitive. The meaning of this apparent lust for competitiveness is somewhat mysterious, given the lavish lifestyles of the rich and nearly bankrupt.

Here in Canada, business had adopted the slogan "Do Something Today to Be More Competitive Tomorrow: Fire Somebody." But if Canada's CEOs took a cut in pay sufficient to hire ten more employees lower down in the corporate food chain, the positive economic results would exceed any combination of recent federal budgets and annual meetings of the Canadian Chamber of Commerce.

Doubtless any such prescription will be drowned out in a chorus of Hey-you-can't-do-that in this here age of international competitiveness. Well, maybe not, but there are other things being done that aren't so competitive either.

Only last week, the vast corporate empire of Edper Bronfman extended $8 million in soft loans to a half-dozen or so of its senior employees to help tide them over a rough patch in their financing of personal stock option deals turned sour in the recession. One wonders where this easy money comes from, but maybe one shouldn't.

An American named Gerald Greenwald wants a $7 million bonus he says is owed him after working a whole year trying to sort out the affairs of Olympia & York Developments Ltd., which only two years ago was everybody's corporate flavour of the month and the corporation judged most likely to prove Canadians knew how to do it. Greenwald's apparent success at O&Y follows the even briefer tenure of one Thomas Johnson (no apparent relation to Nabisco's former president, Canadian Ross Johnson, O.C.) who worked there for two weeks and departed with severance benefits of more than $1 million for his pains.

Where does all that money come from? Is this what they mean by "competitiveness?" And is this why Statscan is measuring the ice floes in the Canadian Arctic?"

Downsizing Empire Builders

MAY 26, 1995

When I was a member of the Ontario Royal Commission on Book Publishing, appointed by John Robarts and chaired by Richard Rohmer, we as a commission argued in vain for public lending rights for Canadian authors.

Considering the threadbare existence of Canadian book publishing at the time (or any other time), the idea that authors should be compensated for their works not only when purchased, but as well when borrowed from the public libraries, was strongly supported by the people in the literary community. And it was not the money—though none despised it—but the principle of the thing. You cannot borrow, for free, someone's invention, patent, software, or song, not even someone else's musical arrangement. So how come an author's private work may be circulated for free by a public library?

Many civilized nations have recognized the public lending rights of authors and have programs in place that provide compensation. Canada, which needed more than most to protect, encourage, and compensate its authors, dithered for years, lacking either the interest or the will to act. Canadians, who enjoy nothing more from time to time than a good rant against foreign publishing and foreign publishers, seemed reluctant to support so modest a proposal as a public lending right for its own authors.

But in the late 1980s, during my three years in Ottawa as the crazy uncle in the attic of the Privy Council Office, culture minister Flora MacDonald and finance minister Michael Wilson finally struck a deal between themselves that provided Canadian writers acknowledgement and compensation for their lending rights. I recall writing them both grateful notes of appreciation, suitable hosannas enclosed.

It was not a big deal; it was never intended as one. But it did recognize an important principle. The Public Lending Right Commission was immediately established, given a modest staff and budget, and we have all lived happily ever after. Until lately.

I say "we all" because, as the author of three books sometimes borrowed from public libraries (according to computer analysis), I receive each year a cheque in some four figures, such as $1,xxx—I forget the amount—a good part of which is returned inevitably to the Department of National Revenue, while the remainder goes into my wine cellar. The architects of the PLR regime placed a cap on the revenues any author might receive, however prolific.

While no one gets rich from having her or his work borrowed from the library, authors do get recognition and respect for their rights, just as songwriters or playwrights do. I have always imagined the Public Lending Right Commission as operating out of some small cranny in the Ottawa bureaucratic infrastructure, a sort of Santa's workshop for writers, peopled by well-adjusted, cheerful, independent-minded, anti-empirialists eager to serve their clientele with as little fuss, as few forms, and as little noise as possible.

Those of us who have been served by the PLR Commission have been profoundly impressed by its humble bearing, its modest stationery, and the ease and facility of its operations. Not only has its budget for operations remained small, by any measurement, but it has customarily come in under budget, to the dismay and discomfort of some of its neighbours in the nooks next door. So that when the commission returned the unused portion of last year's budget, the Canada Council seized it and, as though the PLR were some Bosnian enclave, has now threatened to swallow the commission, its budget, and all its people, whole.

There is some sort of dark impulse that lurks in the unlighted corners of the minds of Ottawa functionaries, which compels them to concentrate vastly disproportionate amounts of their energies upon fixing, changing, and tinkering with things that already work.

In Ottawa, there are people who like to sit in airless, windowless rooms and move lines and blocks about on charts or chalkboards. They are downsizing (though not always), integrating, rationalizing, identifying, condensing, codifying, and generally rearranging the universe. People do this all the time, because they are never satisfied they've got it right, or they've got all there is to get.

It was in the midst of such an operation—over in the war room of the Canada Council—that someone stumbled upon the Public Lending Right Commission and was then confronted by a blinding light of revelation. Since PLR exists on its own, holds few meetings, has no embossed stationery, and serves only one function, it must be powerless. And it really should belong to someone else.

Besides any of that, it is a little thing that works, and the Canada Council, an early sell-out agency to the deficit cult in Debt City, could use a little success story, plus a few more person years and a tad more spending money for administration. Also, keep in mind, the claim that it now nourishes deserving Canadian authors would look good on its resumé.

Swallowing one of the few operations in Ottawa that truly works —quietly, painlessly, and efficiently—will not make the Canada Council look any more impressive to the constituency it will supposedly serve. In the end, if the council gets its way, the commission's budget for lending rights payment to authors will be "globalized" in the council's overall budget, PLR staff will be declared redundant, the cranny will be closed, and—before we know it—Canadian authors will be paid off in supermarket coupons. Write your MP today: Tell him or her to tell the Canada Council to invade Bosnia instead.

And Now a Word from Our Sponsor

SEPTEMBER 6, 1994

Marshall McLuhan, the global guru who came out of Canada, described advertising as "the greatest art form of the twentieth century." David Ogilvy, the British ad man who was the art form's greatest practitioner during the sixties, once observed (in fact, observed more than once) that *political* advertising was "the most dishonest in the world."

Each is saying a lot and both might be right. I speak as one who suffered from static cling during the summer, but not until I saw the ads on TV did I know I had a problem.

Static cling is not a political problem but a social one, like smelling bad. And I go back to the days when pink tooth brush was a social calamity, so there is not anything about the afflictions of humanity I'm not familiar with. When the young woman wrinkles her noise and says on TV "when he gets close and he smells"—I know where she's coming from. Furthermore, I appreciate the fact that, like static cling, the wrong deodorant can lead to the end of a heretofore meaningful relationship.

Ogilvy, you may recall, sold the Hathaway shirt, using as a model a handsome man from New Hampshire who wore a black eye-patch. Ogilvy also promoted Schweppes, the Rolls Royce, and British Travel. But he had never tried his hand at political advertising and had a low opinion of it. I was once obliged to attend a dinner in Ottawa at which he spoke. His ads were better than his speeches; there was an oracular air about him that offered suspense without substance, and a colleague and I left early for the bar and a noggin of vodka and Schweppes.

But was Ogilvy right about political advertising being the most dishonest in the world? If not at the time he said it, likely so now. He spoke before the true epoch of television had begun. Now, having watched commercials aired on CNN by the National Rifle Association and by the American Council for Health Care and kindred fronts for the insurance industry, I see Ogilvy's observation as dire prophecy.

The truth seems to be that no medium is better suited for the propagation of untruths than television; no medium so effective as television, not only for dissembling and distortion, but for inventing reality.

Similarly, television advertising has a blinding effect on common sense and truth. The campaign against a health insurance plan for Americans has been fuelled by advertising expenditures measured by independent studies "in the range of $100 million," according to the *New York Times*. Most of this money went into TV commercials, one of which claimed that Americans who might attempt to buy additional health coverage could face "five years in jail." Canadians who watch CNN on occasion can hardly miss the commercials featuring the anxious couple, worried about the number of pages in the proposed Clinton health plan and vibrantly fearful they may lose their existing coverage, their doctor, and their insurance company.

The edge television holds over other media, especially print, is that only television can use obfuscating smarm and sleaze to such powerful effect. A well-packaged lie can penetrate the thickest skull, given frequency, a modicum of cleverness, and the money avarice can command. Your daily newspaper, alas, is simply not in the race for the big dollars brought to the table by those who have a private self-interest in public policy. This may account for the observation by a movie actress, of all people, which was that, in advertising terms, "an intellectual is anybody who reads a morning newspaper."

Ira Magaziner—an aptly named Clinton appointee partly responsible for planning the health care proposal for which the loving couple cited above act out their minute's worth of alert concern—complains that "never in the history of [America] have modern technology and scare tactics combined to produce the degree and tone of misinformation . . . And never has there been such an extraordinary amount of money spent disseminating that misinformation."

A medium that can be used to convince people who suffer from static cling to buy Bounce can as easily skew a universe of sensibilities and values, even while acting as their custodian. The right to own your own machine gun and choose your own doctor, having been jointly confirmed by the NRA's Charlton Heston and the American Council for Health Care, may soon enough enjoy similar currency in this country, in McLuhan's wired village without walls.

A parliamentary committee is about to "review" the CBC, looking for ways to reposition and reshape the mother corporation in light of the new orthodoxy. Honourable members of the committee should not waste their time and ours. Instead, concentrate on further ways to ensure the public's network remains free of those who would employ television to insult Canadian viewers with their contempt for the truth.

PART V

Tale of Two Cities

Toronto, The What?

APRIL 29, 1994

Let us change the subject and talk about Toronto. There was a time when, for most Canadians, Toronto mattered. Your children went to Toronto and found work. Down at the local train station, there used to be alluring colour posters hung in the waiting rooms, advertising the annual Canadian National Exhibition, "the Ex." Hockey Night in Canada, the same night Canadians also took a bath, was an institution ritually observed at Maple Leaf Gardens. Toronto was headquarters for the T. Eaton Co. mail order house, Canada's merchandiser to middle-class taste and purse.

Almost everyone who could sing, play an instrument, act, or who had an important opinion, paid rent in Toronto; everywhere else was provincial, regional, or less. There were "regional" poets and writers and journalists, but if you worked out of Toronto you were "Canadian" and a foot taller.

It was not only a nice place to visit but a lot of people wanted to live there. Many viewed the city with envy; hatred of Toronto was a commonplace, a national habit. Most immigrants, having imagined Canada, came to Toronto, discovering, as they had imagined, a city of milk, honey, and opportunity. But whether you loved it, hated it, envied it, or were simply grateful, Toronto mattered, as the Maple Leafs mattered to people in Saskatchewan, or the Toronto Stock Exchange mattered to Vancouverites, or the Eaton's catalogue mattered to Maritimers.

It is hard to say, exactly, when the day arrived when Toronto ceased to matter. Possibly the change was incremental, a change in the city itself, become a metropolis, submerged in layers of legislative and bureaucratic authority, become multicultural, cosmopolitan, worldly, still losing it somehow, instant millionaires as suddenly become bankrupts, a social order destabilized by a collapsing merchant class, the failure of oligarchs, the death of titans, and the sudden presence of the socialist hordes at Queen's Park. But ask people what now comes to mind when they think about Toronto, chances are they will say, "Joe Carter." Others say, "Huh?"

And a lot of people no longer want to live there. Corporations and institutions have a hard time "promoting" their employees to positions in Toronto. "You couldn't pay me," I have heard people say, "to move to Toronto." It costs too much to live there; housing is too expensive; you have to lock your doors at night. Besides, "What is the big deal?"

A Toronto friend told me that the crucial moment that marked the decline of the city was when the community gave up on building the opera house to accommodate Canada's national opera company. The land was there, the plans drafted, but not enough will, not enough community spirit.

Nor enough money. But the decision not to build the opera house was the first time, in living memory, that Toronto had blinked at a tab. This is the town that built the dome, built a world-class zoo, and toured the world bidding for more—a World's Fair, failing that, the Olympics—happy to build velodromes or stadiums or entire transit systems in exchange for a few hours in the global TV sun. But the underlying reason for saying no to the opera—and yes to a new playroom for the new basketball team—was that while opera audiences were elitist, basketball was for everybody. Sure.

But the purpose here is not so much to mark the arrival of a Toronto unobserved and immaterial; instead, the purpose is to ponder the effect of its absence on those living elsewhere. Cut adrift from the national consciousness, no longer Canada's eternal city in the mind's eye, but merely a team of some sort—baseball, hockey, basketball—what now will fill the void? Now that we don't have Toronto to kick around anymore, what's left?

It is said that not even Torontonians mark the summer's last hurrah by going to the Ex. Hockey Night in Canada long ago lost Baldy Cotton, Imperial Esso fired the friendly oil dealer, Murray Westgate, and the fires are out in the old hot stove. On hockey nights, an authentic vulgarian now verbally punches out foreigners to the amusement of millions. Eaton's is a mall.

Experienced travellers concede Toronto is toast. But watch Vancouver, they say, a city with an indoor dome, a good hockey team, and now a basketball team. They point out that there is a lot to envy and dislike about Vancouver. The city faces the opposite way, its back to the East, looking towards the new worlds of Asia. It has new money and when immigrants think about Canada these days, many of them imagine Vancouver. It also has its own journalism, as Toronto once had, which outsiders find inscrutable.

What's to become of Toronto? Whither Toronto in the next century? These penetrating questions I asked of sources who have harnessed themselves to "agents of change," who only see the Canada of tomorrow as variables wrapped in sombre hypotheses. Besides, they will say, if you're going to worry about a city, worry about Montréal. Think what you like about Toronto, it will always be there even if largely unnoticed, but Montréal is bleeding to death, losing Anglos, losing capital, losing its patience. The sociology gets heavy, speaking of Montréal, and the economics are worse. It will be like Winnipeg, where—at the turn of the century—a piece of downtown real estate was pricier than land in the midst of Chicago.

The moral of the story is clear enough: Cities have their time, as do empires. Apart from Winnipeg and Montréal as examples, there's also Rome, Carthage, and Pompeii. As for Toronto, it's still a nice place to visit, but you wouldn't want to live there until they build the opera house.

The Last Time I Saw Lawrence Park

OCTOBER 14, 1993

In Toronto, in the comfortable if not commodious community of Lawrence Park, a motorist passing by would note the sea of Reform Party signs decorating the lawns in neighbourhoods once the exclusive domain of Conservatives or Liberals. The rising tide of neo-conservatism, under the testaments of Preston Manning, has now fallen upon the shores of Lake Ontario. In the sweetest dreams or most lurid nightmares—depending upon whose head was on the pillow—no one would figure a Reform invasion of Lawrence Park. The movement might infiltrate rural Ontario, the small towns, but never, not ever, Lawrence Park.

Reports to the contrary come as melancholy news. I once ran for Parliament in Lawrence Park as an undisguised Red Tory whose political heroes were Churchill, Disraeli, and Burke. My signs graced many of the lawns of Lawrence Park then, and I drank gallons of coffee in the homes of the hospitable electors there. It did not occur to me then, and doesn't now, that anyone I met at the door, on the street, or over coffee, would one day—like October 25, 1993—be endorsing a party populated by bigots, racists, and haters, and led by a charismatic authoritarian. Maybe all the people I knew then have since moved away.

It seems to me, despite any of the above, we should not be too surprised. Those whose knowledge of history predates the decline of mix-and-match and the onset of grunge will recall how economic recessions often inspire unrest and upheaval and sharpen the tongues of demagogues. Hard times have spawned a number of curious political movements and even more curious leaders, who marched at their head. In the worst of times, the collapse of traditional politics and of the historic coalitions of interests have heralded the onset of instability and authoritarianism. Those who have forgotten should look it up; they will not need to go back very far.

So that when we speak so glibly today of an oncoming political revolution, of sweeping change and the alignment of new forces, we should be clear about what we mean. The circumstances are familiar. The country is in the grip of recession; all governments are thus at risk, since all are somehow to blame. The door is now open to anyone skilled in the arts of grievance—the politics of recrimination—and who is free of any record or history of service. But the opportunity, as for the opportunist, needs followers. Again, these are not to come from the poor and downtrodden, or from radicals trained for insurgencies, but they come from—as history so painfully records—the middle class, which provides the mass of support, and from the so-called business class, which supplies the political materiel, such as money. It helps as well to have the movement grow and prosper under the idle, diffident gaze of a media distracted by their own penurious condition, in which the projected rise or fall of advertising revenues and circulation is all that matters.

If we examine further the previous revolutions of our time, recall the faceless, nameless thugs who took the incendiary messages to the streets of elsewhere, and the countless apologists and propagandists who worked the salons and gentlemen's clubs, it is worth remembering the gist of their messages. In the most searing and tragic of political upheavals, the new party proclaimed the exclusion of Jews, and then of foreigners, gypsies, Negroes, Poles, and all others who were somehow different. Including homosexuals and artists whose art failed the test of propriety. And, of course, there was general agreement that the process of justice was too slow, too cumbersome, too indulgent of those charged. They should be jailed longer or hung sooner.

There was also a general sense that the political system had become unworkable, that it frustrated and denied the efforts of true reformers. Impatience with a system that was unworkable led to a public demand for leadership with true authority—someone who would "cut through the nonsense," lay down the law, get things done, and make the trains run on time.

Does any of this sound familiar to the good people of Lawrence Park?

Preston Manning, writing in his book, *The New Canada*, writes about "reforming" the political system: "The motivation, values, skills, abilities, and dedication of the people we choose to run our democratic institutions of government are just as important as—*if not more important* than—the rules, procedures, and policies governing those institutions" (emphasis added).

Ah, but they're not and Manning is wrong; his error is a common one among men on horseback who ride into town prepared to dispense their own justice, proclaim their own "rules, procedures, and policies," to make so slothful and dilatory a thing as Parliament more responsive to command.

But what we have done, thus far, drawing upon a long experience, is put our faith in our institutions, not in men with their hastily improvised, often self-serving measures. It is our institutions and not our politicians who must survive the challenges to freedom. Otherwise, all we have is a Manning and his authority granted by people in the streets and behind the drawn blinds in Lawrence Park. Heretofore, Canadians have been rudely dismissive of those who believed themselves as important, "if not more important" than the institutions to which they were elected. But that was yesterday.

And yet, if choosing the people to run our democratic institutions is so important, how do we explain John Beck, the Manning candidate in Toronto's York Centre? The important truth about

Beck and his oddball, abhorrent racist-tainted views is not that he escaped the notice, until now, of his party superiors, but that there are many more just like him out there, babbling on about foreigners, people of colour, queers, those who need hanging, and the sublime consolations in remaining forever unilingual.

Preston Manning is the leader of the party, but John Beck is the party. People ask what will happen after October 25 and the true answer is, no one knows. More interesting is what has already happened, which many know or should know, and it is pitifully sad and unbecoming of us.

. . . And Guess Who's Coming to the Archives?

NOVEMBER 8, 1993

Ottawa: I have come to Ottawa to witness first hand the early days of the new regime and can hardly believe my eyes. You just have no idea, my dear, how much has changed in our national capital. Civil servants these days whistle as they stride purposefully to their offices. The national press gallery hums with activity as journalists turn to cover the real news now that good government once more has been restored and devoted Liberal men and women have taken up their task to rebuild and reunite Canada on this, the very eve, of the twenty-first century, under the firm moral guidance and inspirational leadership of Mitchell Sharp.

Not a moment too soon! There is, about all this strikingly beautiful citadel of national energy, with its spacious, sprawling lawns, parks and tulip beds, under the vast northern sky (recently acquired by Paul Desmarais) and its familiar skyline with the co-mingling of cathedral spires and the towers of power—the Centre Block, the Langevin, the Bank—there is—how shall I say it?—in the wine-laden autumn air (recently optioned to the House of Seagram), a sense of renewal.

So much is happening that journalists, urged on by their editors, can scarcely keep up with the fast-breaking developments. It seems only yesterday (how time flies when all are busy!) that the prime minister cancelled the order for helicopters. Almost the next day—I remem-ber where I was standing, by the counter at Mel's waiting for a booth—when word came that the prime minister was about to cancel the order for submarines. Today, if we are to believe what we hear, he will be cancelling the aircraft carriers and—hold on to your hat—after that, *dirigibles!*

"*Zut, alors!*" I hear you saying. "How can one man do so much in so short a time?"

The answer, according to journalists, as impressed as you and I, is preparation and teamwork. The prime minister has helpers, Big Time. One of the most important of these is Marcel Massé, who will be chiefly responsible for restoring the morale and overall good spirits of federal public servants—already showing remarkable improvement, as noted above—while tidying up federal-provincial relations to allow for a restructuring of a confederation of which we all, as Canadians, can be proud. After that, rumour has it, Massé will be dispatched to the CBC to put down violence while increasing Canadian content and attracting more viewers. There is, as you can see, no end to this man's abilities.

Meanwhile, Ottawa has been absolutely abuzz with talk about the prime minister's decision to review Canadian defence and foreign policy. Newspaper editorials have hailed the move a timely one, and even Flora MacDonald—you remember Flora—returning from a bungee-jumping expedition to the Zambezi Falls, was quoted as saying it was a jolly good idea. The prime minister's initiative has already produced some insightful and meaningful proposals, however tentative, one of which is to contract out Canada's military role to Power Corporation. This shows the value of summoning fresh minds to tackling old problems, does it not?

But I have saved the best for the last: The arts are flourishing once again! At least, great Canadian literary works by great Canadians: Hon. Conrad Black and the Rt. Hon. Pierre Elliot Trudeau, to name two, and not necessarily in that order, have produced volumes of what we hope will be the first of many to come. Even as I write, the nation's capital throbs in anticipation of a visitation from one of these authors, in this case—yes, you guessed!—Himself, himself! Trudeau *today*! *Live*, at the National Archives!

Trudeau's memoirs, Vol. I, is a true literary event not only because of the celebrity of the author, but because it is a ground-breaker in the lengthy and despairing, not to say uneven, relations between Canadian authors and their mendacious Canadian publishers, who so often leave their humble clients dead and remaindered after their pittance of royalties, if any, have been meted out to them. Trudeau will be an inspiration to all those shivering wretches now in their garrets, huddled over their word processors.

If you buy Trudeau's book, published by the legendary Canadian firm of McClelland and Stewart, long known for its settled penurious condition, it will cost you a mere thirty-five dollars. But no one needs to buy the book out of any sense of duty or fealty. This may not be the year of The Book, as it turns out, but it is surely the year of The Author. In this case, The Author has already been paid for his memoirs, of which he has not written so much as a word or two in his own hand out of his own head. He has been paid, in advance of publication, the sum of five hundred thousand dollars. Put otherwise, that is five hundred thousand loonies, a half-million of them, which, if, piled one upon the other, would stand taller than all the books published by M&S stacked one upon the other since the old firm published Charles Templeton's seminal work, *Jesus*, twenty years ago.

Trudeau's book, one might say, is the second in a series begun by Templeton. But no, it is not really a book, as we understand books. What it is, if we follow the old trailblazer, is a twice-edited transcript of television interviews with Trudeau about his life and times, mostly while prime minister, conducted by Ron Graham. The editing was done firstly, for a further sixty thousand dollars, by faithful retainer Tom Axworthy (brother to Lloyd), and secondly, by George Radwanski, a trusted biographer, for considerably less.

But before Ax/Rad, the CBC edited, intercut, and packaged the interviews for its own televised series on the life and times of Trudeau, now to be interspiced with running commentary by the brothers McKenna who have been added to the TV show in order to give the presentation "balance"—i.e., some claim to critical objectivity so as to quiet the country's Trudeauphobes.

People here look upon this publishing venture by the Greatest Living Liberal as the signal of a new Golden Age. What better way to begin the Restoration than a literary bash in the national capital, with Himself on the scene, five hundred thousand dollars richer without raising a sweat, and the CBC about to launch a serial version of his life and times as told by Himself while The Book fills the windows of bookstores from coast to coast to coast? So swept up am I in the excitement, I'm leaving for Montréal to see for myself the Old Lion at his second book promotion event, which is at the Ritz, the home-away-from-home of another one of our prime ministers. You know who I mean—Whatsisname.

Here Today, Gone Tomorrow

NOVEMBER 22, 1994

One of these days, you could wake up in the morning, look out the window and find the country gone. You might think it's a hard thing to do—to lose a country—but busy minds have been working on it.

Some might be inclined to say it's preposterous. How could you lose a country the size of this one? You could lose Luxembourg or mislay Brunei but . . . surely this would be a helluva hard place to lose, most of it rock and much of it frozen. Where would you hide it?

Easy. We could hide it from ourselves. People do that all the time, with the car keys, the family pliers, a borrowed book. Why not Canada?

Well, you might say, Canada is a great country, envied and admired all over the world, which is more than you can say for your car keys. And, of course, that's true. So far as it goes.

But let me be frank about this. As a personal statement, I'd have to say today's Canada doesn't look all that familiar to me. If it weren't for Peter Gzowski and a couple of others, Canada could be anywhere, or nowhere. It could be the northern branch office of the World Bank, at the corner of King and Bay. Or a neo-conservative think tank, on the windswept corner where Pennsylvania Avenue joins Laurier.

It shouldn't be called Canada anymore, anyway. I've been reading my morning paper, looking for a new and more suitable name. The name that comes to mind is Don'tneedit; the capital of Don'tneedit is Can'taffordit. I am writing this from my hotel room in Can'taffordit, formerly Ottawa, from whence I can see the Parliament of Don'tneedit, all of whose members are now redundant, except for the minister of finance, who is in transition.

The movers and shakers here all agree that the country's problems have become insurmountable and nothing can be done except to do nothing. It is generally agreed in the media, and in other opinion circles, that doing nothing becomes us and can be a positive experience, as well as serving to earn the respect of the international banking community, the Business Council on National Issues, the National Citizens' Coalition, and Jesse Helms, everyone's designated neo.

The two major political parties—Reform and Liberal—are in general agreement that doing nothing is the best policy; the major difference between them is only the proper rate of speed at which to do nothing. (Those who flat disagree with doing nothing have the choice of joining the separatist party.)

Reformers, who are now described as "Liberals in a hurry to do nothing," are resolute and uncompromising in their devotion to a decentralized, loose federation based upon family values upheld by greatly enhanced personal firepower. Otherwise, they look like, walk like, and talk like Liberals.

People who visit here, trying to discover what happened to Canada, will find few clues. It is a widely held view that Canada had become more than Canadians deserved, and in today's competitive marketplace, only the leanest and meanest can survive with adequate survivor benefits such as stock options, termination bonuses, drive-by consultant fees, and paid-up pensions.

This can only mean that the major benefits once enjoyed by average Canadians must be taxed back, including old age pensions, the Canada Pension, and family allowances. In the interest of competitiveness, middle-class savings (if any) must be taxed.

There is general agreement on the need to reduce the armed forces yet more, since the cost of outfitting them is excessive and deploying them anywhere for peacekeeping duty even more so. Consideration is being given to their being outfitted with briefcases and sent to the Pacific Rim.

Because of the historic heavy cost of subsidizing the economic growth of Ontario through national tariffs, the onset of free trade at last allows the country to cut its losses by terminating all regional development programs (other than equipment-intensive capital projects). In order to prevent seasonally employed workers in areas east of Montréal from drawing unemployment insurance, the seasonal industries will be closed down and workers inspired to relocate in the editorial offices of central Canadian newspapers.

The truly great thing about living in upper and outer Don'tneedit is that most of the old Canada and its plumbing can be declared unnecessary, along with members of Parliament, as mentioned. The Canadian Broadcasting Corporation is to have its mandate substantially altered since it has become clear to expert consultants in Can't-affordit that there are too many people at the CBC who are musicians, singers, reporters, and actors, while not enough are engaged in international trade. The mandate of the corporation, terminally unaffordable, will be further reviewed and the corporation given responsibility for designing children's programs and selling T-shirts and coffee mugs wherever market forces merit.

Meanwhile, I seem to have become a man without a country, living in exile. Confusing it is, because I haven't left Canada. But it appears to have left me.

He Who Governs Least, Governs Ontario

MAY 19, 1995

I have given considerable thought and attention to the Ontario provincial election, the moment's major political event, one possibly bordering on the momentous. In the process, I have also given dutiful heed to media reports, been nearly faxed blind by Tom Long, the hyperactive Tory campaign chairman, and have actually spent three days on the ground in Ontario, interviewing taxi drivers, bellmen, waiters, and heart surgeons.

Finally, before filing this analysis, I found myself listening to a debate, ostensibly dealing with the issues in the campaign, between a

Ms. Whatsername and a man known as 1-800-MIKE, joined by a third person who identified himself as the premier of Ontario.

I was reminded of a curious fact that emerged from my interviews about the election. Most of those I spoke with assumed the Liberals would win, but concerning name recognition of the party leaders, all knew Bob Rae, most could identify the Tory leader, but no one knew the Liberal leader by name. I realize everyone in Ontario knows that no one knows who is Lyn McLeod. (No one knew Joe Clark either, but he and his party won anyway.) Still, I find it remarkable, in this golden age of communications, when instant celebrity occurs to someone like Kato Kaelin, that millions of Ontarians can't get their heads around the name of the presumptive next premier of Ontario.

The debate among the party leaders, while inconclusive, was nonetheless interesting. And should the voters of Ontario still have a hard time remembering the name of the Liberal leader, they will at least, having heard the debate, know what she sounds like. In the contest of decibels, McLeod was formidable, so that whenever either of her opponents seemed about to deliver some telling rejoinder, the Liberal leader simply bellowed them into submission.

Otherwise, the debate among the three party leaders confirms the widely held view that the Ontario provincial election has been boring, the people little interested, and whoever is to win on June 8 will be swept into office on a wave of ennui. Indeed, it is possible to see in the Ontario campaign the end of politics, if not the end of history. What was and is boring and frustrating about the campaign is the lack of choice, other than in the leaders, all of whom are less than charismatic when not almost invisible.

It is ironic that some in the media, and some politicians, attribute this general lack of enthusiasm now so palpable in Ontario to widespread public cynicism about politics. These dour and oft-repeated sentiments are followed by exampled horror stories about politicians who have failed to keep their promises. But, of course, the most popular politician in the country—the prime minister of Canada—has broken more promises than he has kept, to the entire satisfaction of most of the media and something like 70 percent of the electorate.

Perhaps a better explanation for the lack of public enthusiasm for politics is that there is not much to be enthusiastic about. It is true that Lyn McLeod has a plan, and Mike Harris has a plan, and that both plans deal with reducing the deficit. Each party has sought the advice of various accountants who have provided endorsements that state, in the cautious manner of accountants everywhere, that in the event all the variables remain invariable—and nothing else happens—then the universe will unfold precisely as planned and the deficit will vanish in either three years or six years or, if one follows Bob Rae who does not have an exact plan, vanish sooner or later.

The media, having long since surrendered to becoming propagandists for the Holy Crusade against the deficit, have sought vainly to convince their audiences they should have the same zest and zeal for deficit politics as, say, the Burlington Junior Board of Trade. But having to choose between the deficit reduction plans of Lyn McLeod and Mike Harris requires the same exquisite skill as choosing the superior musicality as between two kazoo players; it would also help if you enjoyed kazoo music.

Oddly enough, we now live in a political environment, as illustrated today in Ontario, where the socialists are the only party without a plan. This is not news but reality, and what I found engaging about Rae's performance was his confessed conversion to pragmatism. But he was also, however grimly, clinging to the belief that governments might yet be of some help to humankind, from time to time, and to the general society.

As against so homely an opinion, both Harris and McLeod stood firm in support of that most sacred codicil of the New Right, the Liberal leader promising to reach the deficit-free Promised Land sooner, the Tory leader promising deliverance a little later but with consolation for the delay in the form of a tax cut. Viewing all this, I found it difficult not to be impressed by Harris's singleness of purpose and by what he described as his "consistency." Admirable qualities for any public man or woman, if not always winning ones.

The voters, according to the polls, are leaning strongly Liberal, drawn by the magnetic pull of Jean Chrétien's popularity, according to some. But it is obviously difficult to get excited about future events at Queen's Park, no matter the result. After a debate relentlessly focused on the question as to who best can govern Ontario least, why should anyone care who wins?

Nothing Thanks, I'm Just Looking

JUNE 6, 1995

The net result of the Tory victory in Ontario's provincial election is that society's losers lost and its winners won. The better off you are, the bigger the victory. The Mike Harris Common Sense Revolution makes a lot of sense to those who are self-sufficient. The Revolution makes no demands upon either their energies or income, but it does reflect their interests as well as their darker view of the general society.

Welfare was a big issue in Ontario. It is a big issue everywhere. It is a striking feature of today's political agenda, wherever politicians hawk their wares, that in the face of unparalleled profits and wealth, the true enemies of the state turn out to be the poor. The middle class, which has been ruthlessly downsized, marginalized, abandoned by the deficiteers, and indeed overtaxed, has turned its fury upon a menacing coalition of welfare mothers, chronic alcoholics, and functional illiterates. Once upon a time the alert guarantor of social justice, the middle class has become today's bullying enforcer of vengeance upon the helpless.

How could this be? Well, it has been largely done by media orchestration and by deploying more mirrors than in all of Versailles. Herewith an example of media musicality, with mirrors: "Mr. Harris would reduce Ontario's unusually high incentives to stay on welfare by reducing average payments ... And he would make those payments conditional on able-bodied people going to school or doing community work."

This does have the virtue of a compelling simplicity. The *Globe and Mail*, swelling with editorial pride, called the idea "entirely sensible and constructive."

It is none of the above. It is a triumph of rhetoric over reality. The talk needs the walk: How many of those on welfare today are able-bodied? What school do we send these able-bodied Ontarians to attend? For how long? At what cost? To what end?

Then, there is the easier part: Put the bums to work. This rises from an old German slogan about the joy of work. But what is "community work" anyway? Well, raking leaves, picking up litter, sweeping sidewalks, standing around. How many leaves can a single-parent welfare mother rake on a November day with the wind blowing? How many old newspapers could she retrieve in mid-January, during an eight-hour day?

These and other vexatious questions will need to be addressed by Premier Harris, provincial authorities, municipal authorities, daycare representatives, Chambers of Commerce, welfare caseworkers, local pastors, and the entire editorial board of Canada's national daily. Clearly, there is not a moment to lose.

Meanwhile, I'm having my own common sense revolution and I say it's bunk. This is not to say the welfare issue, as a chimera, is not part of a winning political strategy these days. Also, it's fair to say that Bob Rae, the outgoing premier, was soft on welfare bums. One of the problems Rae had with welfare, as a political hot-button issue, was that a lot of the public suspected that a lot of those on welfare were also "foreigners"—like Jamaicans or Maritimers—which was an even hotter button. Some of those who pressed the welfare issue knew damn well the passions it aroused in the body politic.

The degree to which political parties should be held responsible for public enlightenment, as against public incitement, cannot be sensibly argued in the wash of a provincial election. But the truth is, or was, the issue of welfare was an exploitative one, and was treated as such by Tories and Liberals alike.

Never mind. While the Ontario election is seen as a defeat for welfare bums and their children, it can be seen as a big win for scabs. The decline in the power and influence of organized labour has been marked throughout North America (and in Britain, where it all began). It is not a phenomenon peculiar to Ontario. Obviously, Ontarians are now on the side of management in the ongoing struggle of industrial relations. While there is nothing new to this, the bias has become more pronounced. Making strike-breaking easier may well make the cost of labour cheaper, but it will not necessarily follow that the price of goods will be any cheaper to Canadians or more competitive abroad. If that is not the result, the Ontario voter will have handed a huge benefit to management in return for lower wages, increased industrial unrest, and lower productivity. As with much of the Common Sense Revolution of Mr. Harris, we shall have to wait and see.

It is surely one of the redeeming features of the Tory triumph that it could have been worse—the Liberals could have won. We have been spared all the ills of so grievous a hegemony, a Liberal lock on central Canada, and suffocating federal-provincial relations.

It is a good thing, anyway, for the Conservatives. Whether in Ottawa, the Maritimes, or the West, Ontario matters in the national scheme of things, and matters materially and philosophically to the Tory party in all its parts. It is one thing to have had Alberta as the prime example of how the New Right works. But it will be something else to see how the Revised Right works in Ontario, in a highly industrialized, pluralist, and diversified society.

Those who doubt profoundly the major precepts of current right-wing policy, and are dubious as to the disinterest of some of its most eloquent champions, will have at last a working model to observe while these precepts are being severely tested. In Ontario, we can all see for ourselves and reach our own conclusions. The talk is over, the walk begins.

PART VI

Neo-Contendere

No White Males Need Apply

JUNE 13, 1995

It is the habit of journalism to render the meanings of great events in generalities. This is for obvious reasons; almost everything in life is too complicated to explain and most people are not that interested in detail. As well, explaining everything in generalities allows everyone to achieve their own level of understanding.

In Ontario, for example, many voters believed most Toronto taxi drivers were also on welfare. According to newspaper reports, people who had not seen help-wanted advertisements reading "No white males need apply" nonetheless knew of others who had. One must assume the election result last Thursday confirms public support for welfare "reform," at least insofar as it would apply to taxi drivers. The result would also be comforting to those who had not seen the offensive "No white males need apply" ad but knew of it, and it explained better than anything else what was wrong with employment equity laws.

It was agreed, on the morning after, that Ontario had, generally speaking, voted for lower taxes and less government. One of the more interesting aspects of the campaign promises made in the Common Sense Revolution is that almost everything can be achieved without calling the Ontario legislature. The new government may cancel programs, reduce taxes, cut spending, and liquidate whole departments without consultation or debate. The Revolution could be half over in a week.

There is something to be said for the advice of Lady Macbeth: If it were to be done, better done quickly. Given the first gush of approval by the establishment press, and the cry from the business community for haste, it should be possible to have this picnic of common sense policy before a single ant arrives, or a cloud to dim the day.

The leader of the Revolution has promised himself a smaller cabinet. David Peterson had a cabinet of thirty, himself included; Bob Rae's cabinet seemed fewer if only because so many of his ministers resigned or were fired or remained anonymous.

Today, to appoint fewer ministers is high political fashion.

Fewer is not necessarily better since the gesture leads, in the end, to more decisions being made by bureaucrats in a vacuum of accountability. But since most neo-conservatives advertise themselves as anti-politics, as well as anti-government, nobody minds much, because the absolute objective is for no government at all. Accountability becomes a frill.

The new masters in the Ontario House have promised a summer session of the legislature. One might express opposition to the proposal in the most poignant and fashionable terms available: too expensive. A legislature summoned in the midst of summer to witness this torrent of common sense revolutionary ardour would be without any substantive part to play in the programs. This would seem contradictory to the declared purposes of the sponsoring regime, one being the practice of frugality. Newt Gingrich, something of a laggard, fulfilled his Contract with America in just less than one hundred days. But Newt needed legislation. Mike needs only to be sworn in.

Many of those who voted against the revolution (about 54 percent) are nonetheless anxious to see it happen. There may be something they missed in the telling of it, but if it turns out to be right, it will assume the miracle properties assigned to it by its creators and bring peace to the suburbs of Toronto. There could be no higher purpose for public policy.

But will it work? We shall see if, in fact, a 30 percent tax cut produces more jobs. There is no evidence the inherent premise is true and there is some evidence the opposite is true. It is also not a sure thing that less government costs less, since it depends whether we consider government spending on conservation and pollution control to be an investment or an expenditure. Obviously, deregulation costs less, as does a decline in consumer protection programs; both policies encourage firm friendships between government and private interests, but at some cost to the public, who pays the difference.mm

There is no doubting the drift of present-day conservatism in Ontario. Its voters have bought into the deficit mania and been titillated by the promise of a tax cut. The seeming contradiction has been glossed over by the acceptance of the welfare myth. An anxious, harried middle class voted the only way it could. It voted for its own interest, as seen from Markham Heights, and nothing makes more common sense than that.

But it is hard to believe this poll-driven, narrowly drawn agenda will do much more than give anger and pessimism a brief public holiday in Ontario. The divisions, meanwhile, between those whose estates are expanding and those whose are shrinking will continue to widen. Every statistic and measure we have confirms the growing gulf between those in power and those in politics, and between the top and the bottom in society—a distance becoming nearly immeasurable—and between those who see what is happening and those who care not to look.

Mr. Manning Goes to Washington

MARCH 7, 1995

Alberta's own Preston Manning has won second prize in the Edmonton Pizza Parlour & Gas Bar annual draw. (First prize: one all-expense-paid scenic tour of the West Virginia coal pits, including clothing allowance.) While Preston didn't win the Big One, the second place ticket is not to be sneezed at. It includes a free guest appearance on National Empowerment Television as a special guest of Newt Gingrich, prominent American historian and America's highest paid author and congressman.

On the day following his joint appearance with Newt Gingrich on real American TV, Preston picks up the rest of his prize, which is an all-expense-paid free meeting with the editorial board of the *Wall Street Journal*. According to Ottawa sources close to Manning's Reform Party branch office, the leader will take the opportunity to reassure American business and political leaders, during his visit, that Canada may survive as a country after all.

Preston's second prize-winning free meeting with the *Wall Street Journal*'s editorial board could not come at a better time. It follows the introduction of the federal government's budget up here in Canada, the continued fall of the Mexican peso, the devaluation of the Spanish peseta and the Portuguese escudo, and the rout of the American dollar on the international money exchanges. Due to arrive at the *Journal* offices next Wednesday, Preston may be one of the first to get through to Wall Street after the world revolt against the Yankee dollar.

His visit, coming as it does at this particular time, requires of Preston that he be properly circumspect. He should bear in mind that the Americans are a proud people—the proudest in the world, some say—and while they have been living "too high on the hog for too long," to coin a phrase, Preston should be prepared to bite off his tongue before saying so in front of the editorial board of the *Wall Street Journal*.

Indeed, the Reform leader would do well to remember where his forelock is and, when in the company of the editorial board, to tug it from time to time. It should be borne in mind that visiting the *Journal* is not a right, but an honour. Board members should be addressed with excruciating unfamiliarity, as in "Your Splendidness." On being introduced, visitors are expected to bend the left knee, however slightly.

Manning's junket to the *Journal* is of interest beyond mere levity, even though there isn't much new in politicians hustling newspaper editors. Besides, it may never be too late for someone to try to improve upon the *Journal*'s knowledge of Mexico. Las Cañadas, someone might tell the editors, is in Mexico, while Canada is—oh—somewhere north of Fargo, most of it anyway. Or, while Mexico is a Third World country, like the Bronx, Canada isn't. But we oughtn't look to Preston for any of this.

The Manning trip to Wall Street is entirely an image-builder: Watch Preston feel at home with America's corporate elite in the world financial heartland. Back home, chests swell with pride; buttons can be heard popping from Edmonton clear to Manyberries. The oracle has landed!

All that, after a night spent with Newt on the National Empowerment Network. Is Preston a great leader or what? What many of us have failed to grasp, in this return of the prophet, is that Gingrich went to school on Manning's career in federal politics. A *Washington Post* piece, written by Charles Trueheart last January, quotes a former Reform Party pollster, now working for Gingrich pollster Frank Luntz, as saying Gingrich "occasionally cited Manning's successes in Canada in speeches and television broadcasts."

The sometime Reform pollster, Dimitri Pantazopoulos, has been described by David Frum, a Canadian columnist and a former editor at the *Wall Street Journal*, as representing "the new North American common market in political consulting," particularly on the right. As Trueheart observed, "The Reform agenda includes a host of issues with American analogs—opposition to abortion rights, gun control and gay rights"—and lower taxes, less government, fewer rights for consumers, and "family values."

This does remind me once again of Senator James M. Inhofe (R. Oklahoma), who has said he campaigned last fall, and won, on "God, gays, and guns." No doubt Preston could arrange through Newt to meet with Inhofe, who is a great admirer of Jesse Helms who is a good friend of Al D'Amato who knows Dick Armey who needs no introduction to Ralph Reed of the Christian Coalition warmly supported by Pat Buchanan who knows Pat Robertson.

Knowing our man Manning has direct access to those guys makes you feel warm all over. Doesn't it?

Luntz of Luck with Newt

MARCH 17, 1995

Having watched Preston Manning's television appearance with Newt Gingrich on NET (National Empowerment Television), I made some notes of my impressions in my journal, something for grandchildren and their grandchildren to read as the hasty scribblings of a forbear present at a historic television occasion.

Since not everyone has a dish, not everyone would have been able to witness this defining moment in Canadian-American relations. My impressions, on reviewing my notes, appear mixed; the program struck me as intriguing and depressing at the same time. Manning himself was interesting—indeed, more so than Gingrich, who appeared throughout as obliging but visibly weary, and suffering from a hacking cough. But Preston did his best; as a verdict on his overall performance, I was reminded of a stirring malapropism once uttered by an ESPN sports announcer, who said of a coach whose team had almost won, "Tonight, he can hang his head high." And so could Manning.

Most of the questions addressed to the Reform leader came from Newt's co-host on the show, Heather Higgins, a woman with a fulsome, incandescent smile sufficient to melt the polar ice cap. Also present as interlocutor, and lending a little verisimilitude, was Frank Luntz, president of Luntz Research, who, according to Higgins, was "very much involved" in helping the Reform Party in its recent Canadian electoral success in 1993. Luntz is something of an overachiever in the polling and consulting business; his clients have included not only Gingrich and Manning, but also Ross Perot and Pat Buchanan.

As made clear in a recent magazine piece, Luntz is a neo-conservative of Gingrichian proportions. He favours the immediate elimination of public funding for the arts, the humanities, and the Public Broadcasting Service. Before eliminating farm subsidies, Luntz would prefer them to be included in a wider range of cuts. "If everyone is giving up something at the same time, it's okay," he is quoted saying. "But if we make the farmers go first, we're going to get killed in the farm community. We've all got to go together."

This sort of pragmatic counselling excites Luntz's colleagues, such as William Kristol, who explains, "That's why Frank gets the big bucks."

While Manning fielded soft rollers from Higgins, and Gingrich struggled to remain conscious, Luntz searched for meaningful connections between the two men. Clearly, both abhorred deficits and "big" government, but when Manning tried to emphasize his party's populist roots, the subject did not appear to ignite Gingrich. But then, nothing did.

The program was interrupted more than once by the offering to viewers of twenty hours of lectures in American history on CDs or tapes, as delivered at Reinhardt College by "Dr. Gingrich"—all for 130 bucks or so, as I recall. But when it was over, and everyone had thanked everyone else, and Manning had observed that perhaps "there are things we can learn from you and you can learn from us" (easily the evening's most chilling thought), I found myself trying to figure what it was all about.

I had been witness to a television production involving the second most powerful politician in America and the leader of the third most populous party in the Canadian Parliament and . . . ? Well, it was a little hard to say—until the last words appeared on the tube, inviting viewers with questions or comments to write "The Progress and Freedom Foundation."

Every totalitarian or authoritarian movement in history co-opts the language of democracy in order to conceal its purpose. The Soviet commissars could scarcely draw a breath without invoking peace or liberty or freedom or progress. Even as the gulags were filling up with their victims, the regime celebrated its legitimacy by claiming itself to be the one true instrument of all the people.

So it is with new-age Republican Gingrich and the populist Manning, each a humble servant of the people's will. What do the people want? Reduced deficits, less government, fewer programs, lower taxes. They want their government run "like a business."

Whose business? The purpose of government is to serve the public interest; the purpose of business is to make a profit, whether selling mustard or mustard gas, firewood or firearms. How can government become a business?

Well, "we can't leave all this debt to our children." Okay, so why do the Republicans talk about cutting spending and cutting taxes, at the same time? Because "tax cuts increase consumer spending" and create a stronger economy. But no empirical evidence exists supporting that assumption; historically, tax cuts have led to debt increases, inflation, and recession. But people "must break the habit of relying on government." So, who should they rely on to protect them from unsafe products, false advertising, usurious interest rates, predatory commerce, and the exploitation of the innocent and gullible? *Caveat emptor*? Oh, sure.

It is clearly the neo-conservative agenda to put the people at a greater distance from their government, by making them powerless and dependent upon the charity of a new corporatism. One wonders if Preston Manning is so dazzled by the celebrity of Newt Gingrich, or so in need of the approval of his friends in Washington and on Wall Street, that he could not see how alien and offensive the Republican message sounds to many Canadians. Or did his presence on the Newt Gingrich Wednesday Night Special signify only that his managers, on both sides of the border, thought it might serve his interests, almost as much as theirs?

Health Care—The $11,865.76 Solution

MAY 9, 1995

As a member of one of Peter Gzowski's *Morningside* political panels awhile ago, I asked a fellow panelist I had identified as a Reform supporter if he preferred the American health care system to Canada's. Yes, he said, he did. Stunned into silence, I never got to ask him why.

Health care is becoming a defining issue in our politics. You can tell a lot about someone's politics once you know their attitude towards health care. The Ultra-Right is perfectly willing to abandon the Canadian system altogether, or as much of it as public opinion and political opportunity will allow. But even the many supporters of our publicly financed Canadian system are prepared to compromise with those who say Canadians can't afford the universal system we now enjoy, that the plan should be limited to catastrophic protection, or—as Preston Manning has argued—the coverage should be limited to "serious" health problems.

Obviously, there are many ways of curtailing the benefits of Canada's universal health care system. And there are many interested parties, such as the insurance companies, willing and anxious to profit from their participation in some new mixed public and private scheme.

The alleged reason for encouraging the dilution of the principles of universality and of the single public carrier and payer is—what else?—the pressing need to reduce the deficit. The imperative of deficit reduction now drives the priorities of government and, it reasonably follows, of Canadian society. The relentless barrage of high-rent economists, underpaid columnists, and bank presidents, all of them hollering about the evils of living in debt, has convinced many Canadians that it would be better to sell the children or give up the country than fail to reduce the deficit.

I don't believe any great number of Canadians has as yet bought into this scam, but some suspect their neighbours have. This leads to the uneasy conclusion that, since the CN has to be privatized to keep the bailiff from the door, then maybe national health care has to be somehow privatized as well.

A sane person who has not been living in the direct line of fire between the editorial boards of some of the world's greatest newspapers (I'm including Canada's family favourite, the *Wall Street Journal*), and the cowering politicians in what was once the national capital, might offer another answer to the alleged dilemma of the unbearable cost of publicly financed health care: Raise taxes. For those who say, speaking through their public affairs vice-presidents and from their southern bunkers, that tax increases are unaffordable in this competitive age, a further answer would be that a tax increase would be cheaper for most Canadians than cutting the insurance companies into the deal.

A man from Greenwich, Connecticut recently underwent a hernia operation at his local hospital. As he told the *New York Times*, he was in the hospital for six hours, two of them in surgery; he was home in time for tea. His surgeon charged him $2,200.00; the anesthesiologist charged him $900.00. The hospital charged him $11,865.76, including sales tax.

What is remarkable about the experience of the man from Greenwich is that it is not at all remarkable in the chaotic and costly American health care system. ("The best in the world," as American Republican politicians oft describe it.) The difference between the Canadian plan and the American experience is that the Canadian health care system is not for profit. Those who argue that competition in the public sector reduces costs have no argument when it comes to public versus private health insurance.

It is interesting to read Manning's rationale for allowing the privatization of Canadian health care: "Reform obviously believes the wisest decision would be to get the deficit to zero as quickly as possible."

To get the deficit to zero, Manning's way, is to get national health care down to about 50 percent of its present coverage. Or less. But first, the great divide must be established between "core services" and "non-core services." Governments, federal and provincial, would cover the costs of "core" services, Manning explains, "up to some minimal national standard." All else would be funded "through a more flexible combination of funding sources, including private insurance and user-pay." Thus, the camel enters the tent.

On the other hand—and in politics, there always is the other hand—Manning insists he is not advocating "abandoning a largely publicly financed, comprehensive, universal, portable and accessible health care insurance program in favour of some American-style system." And anyone who says otherwise, Manning adds, "is not only lying, they are fear-mongering."

At the risk of doing a little mongering, it is plain to me (and should be to you) that Manning's plan would erode the federal government's role in maintaining national health care standards while allowing the provinces to balkanize the present system, dividing medical services and costs and providers however they wished. It would destroy a system that works for the people it serves, replacing it with a patchwork of plans that works largely for shareholders in the private sector. Begging Preston Manning's pardon, that looks to me like America's "best health care system in the world."

Canadians should know more about the world's best system. The man from Greenwich, Connecticut, who has had direct, recent experience with health-care providers of "non-core" needs, told the *New York Times*, "The fundamental wrong [is] an out-of-control health system that is depleting resources that could be used to offer coverage for everyone. Our health care system is a joke."

Buckley Can't Skate,
But He's Good Around de Gaulle

MAY 23, 1995

Harold Macmillan, a former prime minister of Great Britain, once gave a speech on the inevitable decline and fall of all empires and great world powers as observed throughout history, such as the decline and fall of the British Empire, the fall of Rome, and of the Third Reich.

The Macmillan thesis would also have included the fall of the

Berlin Wall and the Soviet Union. And it would pose a question, which may be what Sir Harold had in mind to begin with: Is history's most powerful nation, the United States, now at its apogee, still emergent, or in decline?

As to that, and quite by coincidence, I found myself reading a book of William F. Buckley—for reasons I will later explain—where I found Buckley detailing Charles de Gaulle's view of America following the assassination of John F. Kennedy. "De Gaulle began confiding to his friends that, in his estimate, the erosion of values in America had gone to landslide levels," Buckley writes. "The rifle shot heard in Dallas . . . was just the beginning, the beginning of an age that would see the destruction of the United States by violence."

Buckley goes on: "De Gaulle tells his intimates that we (the U.S.) are through. Our society has broken down . . . because of a confluential collapse of family (see the divorce rate, see the rate of illegitimacy, see the broken homes); of church (see the new skepticism, the playboyism of American theologians); of patriotism . . ."

Buckley's column on de Gaulle on the subject of America was written in 1967. It could have been written yesterday, and the sentiments, most of them, attributed to Newt Gingrich or any number of New Right theologians. Canadians, who may remember de Gaulle for other reasons, might still be impressed by the old boy's prescience. What he was quoted by Buckley as saying to his intimates twenty-eight years ago is today's gospel under the rubric of "family values," in Washington, D.C.

Except, of course, de Gaulle saw America's decline hastened by its impulse for violence and its inability to cope with its racism. The American right today acknowledges the decline of "family values," but sees it more as a winning slogan and as a rebuke to a generation of American liberals.

My reason for rereading Buckley, thus stumbling upon Charles de Gaulle, was an attempt to refresh my memory on the general precepts of the Old Right, and to compare them with those of the New Right. Buckley was, back then, the darling of conservatives, an articulate and literate one. There is, alas, no one like him in the present firmament of the New Right, though there are pretenders.

Buckley remains a delight to read, whether when scolding de Gaulle, mocking Arthur Schlesinger, Jr., or simply getting it wrong.

("The use of limited atomic bombs," Buckley wrote in 1968, "purely for military operations is many times easier to defend on the morality scale than one slit throat of a civilian for terrorism's sake.")

Defining "The New Conservatism" as of 1969, Buckley identifies among the verities: (1) devotion to the democratic process, (2) due process, and (3) upward mobility. As for the latter, he writes, "But now the need for that mobility is more acute than ever, so much so that the new conservatives are giving the free marketplace something of a hand—for instance, by preferential hiring of Negroes." But that was yesterday's conservatism.

Otherwise, most of it was anti-Communism, the ideal anti-Communism, in Frank Underhill's phrase, "in the eyes of God." The loss of Communism as the enemy created an altogether different New Right that is, curiously, more relevant to the Canadian political culture as well as more envied, imitated, and faxed by its Canadian counterparts than anything seen in our politics since the New Deal.

The differences between Old Conservatism and New are apparent and significant. Unlike its predecessor of Buckley's generation, the New Right is self-obsessed, narcissistic, mean-spirited, largely humourless, and about as much fun as a night on the town with Preston Manning. Having lost its most-favoured enemy, the New Right has taken up arms against liberals, welfare mothers, pregnant teenagers, and the dread environmentalists. None of them look like Kremlin world-conspirators; all of them are Americans.

Voting to kill the Clean Water Act, an outrider of the New Right described the Environmental Protection Agency as an "environmental Gestapo." And a supporter of a resolution to cut public subsidies for graduate students observed that those with graduate degrees "earn a lot more." And the same for undergraduates.

Meanwhile, the New Right is unanimous in its support of a tax cut for those in high income brackets and, as well, for a reduced capital gains tax. When a spokesman for Citizens for Tax Justice, an organization not devoted to the political philosophy of the *Wall Street Journal*, maintained that the private and corporate American rich get $456 billion in tax breaks each year, a New Right visionary, Richard Armey (R. Texas), dismissed the complaint as "class warfare rhetoric."

One could say that all this could be anticipated from a political movement whose preferred charity is the National Rifle Association. The bullet that killed John Kennedy was fired from a gun purchased through the mail. Charles de Gaulle did not live to see the violence in Oklahoma or to know of the lunatic "militias." He did not know of the new New Right, but he might have been astonished, as one who assigned a high value to patriotism, to learn how many Canadians think it would suit this country just fine.

Is It Okay for Skokes?

SEPTEMBER 30, 1994

The Liberal member of Parliament for Central Nova, Roseanne Skoke, has declared her opposition to lesbians and gays being protected from discrimination in the Canadian Human Rights Act. In her view, homosexuality is immoral, un-Canadian, un-Christian, and contrary to Canadian values.

Since Skoke's opinion is contrary to the legislative intentions of the Liberal government, the prime minister was pressed to comment, which he did by making allowances. That is to say, homophobia, as a form of self-expression, is an okay thing in a free country; besides, Jean Chrétien cannot assume responsibility for the views of all his supporters in the House, only for a majority of them.

Implicit in the prime minister's endorsement of free speech was the possibility he may have disagreed with Skoke's opinion. This is reassuring, even though, it needs saying, he missed an opportunity to remind the member for Central Nova of the importance of getting it right before declaiming on what's wrong. Skoke's premise is that homosexuals are demanding "special rights" in seeking protection against discrimination in the human rights act. She is wrong and apparently wilfully so.

Skoke has consulted her constituency executive on the issue—the wrong issue—asking its members if they approved of "special rights" for gays and lesbians. Not surprisingly, the executive voted "No." Janet Rosenstock, a member of Skoke's executive, has written to the press to clarify the distinction between what the executive voted on and what the legislation actually proposes, between "special rights" and human-rights.

Skoke is a career anti-abortionist and a devotee of the Religious Right who has fought strenuous battles against the Catholic hierarchy over changes in liturgy and rubric. When her party chose her as its candidate, it did so knowing it was proposing to send a zealot to Parliament. Skoke campaigned, and won, on "family" issues, as she defined them, including the belief that gays and lesbians were threats to "the Canadian family."

Excluding homosexuals from those protected against discrimination appeals to some in the Liberal Party and others elsewhere. For example, half the Tory federal caucus—which is Elsie Wayne, MP for Saint John—would rather the subject hadn't come up.

"Really and truly," Wayne is quoted saying in my morning paper, "you've got the debt and deficit rising as we talk. These [proposals] are things we shouldn't even be talking about."

Notwithstanding, Wayne went on to talk about it, saying among other things, "If two men want to live a certain life, let them go and live a certain life . . . But don't ask the rest of us to consent to it or to condone it."

In Wayne's opinion, human rights legislation creates problems: "Now we're going to redefine what makes a family."

What is interesting in all this is that neither of these public tribunes appears to have grasped the issue, which is not "to consent to" or condone the homosexual lifestyle, much less destroy the foundation of Canadian family life. The issue is whether to make it unlawful to discriminate against people because of their sexual orientation. Those who argue against the right of gays and lesbians to be protected from discrimination by the law are fundamentally supporting gay-bashing and other acts of homophobia, both overt and covert.

In the fullness of time, there will be a more extended and rational debate in Parliament. Elsie Wayne is not the first authoritative voice to claim honourable members have more important business to attend to than ensuring the preservation of a civil, tolerant society. The claim, of course, is always made these days in the name of extenuating circumstances, all of them having to do with debt and deficits.

It would be nice to know that not all hon. members have been gulled into thinking nothing else matters but our alleged financial crisis. Surely, Parliament has no sterner duty than that of protecting the rights of Canadian citizens, especially minorities and others who are somehow different. Members of this House appear to have a problem protecting the public from the addled and uninformed opinion of some of their own. To set matters right, even if only in the context of the facts, may require some political courage. Something a little more proactive, shall we say, than that exampled by the prime minister.

Millionaire's Row in Brampton

MAY 2, 1995

Fortunately for all concerned, and owing to a previous commitment, I was in another country—and another climate—while the Progressive Conservative Party was holding its general meeting and leadership confirmation proceedings in Hull last weekend. Having talked to several Tories present at the deliberations, it seems safe to say media premonitions of the Tory party's early death were premature.

Moreover, the party's supporters appeared to be in a remarkable state of well-being, exuding optimism from every pore. It is a curious thing about optimism in politics. Sometimes the partisans become optimistic because they sense the tides are running for them, or they are optimistic for no apparent reason and then the tides begin to run for them. The power of positive thinking, in politics, can be contagious.

At the end of the day, the young Tories had a meeting of their own to which they invited David Frum to pluck the needle of true meaning from this haystack of Tory euphoria.

Frum obliged. "I promised to speak frankly to you," he told the Tory youth. "You're not going to win the next election." Stunned by this pronouncement, some Tory youths blinked back tears, others clutched their teddy bears. A few young Tories (from the Maritimes) muttered to themselves, "How in hell would he know?"

Let me make it clear that, in my view, what might be called The Frum Intervention at the Tory meeting was a good thing. And no better platform for him, and his message, than one provided by the young Tories, whose notions of politics are idealistic when they are not ideological and who do not suffer from any significant experience with the coarse realities of politics.

Frum is a young conservative beyond his years, which is to say his ideology is considerable, even impressive, but his knowledge of politics is zilch. This allows him the luxury of presenting himself as an incorruptible purist in a political debate about such things as sharing, or caring, or the redistribution of the nation's wealth.

Frum's version of conservatism is a postulate. And while he may be right, all we have as empirical evidence as to the efficacy of right-wing politics is that, where given its opportunity, it has invariably led to repression and internal strife.

So that when Frum says, as he did to the Tory young, that the test of "real humanity" is how the society "looks at the people who produce this country's wealth, do its work and who form the public weal," he is either saying a lot, or nothing.

His is the generality of an idealogue who has previously declared himself opposed to government welfare, public health care, all farm subsidies, student loans, and government support of the arts and humanities. He is thus the ideal spokesman for the peripherally engaged, for the prototype collector of paintings, who doesn't know anything about art but knows what he likes. Or for the reader of the *Wall Street Journal,* who doesn't know anything about politics but knows what he wants.

"The people who produce this country's wealth" are clearly not farmers, but they do, anyway, "form the public weal." In Frum's mind, they are like—he told the young Tories—"a young couple in Brampton." As he depicts this couple, I found myself thinking of Ronald Reagan's "Welfare Queen," the woman who, as he told it, drove to the government office each month in a Cadillac to pick up her welfare cheque.

As for the Brampton couple: "Their income is no higher today than the equivalent person's was in 1973. Now they lose half their income before they even cash their cheque. That money is taken from them for foolish and improper projects. And they're told they're greedy and heartless if they object, and they have children to feed and clothe."

In Frum's example, the Brampton couple both work and may

have children. What immediately strikes me about them is that they need a good accountant. Any married couple with children who are losing half their income even before they cash their pay cheque is being robbed—perhaps by their employer (who, not having raised their pay since 1973, is a prime suspect).

According to Frum, it can only get worse. The Brampton couple "are constantly being told that they're soon going to be asked to pay an even larger proportion of their income." Constantly told by whom? Frum doesn't say.

The heart of the right-wing argument against "big government," and against Canada's social policy, is that it already costs the middle class too much—i.e., the mythical couple from Brampton—and must only cost more. The middle class is indeed overtaxed, but Frum's Brampton couple are no more middle class than the Prince of Monaco. Indeed, the couple would have to be earning $400,000 a year, between them, before their pay cheque would be half-eaten by taxes (in Ontario, they would pay $200,066 in tax, as of 1994, on a joint $400,000 income).

For the rest of us not distracted by the right wing's seeming compassion for the "middle class," the real tax issue becomes one of fairness and equity. Canadians have no idea how many tax havens the wealthy, and the corporate society, now enjoy. Frum, an avowed nonpartisan, is nonetheless a devout supporter of the special interests he has served daily as the voice of an ultimate right-wing fantasy: a world of commerce living in uninterrupted splendour, with neither government nor taxes to disturb its uncommon weal.

Oddly enough, what little talk there was about taxes by Tories over the weekend turned on the latest Republican pipe dream, the so-called "flat tax," meaning the same rate of income tax for a McDonald's hamburger flipper as for a Texas oil tycoon. This wonderfully regressive proposal might best be described as a guaranteed annual income plan for the rich. They would love it in Brampton.

PART VII

Sound Bites

Going Down the Tubes

As I write this, both the San Francisco Giants and the Kim Campbell Tories are still in the hunt. But a betting man might like the Giants as a better investment to win the National League West than are the Tories to win the Canadian Grand Assize on October 25. Harold Wilson, the British politician, once said a fortnight was an eternity in politics. He meant what Yogi Berra, the Yankee catcher, had in mind when he remarked that it ain't over till it's over. Part of the great allure of sports is that public opinion polls cannot predict winners; where sporting analogies fail in politics is in the grim fact that polls can and do foreshadow events, nineteen times out of twenty. As of this day in the campaign of 1993, a betting man would want long odds on the Tories, never mind Yogi Berra or Wilson.

But yes, the Tories are still in it and can still win it. Their problem appears to be the deadliest of the seven deadly sins: the sin of pride. It is hard for a proud Tory to admit things are not going well, partly because things aren't working well at Campaign Central, and not working much better on the campaign trail, where nothing runs on time and no one seems to know what tomorrow will bring.

If there is a strategic plan for this Tory campaign, nobody admits having seen it. Yet the hope of getting by without one, entertained earlier on when all the polls were favourable, is now extinct.

I spent the weekend worrying about the Giants while talking to anxious Tories (and one or two happy Grits and a few bemused journalists). The question frequently asked: "Are the Tories out of it?" Answer: Not yet. Next question: "What should they be doing that they're not doing, or stop doing?" Herewith, a few modest suggestions, humbly offered:

(1) About the campaign slogan, "It's Time." No need to drop the slogan but a pressing need to finish the sentence—time for what? The Tories won an election, in 1957, with the slogan "It's Time for a Diefenbaker Government." My youthful nephew, Peter Atkins, once ran for a Tory nomination with the slogan, "It's Time." He lost.

(2) People I talked with are uneasy about Tory television commercials in which the prime minister's face occupies the entire picture

tube. A journalist I know claims to have been unhinged by them; the visage overwhelms the message, she says. No politician ever lived who could survive a television campaign that close up to the voters, and while Kim Campbell is an intelligent, interesting, appealing politician, Julia Roberts she ain't. Kill the commercials, keep the message, repackage the messenger, and . . .

(3) . . . maybe "it's time" to bring more creative talent to the advertising campaign. The prime minister, TCU on TV from 24 Sussex Drive, is a creative cop-out. What people see and like in Campbell is her openness, candour, and likeability—the person they see moving in crowds and meeting people. Whoever it is who thinks this eyeball to eyeball polispeak about the national debt is a winner should be benched.

(4) While the lack of voter enthusiasm for the Tory single issue is becoming rampant, the Tories continue to press on, as of the start of this week, trying to explain how and why Kim Campbell's projections and forecast, budget-wise, differ from those of Don Mazankowski. *Don Mazankowski?* As manager Casey Stengel once said, looking out from the dugout at his foundering Mets baseball team, "Can't anyone here play this game?"

If, as some ranking Tories claim to believe, their research confirms the wisdom of their campaign, they should stop meeting focus groups and start talking to their own people. While acknowledging this is heresy in Tory power centres (where it remains an article of faith that free trade was the winning issue in 1988), general elections are mostly about politics and less about policies.

The Tories are getting beat up at the political level, despite the fact that they have a clearly superior leader (in the public mind) who is the first woman prime minister in the nation's history, while her principal opponent, the Liberal leader, began the campaign with slight prospects and zero credibility. No one seems to have found a way to pit Tory strength, which is Campbell, against Liberal weakness, which is Jean Chrétien.

(5) Even before they determine what their slogan means, someone should decide who's in charge of the campaign. (Where's Bill Lee?) Taken singly, those ostensibly running the campaign are solid, experienced people. So, what's wrong?

Well, the answer appears to be a lack of clear direction from the top. The campaign chairman is John Tory but there are two co-chairs, one in Québec, the other travelling with the prime minister, that last one being Pat Kinsella. Then there is Allan Gregg, of Decima, who does the polling and, it does appear, also shapes the advertising. In Ottawa, the Tories refer to Gregg as "Waldo," meaning, I guess, he's a hard man to find in the big picture. Anyway, there are daily strategy meetings in Ottawa, under the gavel of John Tory, but the chief strategist remains in Toronto, talking campaign strategy with an advertising person who prefers to work alone and uninterrupted (they all do).

People who have been watching this up close say that Kinsella's job was supposed to be that of maintaining communications between the prime minister and the central campaign committee. This doesn't appear to be happening, but if Campbell is not hearing from Ottawa through Kinsella, she is not hearing anything. And vice versa.

In the living memory of all involved, there has never been a national campaign quite like this one, where no one is truly satisfied with the way things are going but no one seems able to talk about it in a coherent, constructive way.

The prime minister is herself to blame for the lack of communication. If she lacks confidence in the people who are running her campaign, it's not too late to replace them. Otherwise, she should start calling every day, if only to become re-acquainted with those she left behind when she set out to sweep the country. They might even help.

Mr. Chrétien Lacks Company

MAY 27, 1994

A Québec journalist was saying, during the Friday celebration of Canadian politics held weekly on Peter Gzowski's *Morningside*, that all this blunt talk about the possible implications of separatism for Québeckers is counter-productive. If you say, as some of the western premiers have been saying, that the parting may not be such sweet sorrow but instead angry and painful, then you are, says the journalist from *La Presse*, simply adding fuel to the separatist fires. Also: "Jacques Parizeau and Lucien Bouchard are laughing."

It is true that things are now being said, and much more will be said, by Canadians outside of Québec that were previously unmentionable. Some of these comments will sound unpleasant not because they raise unfamiliar issues, but because they have for so long remained unspoken, as though by some sort of shared agreement that limited the discussion to two simple questions: Why shouldn't Québec go its own way? And, how could Canada survive without Québec?

This was never much of a debate since the one side was threatening and aggressive, and the other was passive and accommodating. There were at least two factors that made such a limited debate and discussion possible. The first, and most important, was that most Canadians both believed and *hoped* accommodation would be possible. A second was that the leadership of the country—notably, Prime Minister Pierre Trudeau and the provincial premiers (other than that of Québec)—also believed the threat of Québec separatism could be circumscribed by the promise of accommodation through constitutional reform.

There was a feeling, then, of public optimism that translated into a public confidence in the role of the political leadership. Trudeau spoke seldom but spoke effectively whenever he did. Some premiers came to Québec during the referendum campaign, some did not, but all the first ministers, by and large, were discrete in their comments, positive in their outlook, and supportive of the efforts of the federalist supporters directly engaged in the struggle. Even the leaders of the opposition parties in the federal Parliament were cooperative.

The result of the first referendum on Québec sovereignty, or separatism, or *indépendance*, was a triumph for Canada. The promise of constitutional reform and the strategy of civil restraint were strongly endorsed. Looking back, it may have been the right strategy but with the wrong instrument, because it proved impossible to reform the constitution so as to satisfy either the Québec nationalists, intellectuals, or journalists, or, as it turned out, to satisfy the Canadian people in general.

Obviously, what worked then, in the first referendum in Québec, will not work in the next one. The most glaring reason is already apparent in the tone and temper of the debate. It is the difference between the present Reform leader, Preston Manning, and the then Tory leader, Joe Clark, and between the present premier of Alberta, Ralph Klein, and his predecessor of the day, Peter Lougheed. It is the difference between a public that hoped for the best and a public today genuinely confused as to what is best for the future of the country, a confusion prepared to entertain the prospect of some sort of Canada surviving the loss of the province of Québec.

What strikes one as different from any past crisis is the risk the country's politicians seem cheerfully willing to run, not in the interest of saving the country but for the purpose of jockeying for future position amidst the debris after the country has fallen apart. It is hard to make sense of anything said during the past several days by the premier of British Columbia, Mike Harcourt, or by Manning, or Klein, other than to see their performance as self-serving and opportunistic. The best way to provoke the Canadian people to anger is to address them as though the Québec election had already been won by the separatists and the referendum had already been lost by the federalists. The unhappy truth is that the recent spate of heated rhetoric has worked only because the mood in the country is one of underlying pessimism and uncertainty.

The prime minister, almost alone, remains resolutely optimistic, at least outwardly. But he will have a much more difficult challenge to confront than did Trudeau in 1980. Obviously, public opinion, while supportive, is nonetheless swayed by other forces at play. Unlike Trudeau, Jean Chrétien cannot count on the premiers, certainly not on the leader of the opposition, nor the leader of Reform. Should the issue be lost—which is always a possibility—no better reason will be found for the disaster than the awful weakness of federalism's supporting cast: the premiers and the other party leaders.

How About a Railroad
and a New Opposition Leader?

OCTOBER 20, 1994

"You don't know the country," chided our man Joe Clark, addressing Lucien Bouchard, the leader of the opposition and of the separatist Bloc Québécois party in the Parliament of Canada. I agree.

Bouchard knows little or nothing of his country, outside of Québec.

You can't say that about Clark, whose knowledge of the country could be deemed exquisite. Indeed, the former prime minister's knowledge of Canada once aroused suspicion among his fellow Albertans, who feared he had become tainted by his eastern exposure. So, not only is Clark right about Bouchard—whom he knows as a former cabinet colleague—he is also the right man to say it.

What Clark said of Bouchard could also be said of Preston Manning, the standby leader of the opposition who knows as much about this country as I do about the World Bank. Last week, at his party's pep rally in Ottawa, Manning told his fellow Reformers he expected to be made opposition leader in Bouchard's stead once the top separatist representative in the House officially endorsed separatism.

This would come about through a vote by honourable members who would be so appalled to learn the leader of the opposition would be supporting a resolution passed in the Québec legislature directing the provincial government to separate, they would rise in unison to dismiss Lucien and send for Preston.

It's been a long time since any Parliament in our neighbourhood has ditched its opposition leader merely because of his disagreeable opinion; this should be worth watching. While nothing may come of it, we are these days in the hands of leaders who, along with their followers, remain vividly ignorant of the more elementary political customs and practices. This would apply, in almost equal measure, to both Reformers and separatists for whom either governance or ultimate triumph require both a leap of faith and the suspension of disbelief.

Alert to the strategies of the Reform leader, someone inevitably will take a poll asking Canadians whom they would prefer to serve them as leader of the opposition. Bouchard or Manning? As to the answer, it will depend—as we are learning to say regarding the referendum—on the question. That is, if the question is, "Would you prefer a nice man like Preston Manning, who comes from Alberta, to be your opposition leader, or would you—ughh—prefer a traitorous separatist francophone like Lucien Bouchard, of no fixed address?" chances are the poll will favour Manning.

In advance of the question, I would myself like to be put down in the Bouchard column. First of all, it is important to me that the leader of the opposition be someone taken seriously by the government. He should be someone who puts the fear of God in the benches opposite. This happens to be true of Bouchard (as it would be untrue of Manning), not because the BQ leader is a potential prime minister—he isn't—but because he is engaged daily in gnawing on the government's nerve ends, keeping them awake while delaying the onset of their inevitable lethargy and insolence. This is in recognition of Bouchard's huge constituency located in the midst of the governing party's heartland, where his popularity exceeds that even of the prime minister.

It would be hard to be driven to such choices. The way things are, Canadians have two spokesmen seated opposite the government, both representing provincial or sectional interests in the country, and both either not knowing or not caring enough to represent all of it. What I miss most from past Parliaments, from George Drew to Jean Chrétien, was the unbroken string of opposition leaders who had some idea of Canada, the whole of it, and a commitment to it rooted in understanding, respect, and a mutuality of interest.

That this is no longer so has had, I believe, a profound effect on the public perception of government and of politics. We are often informed by the media of public anger and cynicism; this may be, but how about public confusion or bafflement, or personal—not regional, but private—alienation? Listening to this endless outpouring of hectoring, scolding, and admonitory posturing by our federal politicians—almost all of them—is to drive all to despair or to the familiar comforts of their own neuroses. Are we all as bad as they say? Are we about to go down for the third time?

The minister of finance (for one) has become a mega-bore with his endless recitals of our world-renowned profligacy, our over-indulgence in health care, our near ruinous compassion for the disadvantaged, our naive faith in the benefits of public education—all these having worked great hardship on the capacity of corporations and their shareholders to hold their own in this fiercely competitive world.

Then, too, those with different sexual proclivities and preferences have become more worrisome to our governors. Not that we should hate anyone—saith the latest Reform advisory—but hate what they do or what they are.

Meanwhile, the national round-the-clock government garage sale continues. Bargains abound: the railroad you always wanted, perhaps an airport, to which you can now charge admission. Next: buy a highway. Or a national park. All in a worthy cause. The government wants to be liked in world banking circles. Manning wants to be admired in the Petroleum Club. And Bouchard wants to be recognized at the United Nations. I'd like to keep him where he is.

Furthermore, Larry Zolf Agrees

NOVEMBER 29, 1994

In the exhaustively detailed second volume of *Trudeau and Our Times*, the subject of multiculturalism comes up only once, and peripherally. In the Trudeau government's last speech from the throne, write authors Christina McCall and Stephen Clarkson, there was a "genuflection to multiculturalism," something to do with heritage languages and visible minorities.

Further genuflections followed. But the value of "multicul," as many called it, had been that of counterweight to Trudeau's aggressive push on federal bilingualism. Under the broad umbrella of official multiculturalism, all ethnic minorities would supposedly enjoy special status in the office of the Secretary of State. Status and money. In this celebration of ethnicity, it was hoped it would be possible to distract those critics of bilingualism who had found the government's relentless preferment of the French language as puzzling as it was galling.

As usual, it had been the Ontario Tories, in their dynasty years, who first discovered the true efficacy of multicul. Government ministers made themselves present at ethnic events while government departments advertised regularly in the ethnic press. The symbiosis was palpable. It also made sense, the government would argue, since it was important to inform new Canadians of government services and policies in their own language.

Besides, multiculturalism, Canadian style, lent substance to an important claim, one that separated and distinguished Canadians from Americans: While Americans boasted of their country as a cultural "melting pot," we did not. For one reason, defining society as a melting pot presented a threat to the adherents of bilingualism and biculturalism. To strengthen the Canadian distinction, the government abandoned biculturalism for multicul while locking in on bilingualism.

It is clear that federally approved multiculturalism was no easier a public sell than was biculturalism, even though, on the face of it, the more recent policy included everyone just as the original excluded at least half the country. It is not that multiculturalism will go away; not anymore than will the weather. But the federal expression of it, which was as a cottage industry, has become an embarrassment.

What was important in the government's multicul policy was its patronage, its endowments of selected ethnic fetes and events, its sponsorship of differences that—we were led to believe—were the key to national harmony and unity. It seemed to me, whenever obliged to think about it, that we were all being patronized. And the patronizing and patronage concealed a new reality, which was the coming of a new majority, not English and French, but a truly multicultural majority, and the sooner the federal government ceased to coddle, patronize, and indulge its ethnic clientele, the sooner the rest of us could begin to come to terms with it.

Nearly thirty years ago, in John Porter's depiction of the Canadian establishment in *The Vertical Mosaic*, he spoke of "the charter groups," meaning the French and anglo-Canadians, a different turn of phrase from the "two founding races" found in the report of the Royal Commission on Bilingualism and Biculturalism, published that same year (1965). Writing on the workings of the political parties of that day, Fred Engelmann, a political scientist, and Mildred Schwartz, a sociologist, reported the following: ". . . as far as other ethnic groups are concerned, they are primarily of interest to political parties as voters and not as co-partners in the nation. This does not mean that other ethnic groups are ignored, nor that they are given second-class status. But nonetheless, there is an important difference in the way parties approach these ethnic groups."

Amazing. It was true of yesterday; more amazing, it's true today.

The last one left to turn out the lights on Ottawa's venture into state-sponsored multicul appears to be Sheila Finestone, who is, by eerie coincidence, secretary of state for multiculturalism in the catch-all Department of Canadian Heritage. Finestone represents the view that diversity in society is some sort of trick to be learned and, until we get the hang of it, we need parental guidance.

But parental guidance has served largely to isolate new Canadians and deceive old ones. It has also put limits on the degree to which Canadian citizenship can become a shared experience and increases the time required for mutual adjustment and understanding. This is a lot to pay, in these times, for a failed policy designed to meet another need, which was, to put it mildly, opportunistic if not cynical and a failure if not a disaster. The final irony is that everyone knew it, in the magic circle of policy makers, and the policy was abandoned some time ago. But no one seems able to remember that far back.

If Exxon Can Make Money, Why Can't You?

DECEMBER 2, 1994

Even while the federal government is wandering the countryside hunting down unemployment insurance claimants suspected of over-accessing the fund, the good news gets overlooked. Or, because it's buried in the financial pages, not looked at at all.

If we ignore the gloomsday front page and the editorials, which faithfully recount the tortured cerebral writhings of Paul Martin, the finance minister, and Lloyd Axworthy, minister of everything else, a somewhat different impression is gained as to the condition of the country.

For instance, profits for Canadian corporations are up by 11.6 percent in the third quarter of this year, the highest level achieved since 1989. According to Statistics Canada, profits returned to shareholders are more than double those for last year.

Shareholders in Canadian banks are having a very good year, thank you for asking. Profits for Toronto-Dominion Bank doubled over the previous year. Canadian Imperial Bank of Commerce declared record profits for 1994. Even the lacklustre National Bank of Canada finished the year with a 24 percent rise in earnings.

According to my morning paper, "Imperial Oil Ltd. may give

shareholders another special dividend next year, as it searches for ways to spend $1 billion of the cash in its treasury." Even newspapers are making money: third-quarter profits increased nearly 18 percent (to U.S. $263 million) over last year at the Thomson Corporation, headquarters for the *Globe and Mail,* one of the economy's major, everyday worry-warts.

And if you don't like banking or journalism as an indicator, try travel. Air Canada, mother of airlines, has just racked up the biggest third-quarter profits in its fifty-seven years of flying.

Meanwhile, in related developments, the federal deficit was down more than $5 billion from a year ago, as were—heavens, how could this be?—unemployment insurance payouts, which fell by $1.2 billion, or 14.4 percent, in the first half of the year.

Spokespersons for the Department of Finance and various private sector-endowed think tanks have launched counterstrikes against this attack of positive news on the economy, expressing concern that ordinary Canadians might take to reading the financial pages. Things were, they all said, worse than ever; an "official" at the finance department warned, "We're starting to see the higher interest rate bite." A man named Carmichael at J. P. Morgan warned of interest costs that would "soar" in the next fiscal year.

Notwithstanding veiled threats from the Martin & Axworthy Bad News Bears road show, more than five million taxpaying Canadians put a record of more than $19 billion into RRSPs. The wonder to some of us was that so many (26 percent of all taxpayers) had that kind of dough left over at year's end.

In this month's issue of *Harper's* magazine, Benjamin DeMott writes, "In the space of three years, the total compensation of the average American CEO rises, in the midst of the age of downsizing, from forty times to ninety-three times that of the average factory worker—with no sign of an executive performance leap (or drop in worker productivity) to match the raise."

Corresponding Canadian figures are not available, though at least some of those "American" CEOs are operating in this country; but it would not surprise if the numbers were comparable to our own.

What is available is evidence that the country is moving to a state more profoundly discriminatory than merely a likely two-tier medical system. Those who read their newspapers from front to back may also detect two-tier journalism, reporting on a two-tier economy. Canada may become two nations, after all: the comfortable one, populated by shareholders and their portfolio managers; the second, which we could call Kleinburg, named after its principal founder, prophet, and promulgator, Alberta's Ralph.

In Kleinburg, where parsimony will be practised as a religion and being unemployed will be a matter of ethics, journalism will be comprised of saturation coverage of "The Fifty Year War Against Debt." Such diversions as the CBC might once have offered will have been supplanted by a national twenty-four-hour talk show with host Rafe Mair, featuring spittle-drenched polemics from raving lunatics who alone will know the 1-800 number to call. Full-value family entertainment.

Keeping Canadians in a chronic condition of anxiety and personal insecurity, by sealing them off from the good news, insures a fixed state of outrage sufficient to crush the more ennobling Canadian instincts for fairness and compassion. But such quaint words are now out of political fashion as the Americanization of the Canadian public conscience proceeds.

Mr. Smith Is History

JANUARY 6, 1995

We are all hearing talk about the "revolution" in American politics. For many Americans, all revolutions are salutary if they are of their own making; Americans have the best revolutions in the world.

Because America is the last of the superpowers, the only nation with the nuclear capacity to destroy the world, American politics is more than a mere distraction to neighbours, allies, and adversaries. Apart from that commonplace, the shifting political winds, the passing ideological fashions, and the changings of the guard—all these bring their own message of inspiration or apprehension to those who live beyond the boundaries of the Great Republic.

The Republic is not only capable of bursts of generosity becoming its wealth, but also spasms of fury becoming its power. It is also capable of an overweening, self-serving moralism so painfully evident to its most devoted friends. But the underlying reality in one's relationships with America is the acknowledgement of the power ratio, so great and disparate as to be beyond any meaningful expression in mathematics, but which makes all others subordinate, uncertain, and wary.

With that in mind, when the important American media (CNN, the *Wall Street Journal, Newsweek* magazine) report there has been a "revolution" in the Great Republic, it must be so if they say so.

After all, when Orson Welles reported, in the course of a radio drama, that Martians had landed in the New Jersey marshes, within sight of the New York skyline, thousands of Americans fled their homes or bolted their doors or called the cops. This more recent event has more reliable credentials. We who can only watch and wonder should, however, keep our cool. It is one thing to be eternally patronized and frequently entertained, but another to be propagandized.

All revolutions through history have been carried by minorities. This latest triumph of Republican conservatism is no exception. Less than 39 percent of all eligible voters troubled themselves to go to the polls; somewhat more than half of this number voted for the Republicans. Of those who did vote, 75 percent did not know the names of their members of Congress. (Such is the way of revolutions.)

During the election campaign, Republicans published their platform, calling it a "Contract with America." After the election, a *Newsweek* poll found that only half of those who voted—half of the 39 percent eligible to vote—had ever heard of "Contract with America." Figures were not made available as to how many who had heard about the Contract had any idea what was in it.

Again, this bears the imprint of your average revolution: Not very many showed up at the barricades and even fewer knew what they were doing once they got there. What is more significant about this "uprising" is the fact that 61 percent of those who had a vote did not cast it. There could only be two plausible explanations for this studied neglect of this latest revolution in our time: either a majority who had better things to do—watching television, mulching leaves, dieting—or millions for whom contemporary American politics has no meaning. This growing "silent majority" may represent the true revolution in America.

In Canada, despite our grumblings about political establishments and the whimperings of the self-designated alienated, we would deem our political institutions a failure should a majority of our citizens fail to vote. We would, at least, begin an earnest enquiry in which no special interest or privileged practice would be spared. (Although we might fail to act, as did Parliament after the Fortier Commission.)

To the detached observer, the American democracy has abandoned its idealism and its compelling egalitarian spirit for a predatory acquisitiveness serviced almost entirely by the modern arts of manipulation and the skills of the expert dissembler. In this suppurating concoction of the lobbyists' elixir of money and the exhausted ennui of the journalist, noble words lose their meaning just as worthy sensibilities lose their hold on the public imagination. Cynicism and mendacity conspire in a coalition of interests where the only language is money, huge, incomprehensible amounts of it, enough to buy favour, preference, a senator or two, a Congress, a presidency, while politics is reduced from speech to buzz words, and argument to the artifice of symbols.

Enough to buy any or all of that and, more important, enough to repel the sensible, the caring, and the modest who are at least a few of those who no longer care to vote in the Great American Assizes. One thinks of them as former constitutents of James Stewart whose character, in the film *Mr. Smith Goes to Washington,* was elected to the U.S. Senate where he found corruption, met temptation, and overcame both to the delight of millions of theatregoers.

Today, Mr. Smith would have been found a pinko, tax-and-spend profligate liberal and—lacking the $14 million needed to be a serious candidate—would have been buried beneath the ballots of mobilized Christians rushing to the polls straight from the gospel temple of the Reverend Pat Robertson. As for the movie, Newt Gingrich would have told his mother that Jean Arthur was a bitch.

Between Allan Rock and a Hard Place

JANUARY 10, 1995

Allan Rock has been in Alberta, taking the heat for his efforts, as minister of justice, to oblige gun owners to register their weapons. While the polls inform that most Albertans, and most Canadians, support the minister's proposed legislation, it is apparent that the noisiest ones do not.

Efforts to regulate the toys of big boys are seen in Alberta gun circles as eastern chicanery designed to reduce western testosterone production by cutting it with imported toilette water. The justice minister has been warned to amend his legislation or face retaliation in the form of widespread civil disobedience or Alberta's withdrawal from Canada. No kidding.

Whether or not governments have any sound reason to interfere in the relationships between guns and consenting adults appears to be one of the incendiary issues of our troubled times. Opponents of gun registration are obdurately opposed and see registration leading to confiscation, a troubled vision assiduously promoted by various Canadian models of the National Rifle Association, the American mother of all political pressure groups.

There is—and always has been—a curious correlation between the conservative Hard Right and gun-owning hard liners. Ideologically joined at the hip, the gun lobby and the neo-conservatives have their in-house seminal thinkers to help iron out the wrinkles in their brief. For example, how to explain the fact that public opinion, both here and in the United States, is supportive of gun control measures?

As we all know, public opinion is the guiding light of the Hard Right, crucial to the canon that says that modern conservatism shall represent the final triumph of populism over elitism. Then, how to explain the public preference for more stringent controls over guns?

Well, there is the assertion—bald as a gun barrel—that "the majority of survey polls on 'gun control' are so unreliable and methodologically flawed as to be practically useless as an accurate barometer of public opinion." That, anyway, is the opinion of the Ontario Handgun Association.

As substantiation, there follows the view of James D. Wright, an American authority and presumed archangel of the NRA, who has written, "If the public is in general ill-informed about the existing laws and regulations governing the ownership and use of weapons, then its opinion that the existing measures should be made tougher is rather difficult to interpret meaningfully."

Wright is supported by G. A. Mauser and David Kopel, two more American scholars, who write, "Questions about whether gun laws should be made stricter [*sic*] do not examine whether the respondents understand what the present laws are."

This is interesting stuff. What it says is that public opinion is not to be trusted in areas of public policy where it doesn't understand the problem. No one needs to be told such subversive opinion is profoundly offensive to the sacred tenets of yahoo populism, which would lead to the logical construct that brain surgery could as well be conducted by plebiscite. (Wright, Mauser, and Kopel would have been useful to have had around during the Meech Lake Accord and Charlottetown Accord debates.)

Following this rejection from the Hard Right of the efficacy of public opinion polls, it would be splendid if we now agreed that polls should no longer drive the political agenda. From this day forward, politicians who quote polls to advance their bias should be deemed closet supporters of gun control, guilty of narrow thinking, and docked a day's pay. The sanction includes any citation of polls dealing with capital punishment, taxes, the deficit, foreign aid, and Québec sovereignty. From this day forward, Preston Manning and the rest of us are agreed: Polls don't make policy, politicians do.

It would be seen from so pleasing a result that minister Rock had done us a favour. While one must acknowledge the difficulties of dispensing enlightenment in an atmosphere of so much grievance and bellicosity, the minister has raised the nation's consciousness of his issue (gun control) and shed light on other relevant matters.

Certainly, the sentiment expressed by one of Rock's detractors—vociferously endorsed by audience applause—raises questions sufficient to energize the combined political science faculties of all Albertan schools of higher learning for weeks to come. It was said, amidst tumultuous approval, that if the federal government persisted in its policy of gun registration, Alberta would—or might—take its ball, bat, and shotguns and not only go home but leave the country.

The justice minister remained silent in the face of such dread. Still, as we all know, the other presently difficult Canadian province (Québec) has been told by no less than the prime minister and—as important—by several columnists, that Québec could not leave Canada if it wanted to, referendum or none.

This is further evidence of the growing rejection of majoritarian opinion as being in any way conclusive to the settlement of public policy. Of course, gun registration may be only the beginning of a federal plot leading to the ultimate confiscation of all weapons, including the serpent's tongue. Canadians will then be stuck with one another and will have to get along together for another hundred years, a fate they richly deserve.

This Argument Has Been Blown Up
Beyond All Reason

APRIL 28, 1995

Not much more than a week ago the president of the United States held a news conference and hardly anyone came. Bill Clinton, it was explained, was passé and no longer newsworthy, and whatever he might have to say on anything mattered not. These sentiments excused two of the three commercial television networks from providing live coverage, a decision that allowed viewers another uninterrupted day of Velveeta and vanilla.

Not long after the Oklahoma City bombing, the president spoke out against hatemongerers in the media and became, overnight, the point-man in an emergent debate over the true cause of the awful event that has shaken the composure of millions of Americans. One of the shattering realities of the tragedy in Oklahoma was the revelation that the monstrous deed had been done not by "three Arab-looking men in track suits" who some witnesses had reported seeing fleeing the scene, but was instead the work of white, male Americans who were "right-wing extremists."

The general description of the culprits was further enriched by news they had been provoked and "enraged" by U.S. government gun control measures. With this news, the National Rifle Association went quickly to ground to allow the not-so-far right wing to respond. A congressional sampler of that opinion soon became available to counter Clinton's attack on media hatemongering.

Among those first to speak was Oklahoma Republican Senator James M. Inhofe, who once boasted he had won his recent election to the Senate on the issues of "gay, guns, and God." Inhofe complained that the president "didn't identify who the far right is."

"I don't think it's in good taste," he concluded.

His Republican colleague, Don Nickles, also thought Clinton's comments inappropriate. "This incident wasn't caused by Rush Limbaugh," Nickles said, "[it] wasn't caused by people who think government is too big."

The president, through his office, was quick to deny he had Limbaugh—who is a Republican right-wing media icon—in mind. I don't think he did either. Limbaugh makes a living as the Republican Party's court jester and has a sense of humour perfectly tailored to the mental and intellectual range of his studio audiences. The last time I watched him in concert, it seemed to me his material was becoming shopworn; after all, jokes about liberals in America these days strike some as about as funny as jokes about Trotskyites.

While Limbaugh is harmless—and palpably sane—another suspect could be Gordon Liddy, who did time for the Watergate burglary and who sometimes sets fire to his hand to demonstrate his toughness. A solid Republican on the Hard Right, Liddy has been heard advising his radio audience on how to shoot U.S. federal agents (in the head).

The tragedy in Oklahoma City, however triggered, has been an inconvenience to the National Rifle Association and its Washington agents, who happen also to be the new Republican Party. It had been the plan, prior to Oklahoma City, for House Speaker Newt Gingrich to turn over Congress to the NRA for as long as it would take to repeal the ban on assault weapons. The NRA also hoped for legislation to allow Americans to carry concealed weapons. No problem. But the bombing of the federal building in Oklahoma City postponed the "reforms" for at least a month.

Gingrich withdrew, laying smoke. "I challenge the news media," he said, "to go add up the number of people killed by those [assault] guns this year and come back with a list. And then compare the bombing in Oklahoma City."

Okay, that might be interesting (according to the *Wall Street Journal*, at least 229 homicides were committed by assault weapons in 1992, the latest year of record), but I'd rather compare Gingrich with Aristotle or Archimedes.

Gingrich has made a career promoting mistrust, ridicule, and contempt for government, for people who work in government, and for many who are served by government. Only a man who sees history as a conspiracy could describe a crazed mother's murder of her two young children as reflective of the pathology of the welfare state.

But as the house speaker said, in his carefully drawn non sequitur, domestic terrorism in Oklahoma had nothing to do with the issue of assault weapons control. Still, in the search for evidence against the Oklahoma suspects, the police turned up a private arsenal, including thirty-three firearms, a 9 mm pistol found in the car of the prime suspect and, along with other material and ammunition, a 60 mm anti-tank rocket. The suspected killers were gun collectors, big time.

According to the *New York Times*, "investigators believe all three men may have ties to the Michigan Militia, a paramilitary group that opposes gun control and believes the Federal Government is conspiring to deprive citizens of their rights."

Hell, they sound like modern-day regular right-wing Republicans to me, even allowing for the fact they are likely right-wing extremists, or far-right extremists, or far, far right extreme extremists. There is, however, some correlation between people who love guns and who hate governments. A few of them are those Canadians who have been saying, with the general approval of the Reform Party, that if there is a federal law passed controlling the ownership of guns, they will break it. Such defiance may not sound like much, but it's a start, and it's armed and dangerous.

Mike Scott, MP, Drop Your Gun and Come Out from Behind That Seat

MARCH 2, 1991

Reform Party MP, Mike Scott, fighting out of Skeena, B.C. has written a letter to the *Hill Times*, an Ottawa weekly publication read largely by citizens who work on Parliament Hill, that complains of my column published last January on the subject of gun control. Scott is opposed; I am not.

In defence of his opposition to the measures proposed by justice minister Allan Rock, the Reform Party MP writes: "The major danger of 'democratic' government is unstable, predatory mob rule. And the task of those who promote good government is to find ways of keeping it from getting too big. Naturally, an armed citizenry is an important part of this. Equally naturally, those who seek unlimited power for government fear a citizenry able to resist encroachments on their liberty."

Obviously, Scott includes himself among those who "promote good government" by keeping it small. And he is among those seeking "to find ways" to keep government from growing too big. One way of doing so, he makes clear, is through "an armed citizenry."

It is not entirely certain what this means, though we must surely get the drift of it: Should there come a time when government "gets too big," it can be reduced in size by the combined firepower of "an armed citizenry." Whether these armed citizens fire on the government after first marching on Ottawa, or fire from their upper windows at passing government employees, or perhaps duck out of the house of an evening and nail a few on the street downtown, no one really knows. Scott keeps the order of battle to himself.

Then there is the possibility that Mike Scott himself, acting in the interests of his constituents who feel the need to thin out the herd, could terminate a few government agents by firing from among the cornices of the Centre Block. This is suggested almost every day in America. Whatever works is, I suppose, the modus operandi of Scott's armed citizenry.

I know it's not funny. I think it's serious that a member of Parliament, even one from that party, would preach sedition in an open letter in the *Hill Times* published under the nose of members of Parliament, and that the result would be either silence or simple incredulity.

"We believe," Scott writes in his essay on the evils of gun control, "that the paradox of government is that any government strong enough to protect [the lives, liberty, and property] of its citizens from others is strong enough to threaten them itself."

It is this sort of sentiment that stirs the hearts and heads of those crazed gun-bearing "militias" in the United States. Their excessive patriotism spurs the need to take up arms against the country they profess to love. Of course, the enemy is not America—in the example of the freelance militias—the enemy is America's institutions and those responsible for safeguarding them. And beyond the smell of cordite and of the sweat of their exertions, there is the overwhelming scent of paranoia.

But you do not have to be crazy to imagine that your right to own a gun—or an armoury of guns—is simply confirmation of your inalienable duty to shoot your way into the political discourse as the last means of saving freedom. You could believe as much were you a Republican member of Congress and the crazies were your constituents and, better still, they were all armed and Christian. You could believe the same if you were a member of Canada's Reform Party, a member of the Parliament of Canada, and a follower of Preston Manning.

The trouble may be that we are so overwhelmed by the American experience, that between O. J. Simpson and drive-by shootings and Oklahoma City and talk radio, interactive television and the Internet, we have reached a nearly perfect gravity flow in which we hear everything and listen to nothing. And to imagine we would have someone in our midst so incendiary and menacing as the member of Parliament for Skeena is simply too much for our sensibilities to handle. And it is not even good gossip, because no one knows anything about Mike Scott, a name like that of a hockey player called up from the minors for the playoffs, and coming from Skeena, which is a river when it is not a mountain, and a constituency after that.

Our burdens are already more than enough to bear at this time. The Republicans want us out of Cuba; the National Rifle Association wants its hunters to stay out of Saskatchewan. The member for Skeena, fearing what he calls "predatory mob rule" in a constituency with only one pool hall, wants to be allowed to keep his standing army intact, just in case the government starts upsizing or otherwise gets out of hand. And I suppose, if the combative patriots of Skeena and Preston Manning's Own Irregulars can't prevent government proliferation, reinforcements are not far away in the ranks of the militias of Idaho, Illinois, and Colorado.

"Government exists," Scott informs readers of the *Hill Times*, "to protect the lives, liberties, and property of its citizens." But also to protect the constitution, and peace, order, and good government, of whatever size. The Reform MP's seditious endorsement of private militias as against a people's government offers helpful endorsement of Allan Rock's proposed legislation. The threat is more serious than we had thought.

Ask Not for Whom the Road Tolls,
It Tolls for Dingwall

MAY 29, 1995

The prime minister, I daresay, is much too busy to concern himself with the smaller depredations of his cabinet colleagues, one of them anyway, that constitute yet another assault upon our symbols of nationhood. As a country, we bleed from a thousand cuts, including budget, personnel and program cuts. A capricious, patronage-scented magisterial decision to begin installing toll booths along the Trans-Canada Highway is, I suppose, just another nick in these times, a minor act in a general trashing meant to obliterate the country we have known, admired, and loved.

The magistrate in this latest matter is David Dingwall, the resident federal minister in Nova Scotia and, of greater importance, the province's *chef du patronage*. Dingwall is a Cape Bretoner, a man of rare prophetic profundity; with thrice the prescience of the witches of Cawdor, he foresaw the coming of Jean Chrétien when others were contemplating John Turner as liberalism's man of destiny.

As the result, when Chrétien ultimately moved into the mansion on Sussex Drive, his Cape Breton soothsayer was elevated to become minister of everything in the Maritimes, and responsible for whatever remained there as yet unpaved or unimproved. The prime minister's Maritime Main Man surveyed the needs of Nova Scotians for improved roads and settled upon the priority requirement to improve one of his own—the Fleur-de-Lis Highway—winding through his own constituency and ending, somewhat anticlimatically, nowhere.

Where this otherwise routine matter of familiar ministerial caprice gathered density and hit the fan was over the money appropriated for the Fleur-de-Lis/Dingwall Boulevard. Putting it bluntly, the money had been looted from the federal-provincial highways agreement where it had been allocated for more serious public need. Namely: To improve the portion of the Trans-Canada Highway euphemistically known as Death Valley.

Death Valley, a stretch of road running through Nova Scotia's Wentworth Valley, between Amherst and Truro, needs no further description. People get killed there, year round. The valley offers glorious autumnal foliage and it is a popular winter site for skiing. For purposes of navigating the highway, treacherous in winter because of ice conditions on the elevations, or in summer because of the heavy tourist traffic, or anytime because of the truck traffic, the safest way to travel would be by tank.

However, Chrétien's proconsul in Nova Scotia has decided to pave his own road first, the public interest be damned. Poor Harold Ballard went to jail for less; he merely built a private driveway at the expense of a few shareholders. Dingwall's pillage is big time.

The ministerial response to the need for public safety in Death Valley has been a proposal to rebuild the highway and make it a toll road. The taxpayers thus get a nice, new road in Cape Breton for Nova Scotia's *chef du patronage* and, in the bargain, a toll road on the Trans-Canada between Amherst and Truro.

What's missing in this picture?

Well, the prime minister for one. Jean Charest, the Tory leader, recently visited among the folks in Death Valley and was given a earful on the subject of the toll road proposal. Following up, he wrote a letter to the prime minister seeking intervention; one hopes he enclosed his card.

Certainly, there is nothing in the Red Book—the Liberal Party's widely acclaimed doomsday book—that promised early installation of toll booths along the Trans-Canada. At least, I couldn't find it, though it may be located under the section promoting Canadian culture and the arts, which I skipped.

We need to remind ourselves (every so often) of the importance the prime minister once attached to the question of patronage. Indeed, he has tied himself in knots, to the delight of the legal profession of Toronto, with his heroic stand against patronage at the Toronto airport. But he may also now wish to consider how much he owes David Dingwall, in political coin, compared to what he might owe Nova Scotians who voted for him so resolutely in 1993.

Nova Scotians, other than immediate members of the Dingwall family and several poll chairmen, are in an uproar. The mayor of Amherst has threatened to bolt the province and annex his town to New Brunswick. The premier of Nova Scotia, John Savage, whose recent approval ratings have rivalled those of Idi Amin, has assumed a historic Liberal position: A toll road for Death Valley if Dingwall insists, but otherwise not a toll road. Such are the absolutes of ministerial power these days in Bluenose country that neither a friendly government in Halifax nor an aroused citizenry can break through the barricade of private gratitude that surrounds the prime minister.

Doubtless too, the New Right will hail Dingwall as a visionary, even if by accident. Another good way of getting the government out of the hair of those who prefer jet travel would be to get the government out of the road business. The trend is already apparent in America: private streets in private communities, surrounded by high walls and private police, and toll roads for the public. Toll roads easily turn a profit and those who can't pay the toll can try the back roads.

The original Trans-Canada Highway was built to unify the country, open it up to modern commerce and tourism, and afford Canadians the opportunity to see as much of their country as their time and wanderlust allowed. The Trans-Canada Highway represented a tribute both to Canadian politics and Canadian engineering. And it represented an act of faith at a time in our lives when we believed we could move mountains. Today, the minister gets his indulgent constituency perk; the rest get a toll road. Wow.*

Why Was He in Vietnam?

APRIL 11, 1995

Robert S. (for Strange) McNamara was the U.S. Secretary of Defence from 1961 to 1968, serving under Presidents John Kennedy and

---

* On August 24, 1995, Dingwall put the money back. Who says they don't listen?

Lyndon Johnson. He came to the Pentagon from the Ford Motor Co., where he had been the president, bringing with him a number of bright young men—the media admiringly called them "the whiz kids"—and for seven years presided over the murderous escalation of the Vietnam war which, ultimately ending in defeat, cost the lives of 58,000 American servicemen and women and more than one million Vietnamese.

During his tenure as defence secretary, McNamara was widely admired for his business acumen and efficiency. Those who believed you could run a government like a business were similarly convinced that wars could be waged by businessmen. (I recall John Diefenbaker exulting, on appointing Argus Corporation president Wally McCutcheon to his cabinet, "Kennedy has his McNamara and I have McCutcheon.")

Vietnam was an unpopular war in the United States, especially among the generation of young men designated to fight it. Most white males, like Newt Gingrich and Phil Gramm, assiduously avoided military service; so did Bill Clinton. A disproportionate number of those who fought in Vietnam were either poor or black, or both. But the war was popular with the American right wing, which maintained a belief in "the domino theory": If Vietnam fell to the Communists, one after another non-Communist regime in the region would follow. But after the Communists won Vietnam in 1976, the dominoes didn't fall.

After seven years at the Pentagon, McNamara quit as defence secretary; the Vietnam war would continue for another seven years and twenty thousand more Americans would lose their lives. It was a widely held view, though largely unexpressed, that McNamara had quit because he had come to doubt the war could be won.

This week, McNamara produced his autobiography. In it, he admits to having had more than doubts about the war; indeed, he not only thought it unwinnable, but unnecessary. It was not the sort of war suitable to American military power. Further, the fighting capacity and resolve of the Vietnamese had been seriously underestimated.

I was glad to hear of McNamara's book and his true confessions. I had myself publicly opposed the war in Vietnam, marching in a demonstration against it arm-in-arm with Tommy Douglas, the former CCF and NDP leader. Most Canadians were either neutral or silent on the subject of Vietnam, a notable exception being Mike Pearson, then prime minister of Canada.

Since I have seldom been able to be neutral or silent about anything, I had earlier supported the war despite the objections of my children, including my older son, who had gone to Washington, marched and demonstrated against the war, and returned home smelling of phosgene gas. But although I had criticized Pearson for publicly calling for an end to the American bombing of Hanoi, I began, like McNamara, to have doubts about the war. In the end, I was persuaded by the sensibilities of my children and by what became increasingly obvious—the racist undertones of America's war effort and of the war itself—the war against "the gooks."

Thinking about McNamara and the release of his long confined candour, I am reminded of the ongoing furies and follies of America's right. It is a pity younger Canadian Tories, who seem to find Newt Gingrich, Al D'Amato, and Jesse Helms inspirational political figures, do not have a historic memory much longer than six months. Or six years. Otherwise, they would see this most recent reactionary Republican war against the urban poor and people of colour in the context of a long, historic continuity.

The other evening, I watched New York *Post* editor Eric Breindel being interviewed by Robert Novak. The *Post*, now owned by Rupert Murdoch, has become, under Breindel's editorship, a clarion neo-conservative voice. But as Breindel put it, "The views I express in the New York *Post* are his [Murdoch's]."

Breindel is a handsome, self-possessed man with a resonant baritone voice and eyes colder than any you would find in the New York city morgue. He appeared on TV affecting highly polished black cowboy boots. He said, "[Bill] Clinton believes in government as a remedial institution."

He disapproves of America's intervention in Haiti: "We saw the undermining of a pro-American government in favour of a Marxist one." He complains that Clinton is "willing to bail out Mexico but not Orange County [California]." He speaks well of D'Amato, who recently aired racist slurs intended as wit at the expense of the judge sitting on the Simpson murder trial. D'Amato "is a good man who sometimes says things that do a disservice to his future interests," the editor explained.

He is opposed to affirmative action, a policy that encourages the hiring of women, blacks, and other minorities of colour. It is the firm position of the neo-conservatives that white males should not be discriminated against, even in the face of a century of repression, bias, and bigotry exercised against blacks. I recall once saying to an American ambassador to Canada how unjust it seemed that so much of the war in Vietnam was being fought by poor blacks drafted out of the South and the big cities. His reply was that it had proved a great advantage by providing blacks in the army their first opportunity to occupy leadership roles. How about that for affirmative action?

Straight Arrow Comes to Mother Corp.

APRIL 4, 1995

It is amusing to read the ruminative rumblings on the appointment of Perrin Beatty to the presidency of the Canadian Broadcasting Corporation. He is, commentators insist on reminding us, a politician. This worrying of that old bone does disservice to the fact that the CBC has never had a president who was not a politician. Pierre Juneau, for example: Did he not run in Hochelaga-Maisonneuve in a by-election? The first CBC president I came to know was A. Davidson Dunton, one of the two or three best politicians in the country during the 1950s and early 1960s, the halcyon days of the Mother Corporation when Perrin Beatty was barely a school boy. Beatty became a politician by profession early in life and he was a good one, known to be of impeccable honesty and sound character. People in Ottawa I knew would refer to him as "Straight Arrow."

While remembering that, I also recall what many have overlooked in their reviews of Beatty's political past, which was as the minister of national defence responsible for the White Paper on defence policy proposing the purchase of nuclear-powered submarines. It was about the same time when the national capital seemed overrun with nuclear submarine salesmen that the Tory administration proposed the first deep cuts in CBC funding.

The irony should not have been lost on the nation's deep thinkers, though it apparently was. The cost of one nuclear sub could have run the CBC for several years. The reason we need the CBC, almost everyone agrees, is to help safeguard the country from being overwhelmed by Hollywood cultural imperialists. But the reason we needed nuclear subs was to give Canada a presence in our northern waters, ostensibly because the Russians were up there, under the ice, but also, as important, so were the Americans.

In the end—to conclude this diversion—public opinion was unwilling to protect Canadian sovereignty in the Arctic waters at the price of a fleet of nuclear submarines. And, anyway, the Berlin Wall was falling down, which inhibited the White Paper's strategic premise of the Russians as Canada's designated enemy.

The CBC has since run through four presidents of whom Perrin Beatty is the most recent. His immediate predecessor (the prime minister and his cabinet colleagues would like us to forget), was Anthony Manera, who was a politician, *comme les autres*, but one plagued by scruple. Manera is an engineer by trade and the CBC had been his life, but he resigned the presidency when the government ratted on its commitment to spare the CBC further cuts in its budget.

Since Manera's resignation, the prime minister has been beating the bushes for a replacement. Enter then, Straight Arrow, a CBC president with qualifications earned mostly in the hard school of politics, but also a decent man, plausibly sincere and well-intentioned, with longstanding credentials as a true believer in public broadcasting. He begins his presidency confronting a sea of troubles, armed only with the good wishes, possibly even the prayers, of many Canadians.

At the week's beginning, I listened to the new president being interviewed by Peter Gzowski on *Morningside*. Beatty appeared as himself, articulate, tidy, and on key, a man with perfect pitch. He did not, however, say very much, only that he was prepared "to make the tough decisions."

Later that same day, Tony Manera spoke to the Canadian Club in Toronto. His address had a title: "The CBC: A Canadian Story."

A few salient facts from Manera's speech: CBC government funding in fiscal year 1984–85 was $905 million; in this fiscal year, it is $1,065 million, "a decrease of almost 25 percent when you take into